THE
NOTHINGNESS
BEYOND
GOD

THE
NOTHINGNESS
BEYOND
GOD

*An Introduction to
the Philosophy of
Nishida Kitarō*

Second Edition

ROBERT E. CARTER

PARAGON HOUSE
ST. PAUL, MINNESOTA

Second edition, 1997

Published in the United States by

Paragon House Publishers
2700 University Avenue West
St. Paul, MN 55114

Copyright © 1997 by Paragon House Publishers

Library of Congress Cataloging-in-Publication Data

Carter, Robert Edgar, 1937—

     The nothingness beyond God: an introduction to the philosophy of Nishida Kitarō / by Robert E. Carter.-2nd ed.
     p. cm.
     Bibliography: p.
     Includes index.
     ISBN 1-55778-761-1
     1. Nishida, Kitarō, 1870-1945. 1. Title.
     B5244.N554C37 1989
     181'.12-dc19   88-11458
                                                                CIP
                                                                (Rev.)

Manufactured in the United States of America

DESIGN BY: Stanley S. Drate/Folio Graphics Co. Inc.

To my mother
Dorothy
and to
Scott
and
Meredith

CONTENTS

FOREWORD by Thomas Kasulis   *ix*

ACKNOWLEDGMENTS   *xix*

INTRODUCTION   *xxi*

ONE
Pure Experience   *1*

TWO
The Logic of *Basho*   *16*

THREE
Self-Contradictory Identity   *58*

FOUR
God and Nothingness   *81*

FIVE
The Dialectical World of "Action Intuition"   *100*

SIX
Religion and Morality   *129*

SEVEN
Values, Ethics and Feeling   *162*

NOTES   *178*

BIBLIOGRAPHY   *205*

INDEX   *218*

FOREWORD

This book is a landmark in the exchange between Japanese and Western philosophy. Nishida Kitarō was the single most influential figure in the development of twentieth-century Japanese thought, and this is the first book-length study of his work to appear in the West. That fact alone assures this volume a special place in the history of the dialogue between the Eastern and Western philosophical traditions.

The Nothingness Beyond God represents the fruits of a sustained and extraordinary effort. Robert Carter was already seriously interested in Nishida's philosophy when he sought me out ten years ago at the University of Hawaii. Since then he has made a careful study of every essay on the subject available in the European languages. He has traveled the globe in order to verify significant details with Nishida scholars, gleaning ideas from different interpretations and distilling them into his own analysis. The resultant book is remarkably thorough, balanced, and fair-minded.

As his introduction suggests, Carter does not claim to give a final, authoritative interpretation of Nishida's work. Rather, he invites the reader to enter into a conversation with Nishida's texts, allowing Nishida, finally, the opportunity to be heard outside of his native culture. Through careful translation and commentary, by Carter and other scholars, Nishida's work has become part of the global exchange of ideas for the first time.

Historically, there has been too little work done in Western languages in the area of modern Japanese philosophy, or indeed of Japanese philosophy in general. This has begun to change in the past few years, and the fact that such a book as this is possible and worthwhile attests to Nishida's status as a philosopher of world-wide importance. Carter himself is a philosopher—and not an expert in the Japanese language and has elucidated the cultural and philosophical context, both Eastern and Western, from which flow the ideas of Nishida Kitarō. It takes considerable courage to cross cultural boundaries, particularly when that crossing requires the reassessment of fundamental assumptions and ways of looking at one's self and the world. That Carter would undergo the effort and care to take on such a project is evidence enough that the fields of philosophy and theology are opening themselves up to new, truly global, horizons.

Since this book is a hermeneutic conversation between Carter and the Nishida texts, it is also a text for us, the readers. As readers, we too enter into the conversation, bringing our own concerns and questions. As a specialist in Japanese philosophy, I think it might be useful for me to include some of my responses to the dialogue. In particular, I would like to include in this foreword some philosophical and historical background relevant to the East-West exchange which ensues.

As R.G. Collingwood noted, to evaluate the significance of a philosophical position, we must first understand the question that position tries to answer. What question was Nishida addressing? In focusing on that issue, we should consider the historical and cultural influences on Nishida's thought. Such a discussion may also shed light on why a Western philosopher like Carter would be interested in Nishida's answer at this particular time in Western intellectual history. A few of the basic historical circumstances about Nishida's historical and intellectual context will be helpful.

Nishida Kitarō (1870-1945) was born at the beginning of the Meiji period (1868-1912), when Japan opened its door to Western trade and, by extension, Western culture, after two and a half centuries of isolation. Japan's decision to modernize was not fully autonomous. The immediate cause for initiating full scale exchange with the West was the entrance of Commodore Matthew Perry's American gunboats into Uraga harbor in 1853. Japan naturally felt squeezed and threatened. The United States had expanded across North America and into the Pacific; Britain and France were sweeping across the Asian and African continents; and Japan's nearest mainland neighbors, China and Russia, were countries of continental dimension. So more than anything else, the Japanese underwent technological modernization as a means of self-protection. Japan saw two possible destinies: either to be a pawn in the imperialist power plays of European and North American expansion, or to become an imperialist power in its own right, through extensive economic, political, social, and scientific reconstruction. It chose the latter course.

By the early twentieth century, Japan had achieved a remarkable success. It had defeated both China and Russia in wars and had signed a major pact with Great Britain. There could be no turning back, however. The new Japanese industrial society had enormous needs for natural resources not available within its own archipelago. Modeling itself on its Western imperialist mentors, Japan looked to secure its supply of resources overseas, on the Asian mainland and throughout the Pacific Basin. Japan had truly become an imperialist power, and had set into motion a sequence of events that would result in the Pacific theater of World War II.

The intellectual climate in which Nishida lived developed in relation to those larger sociopolitical upheavals. The earlier Meiji intellectuals had expressed the hope that Japan could modernize without changing its underlying cultural value system, an ideal expressed in the slogan "Western techniques, Eastern morality," popularized by Sakuma Shōsan (1811-1864). The more the Japanese intellectuals studied Western culture, however, the more skeptical they grew about the possibility of changing their country's social, economic, and political systems without also changing its religious and moral values. Toward the end of the nineteenth century, for example, there was even an idea that science and Christianity had developed together so intimately in the West that it might be advisable for the Japanese emperor to convert to Christianity. The pro-Christian contingent did not win out in the end and the emperor remained the chief priest of Shinto, but still, many of the prominent families in the modernization movement did convert. Even today, although Japan is less than one percent Christian, the influence of Christianity among the higher social and economic classes is inordinately strong.

Nishida's first book, *A Study of Good* (1911), was written at the very end of the Meiji period, at a time when Japanese national confidence was on the upswing and the country had the opportunity to reflect seriously on the full implications of Westernization. In that pioneering work, indeed in all the works to follow, Nishida struggled with the great issue of his time the juxtaposition of Western science and technology with traditional Japanese values. If Japanese values were to coexist alongside Western empiricism, there would have to be a common philosophical structure embracing and grounding the two. Otherwise, Japan would, intellectually at least, suffer cultural schizophrenia.

As a first-rate philosopher, Nishida was able to take issue out of its culture-bound form (such as the question of whether the emperor should become Christian in order to help modernization) and universalize it into the classic Western problem of the relation between fact (*is*) and value (*ought*).

In this way, Nishida saw himself addressing a fundamental philosophical question, not just a cultural problem. One option open to Nishida was to follow the route of Hume and Kant, bifurcating fact and value into two separate domains and (as with Kant) two different kinds of reasoning. This approach would, of course, affirm the possibility of separating Western science from Japanese values. But at what cost? Nishida knew that such a separation of is and *ought* was itself a divergence from the Eastern tradition. It was, in the final analysis, a Western approach to the problem and it would indeed seem strange that only a foreign way of thinking could justify preserving Japanese values.

So Nishida tried to bring fact and value, empiricism and morality (or religion or art), back together in a way consonant with the Asian tradition. At the same time, he thought his theory should be Western enough in form to serve the needs of an increasingly Westernized Japanese society. Here Nishida, like his lifelong friend D.T. Suzuki, found the writings of William James particularly provocative. Rather than analyzing science and value as two unrelated systems of reason, Nishida used James's notion of "pure experience" to articulate the common experiential flow toward unity that underlies both the scientific and valuational enterprises. The surface differences notwithstanding, on a deeper level, science, morality, art, and religion share a single preconceptual drive ("the will") to unity, a process Nishida called "the intellectual intuition." At least this was the basic thrust of his maiden philosophical work.

This solution to the fact/value or is/ought dilemma also satisfied Nishida as a practicing Zen Buddhist. Zen's ideal is the achievement of a preconceptual state of experiential purity ("no mind") that becomes enacted pragmatically in various concrete ways, including thought. (For the details of this view, see my book *Zen Action/Zen Person.*) For both James and Zen, thought is the temporary response to a break in the original unity of experience, a response which is itself intended to bring back the original unity of the experience. As Nishida put it, "pure experience is the alpha and omega of thought."

A Study of Good became popular among Japanese intellectuals immediately and is probably still the best known work in modern philosophy among the Japanese. It is questionable how many of those intellectuals actually fathomed the nuances of Nishida's theory, but the major point for them was that Nishida had made philosophy into something Japanese. His writing style had a Western ring to it, yet his fundamental insights were consistent with Japanese tradition. With *A Study of Good,* modern Japanese philosophy—the so-called Kyoto or Nishida School—was born.

As Nishida's philosophical thinking further matured, however, he grew dissatisfied with *A Study of Good*—not with its purpose, but with *its* philosophical form, its structural presuppositions. In particular, he criticized its psychologism (or "mysticism," as he sometimes called it). At the heart of his uneasiness was his belief that *A Study of Good* had attempted to solve the problem of the science/value split by appealing to a kind of experience, asserting it to be the ground of both the is and the *ought*. Nishida's readings in the Neo-Kantians during the period shortly after the publication of *A Study of Good* made him to the problem of how forms of judgment, rather than strata of experience, interrelate. That is, his concerns shifted from philosophical psychology to epistemology.

Throughout his life, Nishida constructed and subsequently razed his own attempts at systematic philosophy. He was an adamant critic of his own work and never seemed satisfied with the mode of explanations he had developed thus far. So the second phase of his thought rejected the idea that *A Study of Good* had explained anything at all; it had simply described the drive of consciousness toward unification. One problem was that the psychologistic standpoint could only trace the evolution of thought in the individual's psychological process. It could, for example, describe how the desire for unity could lead to the emergence of scientific moral, and religious thinking. But what about the fields of science, morality, and religion themselves? How can we analyze the interrelation of their claims without limiting them to modes in the biography of a particular person's own experence? It is, after all, one matter to say my empirical, moral, aesthetic, and religious experiences relate to each other, and quite another matter to say science, morality, art, and religion are related. The former is to connect experiences within myself; the latter to connect kinds of judgments about what is right. Nishida was impressed with the Neo-Kantians' attempts to articulate and explain the rationale of judgments and realized his earlier Jamesian view to be overly subjectivistic.

This new interest led Nishida to examine more closely the structure of judgmental form, what he called its "logic" *(ronri)*. The fundamental insight he explored was that any judgment necessarily arises out of a particular contextual field or place, its *basho*. The purpose of this second phase in Nishida's thought was to explain the logic of these fields *(basho no ronri)*. One way this system came to be formulated was in terms of the three *basho* of being, relative nothingness, and absolute nothingness. Roughly speaking, these corresponded to the judgmental fields of empiricism, idealism, and what he called the field of the "acting intuition" *(kōiteki chokkan)*.

Nishida's "logic of *basho*" is a complex system always in flux and under revision. Still, it represents Nishida's most integrated and systematic attempt to deal with the issues of fact and value. To see the overall structure of Nishida's logic of *basho,* we can consider first a simple empirical judgment, for example, "this table is brown." Scientific statements are generally of this form. They seem to express pure objectivity; the observer is so neutralized that it does not even enter into the judgment *per se.* They are statements about what is, statements about being (hence, the nomenclature *"basho* of being").

Yet, Nishida asked, in what contextual field *(basho)* is such an objective judgment made? Where does one stand in making such a judgment about being? Nishida argued that such a judgment actually also makes judgments about our own consciousness. To neutralize the role of the observer, as ordinary empirical judgments do, is to say something about the observer—its role can be neutralized and ignored. This is an odd thing to say, however, since the larger contextual field of the judgment "the table is brown" is something more like "I see a brown table and since what I see is real and external to my self, I can delete any reference to the self." So, Nishida maintains, the field or place of empirical judgments is really within the encompassing field of judgments about self-consciousness. Empiricism is actually dependent on, stands within, a field of judgments about self. Since empirical judgments, as empirical judgments, ignore the being of the self, treat it as a nothing, this encompassing *basho* can be called the *basho* of relative nothingness." The self is, relative to empirical judgments, treated as a nothing. Of course, from the standpoint of the *basho* of relative nothingness however, the self is very much something, the very thing empiricism assumes yet ignores. This insight, when taken literally, becomes the basis for idealism, theories which maintain all knowledge is based in the mind.

But Nishida was no idealist either. He criticized idealists (including Kant, Hegel, and Husserl) for not recognizing the true character of the *basho* within which their theories were formulated. The mistake of the idealists, according to Nishida, is that they think of the self as a something, either a substance or a transcendental ego. The "I" that is in the previously stated judgment "I see a brown table and . . ." is not an agent, but an action, what Nishida called the "acting intuition." So the *basho* of idealism which sees the self as both subject and object is itself encompassed by a third *basho* the contextual field of "absolute nothingness." The acting intuition is both an active involvement in the world and an intuitive reception of information about that world. It is a process, not a thing, so it can never be either the subject or object of itself. It can never be the gist of judgment—it is absolutely a nothing when it comes to any judgment. Hence, it is called "absolute nothingness."

The acting-intuiting process (the absolute nothingness) is, therefore, the true basis of judgments about both fact and value. On the surface level, fact is, as it were, the intuiting side and value the acting side. Yet, one never exists without the other. The two are moments or profiles of a single process. The facts we discover are influenced by what we value and what we value is influenced by what we discover. Thus, as Yuasa Yasuo has explained in his analysis of Nishida in his book *The Body: Toward an Eastern Mind-Body Theory,* the intuition is also active (informed by value) and the acting is also passive (as response to data received). The two poles of the process are totally inseparable.

How does Nishida respond, then, to the cultural question of Japanese values and Western science? Since the self is, as the Buddhists have noted for 2,500 years, not a thing but a process, we must look at how that process actually functions. It is at once a passive reception and active valuational affirmation, at once an active discovery and a passive absorption of cultural forms. In short, there is no separation of *is* and *ought:* that bifurcation arises from being stuck in one place, in one *basho* (either the idealist or the empiricist), without knowing their common ground as acting intuition, the absolute nothingness. So for Nishida, religion informs science and vice versa; values are objectively discovered and subjectively enacted; knowledge and morality are intimately intertwined. The implications of this position is the theme of the latter part of this book.

This brings us to my final observation. What is Carter's question and why should he find Nishida so provocative in his search for the answer? Many issues Nishida faced in Japan in his time have become, in a different way, issues for us in our time. We are finally feeling the culturally shattering implications of bifurcating fact and value. We live in the age of nuclear armament, genetic engineering, ecological destruction, medical technology, and even computer stock-portfolio management. Technology has vastly enlarged the horizons of what is, or at least, what could be. Yet, we are increasingly sensitive that some of what is ought not to be, some of what could be should not be. In the past couple of decades, the primary repositories of cultural values—morality, religion, and art—have taken a beating and it seems we must somehow recapture some of what we have lost.

But the reactionary attempt to reaffirm the old values exactly as before will not do, any more than early twentieth century Japan could have retreated to an earlier age. We cannot pound in the wedge further that separates *is* and *ought,* science and value. Nor do we need a religious pseudoscience to oppose actual science, or an outdated morality that breeds only intolerance. Rather, we must pull out the wedge between *is* and *ought,* rediscovering in ourselves a mode of affirmation that unifies rather than divides.

I think that is what Carter admires in Nishida's philosophy. From this point, I will let Carter speak for himself. Let us enter the conversation between this late twentieth-century Canadian and an early twentieth-century Japanese. Let us see what this conversation between East and West can teach us about ourselves—what is and what ought to be.

Thomas Kasulis
Professor of Comparative Studies
The Ohio State University

ACKNOWLEDGMENTS

Assistance in finding my way through the complexities of the Japanese language and culture, and of the vast expanse of distinct types of Buddhist thought, requires a special expression of thanks to Professor Thomas Kasulis of The Ohio State University, whose painstaking reading of this manuscript yielded invaluable suggestions for improvement. Professor Jan Van Bragt of the Nanzan Institute for Religion and Culture, in Nagoya, Japan, and Professor David A. Dilworth of the State University of New York at Stony Brook also gave freely of their time, made helpful suggestions, and provided access to various unpublished manuscripts of importance. Tomio Nitto, Toronto artist and friend, undertook a distinctive and modern rendering of the "ten ox-herding pictures" which appear in this volume for the first time. In Zen fashion, they have the quality of direct communication. Paul Suttie, a philosophy major at Trent University, spent untold hours laboring over an index that he wished to be both thorough and useful for future Nishida enthusiasts. Tom Hino, a former student, translated a selection of Nishida's writings that I found essential to my understanding of Nishida the scholar, in communication with friends and colleagues over the precise meaning of terms. Marg Tully, Secretary to Peter Robinson College, Trent University, processed and re-processed the manuscript for this book more times than either of us cares to remember. And finally, to Marjorie Haughn, whose editorial advice was both painstaking and invaluable, and who allowed me to talk out some of the more esoteric notions of Nishidan thought, while calmly remaining "post-modern" in disallowing "premature closure," I am grateful both for the sounding board provided, and for the love and support.

To all those mentioned, and to the others not named, but who engaged me in and out of class on relevant issues in East Asian Philosophy 282 at Trent University over the years, I extend my heartfelt thanks. None of them, named or unnamed, are responsible for any deficiencies, shortcomings, or errors in interpretation which appear in these pages. Indeed, not all of them will agree with my conclusions. Whatever criticism is elicited by the publication of this endeavor is mine, while any praise will have to be shared.

Financial assistance for the research for this study has come from several quarters; the Trent University Research and Travel Grants Committees have provided funds for the preparation of this manuscript, for consultations with scholars in the field, and for travel assistance while in Japan, and to allow me to visit Japan again as part of a research stay in Korea. A Social Sciences and Humanities Research Council Research Fellowship provided an extended period of research in Japan in 1978. Nishitani Keiji, Abe Masao, Noda Matao, Bandō Shōjun, Nakamura Hajime, and Ohe Seizo, and many other typically busy Japanese scholars took whatever time I needed to examine Nishida's perspective with me.

I have drawn on material, previously published, in chapter 4. "The Nothingness Beyond God" first appeared in *The Eastern Buddhist*, vol. 18, no. 1 (Spring 1985), pp. 120-130, and again in *Dialogue and Alliance*, vol. 1, no. 3 (Fall 1987), pp. 70-76. Grateful acknowledgment is made for permission to draw on that article.

INTRODUCTION

In the time of Plato and Aristotle and even before, the Greek verb *eisagō* carried the meaning "to import new, strange, or foreign ideas." Such introductions (*eisagōgai*) provided *entry* into hitherto often inaccessible fields of inquiry. It is in this sense of "introduction"—the English rendering of *eisagōgē*—that I offer this study.

Nishida Kitarō achieved a rare blending of his own Japanese heritage, and an incredible sensitivity to and understanding of a wide spectrum of Western philosophic and religious traditions. In an age such as our own with hermeneutic interest now everywhere apparent, and with deconstruction an ever-present reminder that no interpretation is an "objective," "right," or "final" one, what is vital in encountering a foreign understanding of our own intellectual texts is the discovery of the extent and the range of our own assumptions exposed en route. It is not to be assumed that all readings are equal, even given the postmodernist radical critique of objectivity, but rather that every major and systematic reading of a text aims to establish its own text as superior. Given the perspective or standpoint of the new reader, what he or she says does rule, and except for occasional slips into inconsistency, or factual inadequacy, must be taken as a pronouncement of a self-consistent philosophic reading. To criticize this new reading, or any other, requires that one present one's own text as the norm, and it, in turn, must be judged as adequate or acceptable, or not, by other readers having their own texts. On this view—which announces my text with its implied array of assumptions—one cannot show another's text to be "wrong," but only inconsistent, not sufficiently developed (fragmentary), factually inadequate, or one can simply be unwilling or unable to accept ingredients in another's system of thought. Walter Watson refers to the entire array of foundational presuppositions as "archic variables," and those specific "values assumed in a particular text are the *archic elements* of that text."[1] There is a plurality of great texts, and each is more or less complete in its archic foundations.

Great texts are, by and large, systematically developed and, therefore, whole as perspectives. As such, they are self-legislating. It is important to get inside the point of view being investigated, for otherwise, one would be guilty of distorting the text by unsympathetically imposing one's own archic elements on the text in question. At the same time, it is well to be aware that one can never be sure that one's sympathetic reading is not just another imposition that distorts. One does one's best, and the public forum comes to the interpreter's aid in the neverending attempt to grasp the system and import of a text.

The interpretation of Nishida's lifelong text which follows is necessarily partial and selective. It does not pretend to survey the subtle and not so subtle evolution of his thought with the corresponding alterations in linguistic expression. Instead, it dwells on Nishida's complex theory of universals, if only because it helps to lay bare the logical foundations of his work. This focus clearly appears about 1926, together with his introduction of the concept *basho* (nothingness as field, place, or *topos* as borrowed from Plato's *Timaeus*). Taking these elements together, the *logic of basho* was formed. With the completed translation of Nishida's final essay, "The Logic of the Place Nothingness and the Religious Worldview," only completed in 1945, and Professor Dilworth's translations of six of the essays in *Philosophical Essays*, also first published in 1945, the logic of *basho* is now accessible to the English reader, providing Nishida's final text. Nishida surveys his life-text, and attempts to make clear what he had been intending throughout. One can read his earlier account of "pure experience" as a constant that was transformed by the logic of *basho* such that any of the nine *bashos* (described below) take on the transparency of nothingness which characterizes pure experience.

While my concentration is on the logical foundations and archic elements and concepts as a strategy aiming at a hermeneutical transparency that will allow Nishida to be understood faithfully, the reader of my text will already be acutely aware of the complexity of Nishida's philosophizing, the vagaries of translation, and the added difficulty of interpreting a thinker who straddles the major literature of both the West and the Far East. Indeed, this fact may make him more of a bona fide world philosopher than his esoteric Japanese heritage may suggest. It is true that Nishida is Japan's outstanding modern philosopher, and he may be as great a philosopher as Japan has ever produced. Dōgen, too, stands high, but as a twelfth and thirteenth century thinker he was obviously less preoccupied with what Western philosophizing considers central to its work.[2] Nishida philosophized by taking seriously the range of problems encountered within the Western philosophical tradition. As such, Nishida was adept in Western philosophy's terms, and well versed in the philosophical literature of the West. At the time that he wrote, nothing could have been less Japanese than to focus upon the problems, concepts, and methodologies of Western thinkers. To be sure, his aim was to understand his own cultural influences as dissected by previous and current philosophizing in the Western world. What distinguished him, however, was his passion for rendering Buddhist paradoxical utterance, or the Zen experience of immediacy, understandable in the several "languages" of Western philosophy. He did not merely recognize the paradoxicality of Buddhist utterance: he attempted to elucidate its logical structure in a way that would contrast it with the logical strategies and regularities of Aristotle, Kant, or Hegel. To say that Nishida was the exemplar of Japanese philosophy, then, would be like claiming that Santayana exemplified America, or G.E. Moore, England. The fact is that there are many traditions of philosophizing in any cultural tradition and language, as the sweep of thought from Meister Eckhart, to Kant, Hegel, and Nietzsche in Germany makes abundantly clear. Nishida, like Santayana and Kant, was deeply influenced by the problems, insights, texts, and forms of expression of his indigenous cultural heritage. His true text was, however, his own, and its sources were, in fact, more heavily Western than Eastern, if only because his project was to understand his perspective in Western philosophical terms. His work is as much of world status, and of world significance, as is the sweep of minor-to-major thinkers regularly studied in Western philosophy. Nishida's background is Japanese, but his foreground is the struggle towards philosophical understanding of a kind that would be recognized as universally significant because of the nature of the problems raised, and the way he came to deal with them. Nishida was, first and foremost, a practicing philosopher.

The texts of Nishida with which I must work are provided in English translations. My Japanese is limited, and it will be for those more skilled to decide whether I have been led astray by a nuance missed or misdirected. Furthermore, as Martin Heidegger ponders in "A Dialogue on Language between a Japanese and an Inquirer," in *On the Way to Language*, it may be that we Europeans "dwell in an entirely different house [of Being, i.e., language system] than East Asian man."[3] He further warns that dialogue from "house to house remains nearly impossible" because it is difficult in the extreme to put one's own house or language perspective at risk such that one could enter a foreign house and begin to see from that perspective.[4] It is my aim to try to glimpse something of another culture's perspective in this study, and to do so by putting at risk as many of my own assumptions as I can. Yet, it will be only those assumptions that I come to recognize as assumptions that will be carefully watched. The others, so much a part of my way of being in and seeing the world as I do, will need to be spotted by others and called to my attention. Interpretation *and* translation alike suffer the same possibility of distortion and deep cultural bias.

The reader will form his/her opinion as to the success of Nishida's project, but it will be *my* project to show sympathetically that he reached remarkable insights, without parochial claims of final truth. Indeed, I am not a believer in the philosophical position that assumes that philosophy can "settle" philosophical issues in anything like a conclusive manner. Rather, my text is pluralistic in recognizing that *major* systematic thinking has a plurality of forms, and arrives at differing conclusions. One can much more easily distinguish inferior from superior thinking by noting fragmentary, unsystematic, or narrow content. Even these values are imposed by me, of course, and completeness would require that I make a case for accepting the holistic over the fragmentary, for example. While not pretending that this would be easy or even conclusive, I do assume that most readers have already decided in favor of these rock-bottom assumptions of systematic, linguistically univocal, and logically coherent pronouncements about a whole subject.

We must be prepared to *deconstruct* such constructions, our own post-modern thinkers warn us, but not in order to render us hopelessly catatonic. The aim of deconstruction is to prevent premature closure by assuming that a perspective is objective, final, or intrinsically superior to all others. In my terms, all positions are *myopic*. Myopia, or nearsightedness results from the imperfect curve of the eye, causing parallel rays to come to focus in front of the retina, rather than on it. One's vision is, in such cases, better for near objects than for far—that is, defective with respect to objects at a distance. A myopic intellect is one narrowed to new or conflicting ideas, and able to focus only on that which is at hand, recognizing only the familiar, habitual, or congruent. In rejecting intellectual closedness, I advocate an intellectual myopia that encourages the openness that results from the (for me) liberating recognition that, as humans, we don't know with apodictic certainty. Nishida's life-work is, for me, an ongoing search for better, fuller, deeper understanding. His writings challenge many firmly held and unquestioned assumptions, and his various critiques serve as occasions for our own reexamination of strongly held principles and presumptions. Recognition of one's myopia is inevitably a prod to critical reflection and revaluation.

Nishida's life-text is his "whole story" of metaphysical/logical/psychological/ethical/religious assumptions which together form an entire and internally consistent perspective. It is normative for the one who holds it, and powerful in its work of systematic integration. Since the same can be said for Plato, Aristotle, Kant, Hegel, and Wittgenstein, however, the historian of philosophy must take a more dispassionate stance with regard to any one perspective. The actual lifeblood of philosophy is the problem cluster which a philosopher or philosophic tradition inherits or encounters, along with the response worked out in an attempt to settle the problems, or at least come to grips with them. For example, to say that Plato held a view called the "theory of forms" is by itself only marginally informative. To understand that he maintained such a theory because, as he saw it, it would otherwise be impossible to show that knowledge of any kind was achievable, is informative. More important still is his own recognition that the theory of forms itself was fraught with difficulties, ambiguities, and possible inconsistencies, and that there remained a vast darkness that the theory was unable to illuminate.[5] This is philosophic humility in action, and represents a central aspect of the myopic view. Knowledge, or even "wisdom," to a myopist, is not taken as final, ultimately revelatory, or sacrosanct, but as a perspectival achievement of the first rank, a set of well-honed lenses to see through and possibly to reject as inadequate for one's own tasks. It is such active and continuing response to one's initial viewpoint, or to someone else's response to it, that keeps alive that original creativity that fostered it in the first place. An idea can only remain alive if it elicits a response. If it is passively received, it is already a dead issue. The myopic perspective itself is but one perspective, of course, and it may be that the reader will wish to question my understanding of what philosophizing is, or ought to be. A dialogue between us might resolve the issue between us, or it might simply make clear our basic disagreement.

This introduction to Nishida's thought is a substitute for such a dialogue, and should be seen as an opening statement of my approach in the pages of interpretation which follow. I write not as an advocate, but as a sympathetic philosophic unraveler of texts, who wishes to see as Nishida saw, at least to the limited extent that that is possible. The reader will, if the work is at all an aid, engage in dialogue with Nishida, and occasionally with me, about the adequacy, or bias, or manner of expression of an idea or claim. If this happens, then I shall be encouraged that philosophic interaction and reaction is occurring, with Nishida's provocative perspective as its occasion and focus. Interaction and reaction impel the trajectory of this work, not uncritical advocacy anywhere along the line. Myopic understanding warns that I will inevitably fail in this task, but I trust that there will be successes along the way as well. Be that as it may, the encounter with a major philosophical figure from an exotically different cultural background than those of the West ought to do much to make us aware of a range of assumptions which we have long since taken for granted. Whatever our reaction to Nishida's claims, his critique of our heritage should at least open to us a vision of several new "lines of flight" to be fruitfully undertaken.[6]

ONE

Pure Experience

A Study of Good is Nishida's first book, and the central notion of that work is "pure experience." Borrowing the term from William James, Nishida explains that the qualifier "pure" is "used to signify a condition of true experience itself without the addition of the least thought or reflection."[1] It is experience prior to judgment of any kind; it is direct experience with nothing added. And such direct awareness is prior to any distinguishing of subjective and objective strands in experience:

> When one experiences directly one's conscious state there is as yet neither subject nor object, and knowledge and its object are completely united. This is the purest form of experience.... True, pure experience can exist only in present consciousness of events as they are without attaching any meaning to them at all.[2]

The focus of pure experience is always in the present, in the now as "a certain continuation of time."[3] It is not a single, atomic sense awareness in a single, atomic instant of time, but an interval of immediacy, likely viewed as a manifold to the later analyzing mind, yet without there being "the slightest crack wherein thought can enter."[4] The "now" of immediacy is always a "here" as well. Joseph Flay, in his scrutiny of James's notion of pure experience, has argued that experience implies "some privileged place from which to determine what is temporally now or then and what is spatially here or there."[5] Within any system of objective coordinates there is no privileged place or time. An event may be "prior" to one event and "subsequent" to another; a specific location may be south of Canada, but north of Puerto Rico. But each person, as a subjective awareness, "is a privileged center of indexicality."[6] Indeed,

... there is a complete invariance of place in the case of each experiencing person. In other words, whatever I am doing, in whatever space (wherever) and at whatever time (whenever), it is always "here and now."[7]

The self, as the place where experience arises, is always here and now. Flay's language is striking in that it anticipates Nishida's logic of place, while itself being grounded in James's "pure experience":

> . . . *there is an absolute invariance of place in the case of each* self. In other words, whatever I am doing, in whatever space and at whatever time, it is always here and now.
>
> *It is in this sense that the self is place* and that what is "in" my experience is experienced as belonging uniquely to me and as having continuity.... Here and now is primordially always the place *in which I am*, and it is the place *in which* I am derivatively from the pure, primordial place *which I am*.[8]

It is important to remember that James called himself a "radical" empiricist in order to call attention to the fact that he wished to base his philosophy on the foundational raw material of experience as given. He writes, "The postulate is that the only things that shall be debatable among philosophers shall be things definable in terms drawn from experience."[9] For our purposes, what is given in experience is the flux of time, location, things and their properties, *and* "a kind of eternity and omnipresence to the self as place."[10] While all things change in a changing, flowing time, one also experiences "that the self is permanent in the sense of preserving identity over time and space *and* that the self is ephemeral in the sense of changing identity

> over time and space—it is rooted in the double sense of place which constitutes experience. It is in reality not puzzle, but simply a fact, an important characteristic, an identifying ambiguity or contradiction which must be accepted as the truth about the self.[11]

It would be pressing too hard, perhaps, to stress the *identity of contradictoriness* by which Flay identifies the essential features of self, but it will do no harm to anticipate by remarking that Nishida would welcome such an analysis as *prima facie* correct precisely because the self-contradictoriness is recognized as constituent of the self-as-experienced. Nishida himself confirms that "All unity of consciousness transcends change and must be clearly unchanging; and change comes to arise from this, i.e., it is that which moves and does not move."[12]

Nishida describes pure experience as a unity of experience, with no opposing or complementary polarities present.[13] All things are unified by/in the "true self," which is not something apart from this unification, but which is nothing more than this unification: "The self does not exist apart from this."[14] Such a functional account of the self would likely have pleased William James, who similarly held that the self-as-consciousness is but a function, rather than a thing: "Consciousness is at all times primarily a selecting agency."[15] But Nishida refers to this unitive functionality as an *intuition*, and then goes on to add that authentic religious enlightenment "is the apprehension of that profound unity which lies at the foundation of intelligence and the will, namely a kind of intellectual intuition, a deep grasp of life."[16] He concludes the chapter on pure experience by remarking that "at the root of learning and morality there must be religion, for both of these are constructed according to it."[17] While James was profoundly interested in the phenomena of religiosity as experience, it is easy to discern a more diaphanous perspective in Nishida's philosophy. His philosophy begins and ends as a religious philosophy, whereas James is the psychologist and epistemologist who includes religious experience within his research domain.

ONE PRIMAL STUFF

In what is perhaps the only article in English to seriously compare Nishida's appropriation of James's "pure experience" to James's own account, David Dilworth urges that Nishida sought "a richer unity behind the thinner and more abstract editions of perception and thought," whereas James had no such purpose, but merely sought to guarantee the reality of concrete perceptual and intellectual contents themselves."[18] These contents were "plural," and included transitive relations in his account of the directly experienced. In fact, I think it can be shown that James, with Nishida, exhibited both the aim of seeking a richer unity behind experience, language, and conceptual thought, *and* sought to preserve the reality of the concrete within experience. In James's own words,

> My thesis is that if we start with the supposition that there is only one primal stuff or material in the world, a stuff of which everything is composed, and if we call that stuff "pure experience," then knowing can easily be explained as a particular sort of relation towards one another into which portions of pure experience may enter.[19]

Neither consciousness nor matter are ultimate, but both arise out of, or are distinctions makable from within the aboriginal "stuff" of being. Consciousness is but one function of this stuff, and matter is a conscious fixation or an *aspect* of this primal stuff. James also warns, in the same essay, that "there is no *general* stuff of which experience at large is made,"[20] to avoid being mistakenly thought to be positing some metaphysical substratum:

> James's thesis of "one primal stuff or material in the world" is meant as a counter-assertion to those who hold to an aboriginal dualism of consciousness. James is not asserting a metaphysical sub-stratum, but he is denying the subject-object distinction as irreducible. Pure experience is neither monistic nor dualistic, it is undifferentiated.[21]

Reality is "a that, an Absolute, a 'pure' experience on an enormous scale, undifferentiated and undifferentiable into thought and thing."[22] It is precisely this sense of pure experience as undifferentiated, undichotomized, conceptually neutral, ambiguous, and prior to the subject/object distinction that Nishida intended by his unity of the undifferentiated. It is a fact of conscious awareness prior to all cognition and to all physical traits. "It is plain, unqualified actuality, or existence, a simple *that.*"[23]

Thomas R. Maitland, Jr., amplifies the point that for James pure experience is a unity underlying conceptual distinction making:

Another revealing but difficult to understand characteristic of pure experience is its "much at onceness" that transcends all separation. As such it is similar to the impression made on the conscious level if a number of impressions, from any number of sensory sources, fall simultaneously on a mind which had not yet experienced them separately. Such a mind would fuse them into a single undivided object. In this case, and in that of pure experience there is no meaning, only a "big blooming buzzing confusion." But in another sense there is meaning because all there is in each case is pure experience... on the level of pure experience they mean everything they are. On that level things compenetrate each other, are alive and fuse into each other....[24]

On the question of *meaning*, and its relation to pure experience, Nishida contends that when the unity-as-undifferentiated-pure-experience is broken, "i.e., when one enters into relationship with something else, meaning is born, judgment is created."[25] Meaning and judgment are always and necessarily states of disunity. In the state of pure experience, self and other, subject and object, true and false, meaning and the meaningless, "are mutually submerged, and the universe [as unity] is the only reality...."[26]

Building on what has been said thus far about James's notion of pure experience, we are now in a position to show why it does seem evident that he presupposes a "richer unity behind the thinner and more abstract editions of perception and thought." Quite explicitly James maintains that the division of pure experience into consciousness and content "*comes, not by way of subtraction, but by way of addition....*"[27] Edward I. Moore summarizes James's position when he writes,

For James the world consists of a flux of pure experience out of which man—by observation and inspiration—carves isolable chunks to which he gives names. These chunks have no identity in reality as chunks. They are simply artificial cuts out of what is in reality a continuum. Man cuts them out for purposes of thought and purposes of behavior. But the cuts are *his* cuts, not nature's.[28]

In James's own picturesque words,

> Out of this aboriginal sensible muchness attention carves out objects, which conception then names and identifies forever—in the sky "constellations," on the earth "beach," "sea," "cliff," "bushes," "grass." Out of time we cut "days" and "nights," "summers" and "winters." We say *what* each part of the sensible continuum is, and all these abstracted *whats* are concepts.[29]

What was once a unified and undivided whole of experience becomes separated into parts, concepts, relations, according to human needs and purposes. But pure experience is never so divided. It is always and everywhere "the instant field of the present."[30] So it is that we discover that reality and the immediately sensible are one and the same: "Reality is apperception itself."[31] Experience is reality as it presents itself to us. Conception halts the flow of pure experience, isolates one or more aspects of it, abstracts these from the whole for practical purposes, and thereby harnesses reality.[32] These selective abstractions "must never be taken as the full equivalent of reality,"[33] partly because they are partial selections from the whole, and partly because they are static fixations of a reality which is always and everywhere a flux, a changing flow. James presupposes the eternal flux of reality as apprehended in pure experience, much as the typical Buddhist affirms that reality, even the Buddha, is impermanence. James stresses that concepts cannot change, they can only cease to be: "They form an essentially discontinuous system, and translate the process of our perceptual experience, which is naturally a flux into a set of stagnant and petrified terms."[34]

In one sense, conception adds to reality as perceived, for concepts "bring new values into our perceptual life,"[35] e.g., sublimity, power, admiration. Nevertheless, the "shortcomings" of the "conceptual transformation" include the rendering of a map "superficial through the abstractness, and false through the discreteness of its elements.... Conceptual knowledge is forever inadequate to the fulness of the reality to be known."[36] Concepts are just "secondary formations, inadequate, and only ministerial."[37] Still, concepts are as real as perceptual experience, but "the 'eternal' kind of being which they enjoy is inferior to the temporal kind, because it is so static and schematic and lacks so many characteristics which temporal reality possesses."[38] Thus James concludes that "the deeper features of reality are found only in perceptual experience."[39]

> Here alone do we acquaint ourselves with continuity, or the immersion of one thing in another, here alone with self, with substance, with qualities, with activity in its various modes, with time, with cause, with change, with novelty, with tendency, and with freedom. Against all such features of reality the method of conceptual translation, when candidly and critically followed out, can only raise its *non possumus*, and brand them as unreal or absurd.[40]

Still, James warns that as finite beings, we are able to encompass but a few passing moments of pure experience. But in a footnote he adds that in "'mystical' ways, he may extend his vision to an even wider perceptual panorama than that usually open to the scientific mind."[41] And while Nishida resists the "mystical" label, he does assume that such extensions of vision are readily open to us, and that it is in the religious life that they are most distinctively found.

James and Nishida appear to share the insight that the rational or transcendental attempts, in the history of philosophical thought, to understand or grasp reality-as-experience in conceptual and linguistic systems, "draws the dynamic continuity out of nature as you draw the thread out of a string of beads."[42] In words that would gain immediate endorsement from Nishida, James writes that if this "continuity and flow mean logical self contradiction, the logic must go."[43]

The human mind draws out of pure experience what it needs, or prefers, to achieve certain practical ends. It does this by making distinctions within the undifferentiated whole of pure experience. Such drawing out, fixing, staying the flow of lived experience, and "holding fast to meanings, has no significance apart from the fact that the conceiver is a creature with a partial purpose and private ends."[44] We are responsible for carving out this partial practical truth from the richer unity behind our pragmatic purposes, concepts, and conscious experiences.

A LIMIT CONCEPT

As soon as we are able to talk about pure experience, to conceptualize and "language" it, it thereby becomes a mixture of perceptual and conceptual awareness. This, of course, leads us to more sharply distinguish the conceptual as subjective, and the perceptual as objective. Yet, the worrisome question remains: Can we, in fact, speak philosophically meaningfully about non-experiential experience? "If pure experience is never pure as experienced, then in what sense can it be spoken of meaningfully at all?"[45] Siegfried answers this question by taking pure experience to be itself a *posited* limit concept "which enables James to dethrone dualism as the primordial beginning of all experience."[46] Ontological dualism is perhaps the key assumption that Zen Buddhists seek to question and undermine in the attempt to push back behind conceptualization and thought to the immediately given. "This temptingly plausible dualistic explanation can be overcome by hypothesizing that the primary reality is of a neutral nature and can be designated by an ambiguous name like 'phenomenon' or 'datum'."[47] It is interesting to note how often the term "field" is used in Jamesian interpretation, for Nishida, too, writes of the field of the immediate:

> Pure experience can be defined as the instant field of the present, the immediate flux of life before categorization. Its purity is a relative term, denoting the proportion of unverbalized absorption in the present sensation.[48]

Pure experience is an heuristic limiting concept for James, whereas it appears to be an actual and direct experience for Nishida. Indeed, a culture of meditation, of silence and emptiness would not find pure experience a speculative fact, but an original experience out of which conceptual experience is carved. As Nishida observes, "that within meaning or judgment is a part which has been abstracted from the original experience, and in its content it is, on the contrary, a poorer thing than the original experience."[49] Yet it is not to be concluded so quickly that James, unlike Nishida, was unable to find a direct experience of pure experience. He does not state that it is not experienced, but only that it is not conceptually graspable and communicable, for to do so is already to break it up into categories. Instead, as Siegfried remarks, it is "the immediate flux of life which furnishes the raw material to later reflection."[50] Nevertheless, James does hedge his bet in concluding that

> only new-born babes, or men in semi-coma from sleep, drugs, illnesses, or blows, may be assumed to have an experience pure in the literal sense of a *that* which is not yet any definite what....[51]

Yet, even though James assumes that totally pure experience is rare, and at that available only to those whose intellectual activity is reduced or damaged, he also states that "namelessness is compatible with experience," and in his study of religious experience he lists ineffability as one of the characteristics of mystical experience.[52] Furthermore, in his *The Varieties of Religious Experience*, he clearly leaves open the door for pure experience to enter in, warning that

> ... our normal waking consciousness, rational consciousness as we call it, is but one special type of consciousness, whilst all about it, parted from it by the filmiest of screens, there lie potential forms of consciousness entirely different.... No account of the universe in its totality can be final which leaves these other forms of consciousness quite disregarded.[53]

Then, as if speaking directly to our point, he reflects autobiographically that,

> Looking back on my own experiences [with nitrous oxide], they all converge towards a kind of insight to which I cannot help ascribing some metaphysical significance. The keynote of it is invariably a reconciliation. It is as if the opposites of the world, whose contradictoriness and conflict make all our difficulties and troubles, were melted into unity.[54]

A NORMATIVELY "RICHEST" EXPERIENCE

It may well be that the greatest difference between James and Nishida is what Dilworth correctly describes as "the concept of a 'richest' experience in Nishida's mind which might best be understood in terms of the Zen notions of 'emptiness' or 'nothingness'."[55] Nishida began *A Study of Good* with the claim that to experience means to know events precisely as they are."[56] Reality, as it is in itself, can be directly apprehended, and without distortion, so long as the experiencer keeps out of the way, and passively *mirrors* reality. James is an advocate of the active mind, and in addition to the inclusion of the activities of the mind in virtually all "somewhat" pure experience, he warns that "all present beliefs are subject to revision in the light of future experiences,"[57] including pure experience, precisely because it is never completely pure. Inescapably, experience is filtered through the categories of intellection and distinction. Still, it is the uncut "big blooming buzzing confusion" which is the methodological whole out of which the parts are cut.

James was emphatic in pointing out that relations among things in experience are "just as much matters of direct particular experience, neither more so nor less so, than the things themselves."[58] We experience the "and" of two things in relation, and the "if" of uncertainty (or potential sequence as in "if-then"), just as much as we do the substantive matters being related. In short, "the relations that connect experiences must themselves be experienced relations, and any kind of relation experienced must be accounted as 'real' as anything else in the system."[59] As immediately apprehended, experience is not a dualism composed of thought and thing, subjective and objective elements, but is undifferentiated, as we have seen. Even in his early *Principles of Psychology*, James compares the flow or stream of conscious awareness (stream of thought; stream of consciousness) to the pattern or flight of a bird. "Like a bird's life, it seems to be made of an alternation of flights and perchings."[60] The "resting-places" are the "sensorial imaginations," arresting the flow-of-flight and providing images which are capable of being held before the mind indefinitely, and contemplated without change occurring. The flow-of-flight is filled with "thoughts of relations" which apply between the fixed matters for contemplation. We can experience "if," "but," and "by" as readily as "blue" or "cold"[61] But we are habituated, for whatever reason, to "pay attention to, or focus on ('perch on'), the substantive parts."[62] We select from the undifferentiated broth of experience, what we wish to attend to, and "actually *ignore* most of the [rest of the] things before us."[63] Perchings and flight together add up to our awareness of the whole life-activity of our own life as, metaphorically, a bird. Perception and transitive relations together add up to our life of experience. And both are cut out of the infinitely rich flow called pure experience. Substantive "things" and their relations are not ultimately different, but arise from the same aboriginal source. "Mental content and object" are identical,[64] simply different aspects abstracted out of pure experience for practical purposes. "Subject" and "object" denote different aspects of the same primal flow. The distinction is real enough, for functional purposes, but not ultimate.

Nishida, too, stresses that at the background of any judgment "there is always an event of pure experience."[65] Indeed, pure experience is proposed to rest behind all experience, even the experience of thinking. Relations, thought, willing, feeling are all aspects of direct experience and dimensions of pure experience. Nishida concludes that, "Pure experience and thought are basically the same event seen from different points of view."[66] Perception, intelligence, and will are all processes of our own self-expression and realization, directly experienced. In fact, "the distinction between the intelligence and the will [or either from perception] arises when subjectivity and objectivity are separated and when one loses the unifying state of pure experience."[67] But direct apprehension of the "source," the aboriginal flow, is not simply available to babies and men in sleep-coma, nor is it a limiting concept with heuristic value only; as it was for James. Rather it is itself a directly experienced recognition of this very (pre-all-distinctions) oneness, an *intellectual* perception, "but in content it is infinitely richer and more profound."[68] By describing it as akin to intellectual intuition, differing only in richness of experienced content, Nishida apparently breaks with James, who urged that all direct experience was already post pure experience, and therefore already contained distinctions. Nishida seemingly parts with James's radical empiricism when he states that

If our consciousness were merely a thing of sensory characteristics, it would probably stop at a state of ordinary, intellectually perceived intuition, but an ideal spirit demands infinite unity, and this unity is given in the form of so-called intellectual intuition. Intellectual intuition, like intellectual perception, is the most unified state of the consciousness.[69]

Nishida seemingly parts with James on this issue, for Nishida's stress on intellectual intuition and ideal spirit seems to move away from James's emphasis on experience. It is a movement toward a unified awareness as a contemplative-like state, which yet is supremely active. In this state of pure and immediate experience, such activities as intellection, forming relations, perception, feeling, and willing are not distinct and separate. Indeed, Nishida even writes of "intellectual perception" in order to emphasize the fact that the usual boundaries are inadequate.[70] He sums up by articulating clearly that "true intellectual intuition is the unifying activity itself in pure experience; it is the grasping of life...."[71] There is only one world, only experience flowing. To be sure, "intellectual intuition" sounds as though it refers to a subjective state of human rational or intellectual activity,

but actually it is a state which has transcended subject and object, and one rather can say that the opposition of subject and object is established by this unity, and such things as inspired art will attain this realm. Also intellectual intuition does not refer to the direct perception of an abstract generality separated from actuality.[72]

Generality and individuality both are moments within pure experience, as are subject and object. All distinctions rest in pure experience, as perchings (distinctions) in the course of a line of flight. Thought itself is a system, "and at the base of a system there must be an intuition of unity."[73] It follows that the ground of all systems and of all unities is pure experience. The true self is precisely this unifying intuition.[74] Intuition transcends the will, intelligence (thought), emotion, perception—but is the basis of them all. Nishida calls this awareness "religious," and defines it as "the apprehension of that profound unity which lies at the foundation of intelligence and the will, namely a kind of intellectual intuition, a deep grasp of life."[75] Logic is incapable of going "towards it," nor can human desire "move it."[76] It must be present in all religion. The concluding section of the chapter on "pure experience" also points ahead to the "final essay," finished just days before his death, and with which the second half of the present study is concerned. Nishida places religion at the foundation of morality, as we shall see:

> At the root of learning and morality there must be religion, for both of these are constructed according to it.[77]

What happens to most of us, in our intellectual journey towards understanding, is that we lose touch with our connectedness with the unity given in pure experience, and retreat into the defined and purposeful realm of the intellect alone. In James's words:

> The intellectual life of man consists almost wholly in his substitution of a conceptual order in which his experience originally courses.

Nishida would no doubt agree. For Nishida, to be aware of pure experience is not to deny conception and the various systematizations resulting from thinking, but to ground them all in the original undifferentiated flow of pure flight. They are all perchings, and the only real error we make is to focus so fully on the perchings—the stable, fixed resting places—that we forget altogether how to fly. To keep both perspectives alive in a single consciousness, is to understand the true depths of the conscious self, for we are both capable of self awareness of ourselves as distinct from the whole, and aware of the whole as ourselves. We, too, are but temporary perchings in the cosmic flight, the cosmic flow of life.

INTELLECTUAL INTUITION

Both William James and Nishida reject dualistic consciousness as either necessary or ultimate. Pure experience is undifferentiated, and as such is beyond all distinctions, including monism and dualism. Simply, no distinctions apply, for pure experience is beyond any and all distinctions, of whatever kind. The self is the place where experience occurs, and is the theater for both pure and ordinary experience.

Pure experience is carved up, according to our practical needs and purposes, in the myriad ways that constitute ordinary distinction-filled experience, but we should not hold fast to these divisions and distinctions, for they are at best partial glimpses, and at worst distortions of the "aboriginal sensible muchness." Reality presents itself to us as a flow, and as a seamless web, which we then divide up in accordance with whatever principles of focus are important to us. We form concepts of such fixed focuses, and these perchings are not unreal, but proper portions apportioned from the original wholeness.

While James is unsure whether we actually ever have "pure" experience, Nishida takes it as given that we do, and that analysis will reveal that all distinctions arise out of an original distinctionlessness. "Intellectual intuition" for Nishida is a name given to our ability to apprehend the original "unity," this aboriginal flow of life. James wonders whether we can ever have pure experience as normal adults whose intellectual activity is laminated to experience of whatever kind, while Nishida begins with the assumption that both logically and experientially, pure experience lies behind all possible and actual distinctions. It may be that a tradition of analysis and verbalization finds it less obvious that preconceptional and prelinguistic awareness is possible, and that a tradition of meditative silence, and skepticism with respect to the adequacy of language, would find the preconceptual and prelinguistic necessary to a correct understanding of any and all discursive activities.

Intellectual intuition exposes the unity of experience-as-lived, and such unity is the ground of religious awareness that sees the oneness of all things as given in pure experience. Reality, in its ultimate form as pure experience, is undifferentiated. All partial awareness, revealed via the separating out of distinctions of any kind, is less ultimate and less real. Distinctions are empty of ultimate reality precisely because they are distinctions. Even the designation "oneness" or "unity" is but a metaphor, for pure experience arises even before, and is always already there. It is, therefore, apart from even such distinctions as these. Thus, to speak of it at all is already to have lost it, to have distorted it. It is, quite naturally, beyond words and ineffable, because it is that, before words, out of which word references are cut.

TWO

The Logic of Basho

Nishida's philosophy culminates in an analysis of religious experience, yet the path to this finale leads from logic and epistemology, through metaphysics, ontology, value theory, and ethics. In the grand style of philosophy, he offers a comprehensive vision that, nonetheless, is meticulous in its detailed analysis of the foundations of system. Thoroughly studied in Western philosophical and much theological scholarship—primarily in the original languages—he sought to re-think the traditions of the West in order to account for the perspectival differences of the East. Nishida remained, to the end, unconvinced that there was a barrier between philosophers, Western or Eastern, that philosophy itself could not penetrate. His method was not to throw out the achievements of previous thinkers, but rather to accept them as profound expressions of genius which, nevertheless, either did not push quite far enough, or because of a degree of cultural blindness or bias, moved in directions other than those of the major traditions with which he identified. We might say that it was not that Ptolemy was not a keen thinker and observer, but that he fixated on the assurance that the earth was stationary. The philosophic "assurance" of many in the several Western philosophical traditions has been the desirability of *objectivity,* and the primacy of the *grammatical subject* in logic. Yet the decision as to whether the assurance is justified can only be made as a result of an examination of the several traditions in Western logic and epistemology, and by using the tools of these activities to examine them.

Nishida seeks only to think through the history of the Western intellectual heritage once more in order to see whether his own Buddhist philosophical tradition can find its proper place, or shed light on blind spots in the works of major philosophers of the West.

Remarkably, he assumes that it is the Western philosophical tradition that provides the tools for analyzing and clarifying the central concerns that he gleans from Eastern thought. Insofar as "Logic is the form of our thinking,"[1] we should not be surprised to find that the logical analysis of several central Buddhist philosophical texts will yield a logic peculiar to Buddhist ways of thinking, while perfectly locatable in some of the logic texts of Western philosophers. The differences will not be slight, but they will be capable of being handled via familiar Western philosophical terms and methods. Just as the logics of Kant and Hegel markedly depart from the logic of Aristotle, yet presuppose and arise out of it, so Nishida stands on the heights of the historical sweep of logic and philosophy in order to formulate the "logic of the East." Even partial success in this endeavor has resulted in the building of a conceptual bridge between Eastern and Western thinking. By dissolving the alleged difference between the two, Nishida is able to focus on the range of Western problems of particular interest to the thinkers of several Eastern traditions.

THE HERMENEUTIC PROJECT

A common, but certainly not universal philosophical perspective in the West has been that language is adequate to the task of capturing reality "truthfully" or "objectively." This perspective is a semiotic one, and assumes that signs (words, grammar, logic) are adequate to describe the world, certainly the world of experience, if not reality itself. In general, the traditions of the Far East have from the very beginning viewed this thesis as inadequate, uninteresting, or both. Taoism's warning that those who know don't speak, and that those who speak don't know is given in the very first paragraph of the opening chapter of the *Tao Te Ching*:

> The way that can be spoken of
> Is not the constant way;
> The name that can be named
> Is not the constant name.[2]

Indeed, the ultimate ground or origin of things is, necessarily, "nameless."[3] Similarly, in Japan, as C. A. Moore observes, Zen Buddhism's "anti-intellectualism" is popular "because of its positive attitude toward living naturally rather than intellectualizing life, since such intellectualizing falsifies and distorts life."[4] We have already noted a congruence between James and Nishida on the distortion and impoverishment of pure experience by conceptualization, in chapter 1. Izutsu discusses the Zen dilemma of realizing that language is not adequate to describe reality, and that silence is also inadequate. We need to accept the inadequacy of language, yet continue to employ it with the warning in hand, while remaining silent at appropriate times in order to emphasize that any attempt to name the nameless, or to articulate the non-articulatable, is bound to fail. Nevertheless, if

> we refrain from using language in order to avoid this difficulty, we fall into another pitfall. Certainly, by not using language we could make silence function as a symbol of the non-articulated; but, then, the articulated aspect of that non-articulated will totally be lost sight of. In other words, the non-articulated will be presented as sheer "nothing" in the negative sense of the word, which is exactly the contrary of what Zen holds to be true.[5]

Neither language nor silence can express the real, and so one is pushed beyond *both* language *and* intellectualization. Even the fourth century BC logicians and linguists of ancient China had a brief fling with such a position, but concluded that the fruitfulness of such a thesis was limited.[6] It is not simply that another theory won out (or at least, this is far from the whole story), but that language and logic were *perceived* to be inadequate to describe and to recreate even the most everyday experience. Indeed, the chief results of "The School of Names" was a sophistical play of paradoxes which demonstrated that language was inadequate as an accurate purveyor of even simple experiences. The early Chinese have long been characterized as pragmatists who were keen observers, although often unwilling or unable to ask the "whys" of experience, but instead focused on the "how" of things. This should not be taken to show that philosophy was not occurring there, but rather that the instinctive approach was to shy away from "why" questions, since these questions lead to theory and logic which are inescapably verbal and inevitably yield hopeless paradox. By contrast, "how" questions plunge one back into the richness of experience, i.e., the observation of nature, out of which better answers must come, *even if they are not always systematically verbalizable.* In other words, "how" questions keep us closer to the flow that Nishida and James term "pure experience." Words, acupuncture manuals, the divination of the *I Ching,* "scripture," and guides to rulership—all are taken only as surface pointers which must not be thought to exhaust the depths of the actual experiences encountered. At best, they lead beneath the surface "hows," to the deeper causes and regularities of things and events, which only the keenest and most experienced observer will have noticed. Ironically, a deep "how" functions much like a "why," for it probes beneath the surface of appearances, to deeper and deeper levels of regularity and sequence, cause, and effect. It does so, however, on an experiential and observational basis, and without the assumption that such findings can be directly passed on through language. The model is that of apprenticeship, or even that of monk and master. When it ripens and becomes one of scholar and student in the strict sense of manuals and verbal formulae, it is as though Confucianism, or any other ism, has lost its initial mystery and depth, and has given way to orthodoxy, priest-scholars, and dry-as-dust edification of that which is intrinsically uncodifiable. Still, it has not been less frequent for the Chinese to have forgotten the distinction between sign and the richness of intuition or actual experience, but only that they have had also a living tradition of dissent that has nearly as often gained the right of being termed major opposition. If there is a contrast to be drawn between the over-generalized summary of the strands of schools and thinkers in East and West, it is at most one of degree and not of exclusive difference. Indeed, Plato serves as an example at the beginning of philosophy in the West of one who doubted the adequacy of words to convey "essential reality":

> ...these four [names, descriptions, bodily forms, concepts] do as much to illustrate its essential reality because of the inadequacy of language. Hence no intelligent man will ever be so bold as to put into language these things

which his reason has contemplated, especially not into a form that is unalterable—which must be the case with what is expressed in written symbols.[7]

As well, virtually the entire mystical tradition in the West has doubted the adequacy of language in expressing experiential truth.

Nevertheless, Aristotle, with his scientific requirement of univocal precision, tended to take language as the only real route to knowledge and reality, with practical (especially ethical) knowledge *(phrónēsis)* more likely to be called "wisdom," or "practical wisdom," while epistemological and clearly theoretical matters are associated with *sophía* (knowledge). At least this has been the more or less standard interpretation of Aristotle's *phrónēsis,* as can be seen in Jaeger's claim that Aristotle "deprives it of all theoretical significance, and sharply distinguishes its sphere from those of *sophía* and *nous.*"[8] Recently, however, the distinction of an alleged radical separation between *sophía* and *phrónēsis* has been taken up, and thoroughly revised. Indeed, Father Joseph Owens concludes that Jaeger's exclusive distinction between theoretical and practical knowledge is nowhere to be found in Aristotle: *phrónēsis,* too, is theoretical knowledge, applied to specifically practical ends.[9] Nishida, however, viewed Aristotle as seeking linguistic precision as the exclusive and direct road to knowledge, and neglected to consider Aristotle's practical (acting) knowledge as genuine knowledge even though action-in-history becomes a central emphasis in his later work.

Most scholars, even the physicist and sociologist, work from mathematical signs and documents, and not directly from experience. Observations are to be written down, turned into data, before they can be accurately handled. And there is hardly a whiff of doubt entertained about whether the translation from observation to paper, or to symbols on a blackboard, adequately captures the richness of the immediate. Quite the contrary, the common assumption is that it is not genuine data *until* it is verbalized, organized, or rendered precise through translation to yet more precise formulae. Yet if the assumption was that all such translations are extremely helpful and informative for certain specific purposes, but are incapable of either exhausting the real-in-experience, or unable to grasp the flow of living experience, then our philosophical approach would be radically different.

THE ARISTOTELIAN BACKGROUND

It was Nishida's conviction that by analyzing ordinary experience one will come to see that something more is required than our existing theories provide, if we are truly to account for the rich content of our experiences. It is as though the unrecognized yet profound lies in the depths of the ordinary, awaiting recognition of the fact that without reference to it we cannot give a satisfactory account of what is implied by our ordinary experience. In ferreting out the *implicit,* we must return to experience itself and to our theories of experience, more or less from the beginning. It is Aristotle whom Nishida takes as the substantive beginning of the Western approach to knowledge.

Aristotle's description of knowledge assumes that "the world lends itself to the grasp of language, it has a 'logical' or 'discursive' character, a systematic structure."[10] Knowledge becomes, on this view, a linguistic matter, and not a matter of sensation. To know is to define, and definition occurs insofar as any one of a series of general classifications is applied to the "what" of a thing, thereby rendering the "what" or "this" *(tóde)* of a thing a "this somewhat" *(tóde ti)*. To define, i.e., to know, a thing is to *say* what kind of a thing it is. The series of general classes, or universals, increases in generality "until we reach the last answer possible for that kind of something, and this last answer is the category in question."[11] Even the "what" or "this" of a thing is grasped as one or more attributes belonging necessarily and uniquely to certain kinds of things—i.e., what that thing essentially is. The "being-what-it-is" of anything is what is knowable, both essentially and accidentally, and not the thing itself. This, at least, is the complaint that Nishida and, from a quite different perspective, Hegel, raise in common against Aristotle. The complaint is really twofold: (1) that Aristotle maintains, perhaps even against the evidence from experience, that language and definition are strictly adequate to grasping reality as it is, and (2) that which is knowable in Aristotle's logic is the general or universal, but never the particular. The second issue is the starting point for Nishida, and the language-as-adequate-to-reality issue is not directly attended to until later on.

THE TROUBLE WITH ARISTOTLE

It would be difficult to say with any assurance whether Nishida is correct in his assessment that Aristotle neglects the individual (or particular) in his account of the knowable. In a way, the single thing is the primary thing for Aristotle, for the universal is only seen or known in the particular. Nevertheless, "though the act of sense-perception is of the particular, its content is universal—is man, for example not the man Callias."[12] The individual gets lost in the very process of coming to know what it is. Put in different terms, the modern distinction of being as existence (or identity), and as predication, tends to be absent in Aristotle both because, for him, "essential predications are in a sense identities,"[13] i.e., universals-as-predicates are treated existentially, and because the existential is regularly subordinated to predication. Charles H. Kahn concludes that both Plato and Aristotle

> ...systematically subordinate the notion of existence to predication; and both tend to express the former by means of the latter. In their view *to be* is always to be a definite kind of thing: for a man to exist is to be human and alive, for a dog to exist is to be enjoying a canine life.[14]

Emphasis on predication is tied, continues Kahn, to emphasis on truth and falsity which, for the Greeks, centered on the question, "what must reality be like for knowledge and informative discourse to be possible, and for the statements and beliefs of the form X is Y to be true?"[15] In a real sense, Aristotle ends up conflating the essence of a thing with its individual existence.[16] All of this appeared odd to Nishida who pounced on the apparent emphasis on the universal as the only truly knowable thing, while Aristotle professed the basic reality of the individual.

Aristotle's project was simply quite different from Nishida's. It would have made no sense at all to have asked Aristotle why he did not ask how the individual was knowable *qua* individual, or, if not, why

Aristotle was not bothered by this fact. Indeed, Nishida himself readily asserts that "Aristotle, in opposition to Plato, sought the ground of truth in individual things."[17] Yet, Nishida wants a special sort of attention paid to the individual, for "the true individual must be an acting individual."[18] The extreme limit of a universal is the individual, and, for Aristotle, it is a subject that cannot become predicate. The crux of Nishida's disagreement rests in the realization that "Aristotle's concept of the individual was not a truly moving thing."[19] To be sure, Aristotle sought truth in individual things, but such things were fixed, unmoving, unchanging, and eternal. In Nishida's reconstruction of Aristotle and the Greek tradition,

> ...reality in Greek philosophy was *logos*. In contrast to modern science, Greek philosophy considered that which transcends time, the eternal, to be true reality, and, on the contrary, that which moves in time to be imperfect.[20]

Aristotle was Platonist enough to fear the changing which, by definition, was thought to be intrinsically *unknowable*. Laws, trajectories, and the sequence of Zeno's arrow were needed in order to account for change, and all of these against the fixed center of an unchanging and fixed *substance*. As will be seen, Aristotle's *hypokeímenon* (substrate, substance) is the fixed background against which change is measured. For Nishida, however, the background must change as well, for otherwise there is no mutuality of influence. In his words, "the true individual must be an acting individual,"[21] and it is time itself that is the "form of the self-determination of being."[22] Put simply, genuine change requires alteration of *both* subject and predicate components of a judgment, both *hypokeímenon* and predicates.

While Nishida does not explicitly say so, the background of continuity must now be the self-as-consciousness-in-time which always wherever and whenever is the "privileged" place or center from which change is marked.[23] Action remains the factuality of experience, for all things flow, but they flow for an individual who is always the measure, wherever, whenever. Thus it is that Nishida speaks paradoxically about the self, which "lives by dying,"[24] for it is a continuity of discontinuity. It flows, and yet in flowing, flows not (for it is ever the privileged marker of all flowing). It is not substantive, for that would be too Aristotelian, but rather a function in James's sense, or an activity. It is the place *(basho)*, i.e., "A unity of absolute contradictories."[25]

It has been noted that the Greeks tended to fixate on the unchanging, making the unmoved real, and the changing subsidiary to it. Heraclitus was the clear exception. Philip Wheelwright speaks of him in terms reminiscent of Nishida:

> The most characteristic difficulty in Heraclitus's Philosophy lies in the demand which it makes upon its hearers to transcend the "either-or" type of thinking and recognize in each phase of experience that a relationship of "both-and" may be present in subtle ways that escape a dulled intelligence.... To him nothing is exclusively this or that; in various ways he affirms something to be *both* of two disparates or two contraries, leaving the reader to contemplate the paradox, the full semantic possibilities of which can never be exhausted by plain prose statements.[26]

Wheelwright adds that it is Heraclitus's acceptance of "the ontological status of paradox," i.e., his view "that paradox lies inextricably at the very heart of reality" that caused him to be thought of as obscure and inscrutable.[27] It is of special importance to see clearly that Heraclitus spoke paradoxically not in order to resolve paradoxicality, but to affirm it as the only way that logic, words, and thought can do *fuller* justice to the richness of reality as it is given in experience. In Fragment 108 he tells us that "the way up and the way down are one and the same."[28] Taken literally, we have absurdity, as we do with "living is dying," but taken as a metaphorical way of pointing towards the mutuality of effect given in flux, there is no other way of saying it. A river is what it is and is recognizable as a "static" entity. And yet, as a river it is never static, but is always becoming other than what it is at any one moment. Thus, the river is a river by virtue of its not being a river, or by becoming not-a-river. Is this not a helpful way of pointing to change? In fact, does it not protect against an Aristotelian reification of some unchanging substance, a fixed "something I know not what" to which predicates are attached? Instead, paradoxical utterance announces that we are aware only of processes-in-experience, and that "two contrary processes are both going on all the time, and that their continual and varying tension is what makes existence and life possible."[29] In addition to William James, Nishida might also have found another kindred spirit in the Western tradition in Heraclitus, except for the fact that so little is left of his writings, and those that are extant are so cryptic.

Aristotle's emphasis on predicative universals arose because of the "Parmenidean" thirst for the fixed, eternal, and unchanging, and no doubt Aristotle's emphasis on grasping the *essence* of a thing was his attempt to fix the flow by finding the universal in the particular. In the famous rout in battle analogy in the *Posterior Analytics,* we read that "though the act of sense-perception is of the particular, its content is universal," and that "the soul is so constituted as to be capable of this process."[30] It is little wonder that the highest state of intellectual achievement for Aristotle is contemplation of the fixed essence of the unmoved mover, for "there is a substance which is eternal and unmovable and separate from sensible things."[31] Human happiness is fulfilled only when we contemplate as does God, since "that among human activities…which is most akin to God's will bring us the greatest happiness."[32] God is pure *nous,* pure understanding, and "for Aristotle, there is no slightest doubt that *nous,* the power to know and understand, is the 'highest' power in the world."[33] Its thinking, at its best, is a thinking of thinking eternally.[34] Individuation, by contrast, is not of the "forms" (i.e., the formal aspects of substance), but, likely, associated with matter *(hŷlē)* Matter itself, however, has no individual character, and so is unstable in words. Matter by itself is unintelligible, and so, we must assume, is the individual *qua* individual, as distinct from its universal predicated forms. It is knowable not *qua* individual, but as *intersection* of universal predicates! To know a thing is to name it, and to name it is to attach one or usually more universal predicates to it. Not only is the fixed within the flow alone knowable, but the universal in the individual as well. There is no place for the flow to be known as flow, nor the individual as individual. These defects Nishida set about to repair.

The primary category of the *Categories* is substance. First substance *(proto ousía)* is that which is neither predicated of a subject, nor present in a subject.[35] To predicate is to speak or say of something that it is this kind of thing. All predicates, therefore, have some degree of generality (not just "this is this"), so as to be applicable other than just once, in this unique case. Whatever is predicable of a grammatical subject of a definition, then, is always non-individual. And what is never predicable of a grammatical subject is what is non-general, individual, particular, unique. "Present in" applies to the sort of thing which by its nature cannot exist independently of the subject—i.e., it is dependent on the subject in that it cannot exist by itself. What is independent is the subject: that to which the predicates attach. Yet, how is it that we come to "know" the subject? For example, in the sentence, "This wine is red," "wine" is a general term (second substances are, for Aristotle, kinds of first substances) and "red" is not only general, but refers to a species of the genus "wine." We are left with the "this." How do we come to know the "this," and what is the precise relation between the "this" of the judgment, and the actual individual object of knowledge which, presumably in this case, is what the utterance is about? We generally assume that Aristotle holds that the subject of a sentence/judgment, and the actual object of knowledge in nature, are identical. But what is the principle of individuation? If the species-genus relationship is the model of definitional utterance, then the subject of a judgment must always itself be a universal, and never a particular.[36] Unless one grunts and points, all speaking is speaking of kinds, or universals. Yet Aristotle is confident in what Marjorie Grene calls his discovery, that the world sorts itself out into kinds, but the kinds are kinds of individuals.[37] Forms cannot be found separate from individual substances, as in Plato's world of forms, but are always to be found in individuals. Yet judgments are particular relations of universals, and not ever of genuine individuals. If all knowledge is of universals, then it must be concluded that individuals cannot be known. Yet if the world can be said to sort itself out, there must be some sense in which we know this of the individual things of the world. The answer seems to be that all judgments are the amplification and articulation of what are taken to be the parts of an intuition. So, if I say "this wine is convex," you will not tell me that there is something about the string of terms that offends you, but that your intuition of wines of all sorts make it impossible for such a uniting of terms to be a genuine judgment. The standard is one's initial intuition, in this case, of this wine, but in general of any and all wine.

Judgment is the form of conceptual knowledge. It consists of a subject and a predicate. The standard form of judgment is that of *subsumption:* the subsumption (or envelopment) of a subject by a universal predicate. However, to say anything at all is to speak of a kind, and therefore the subsumptive model is really the enveloping of a less general universal by a more general universal. All speaking and judging is of kinds. A concrete individual cannot actually become the grammatical subject of a subsumptive judgment. What, then, is the link between the grammatical subject and predicate? Nishida's "Copernican revolution," to so name it, is in hypothesizing that the proper question is not "how are these two universal concepts unified or linked?" but "how can such specification of the wider (more general) universal occur?" The initial intuition already contains, at least implicitly, the structure of the relationship. To say that one's glass of wine is red, then, is to have already "bought into" the system of wines and their types. To say that "wine is blue" is to be in error, for wine, i.e., the system or class of wines, does not include "blue," unless it has been artificially prepared or has gone bad. Perhaps the point can be better made by switching examples to one of Nishida's own.

What is primary in the judgment "red is a color," is not the grammatical subject. To be able to say that red is a color, one must understand what "color" means, and to some degree one must also know of the system of colors (red is not black, or green, or...). Wargo articulates this point precisely when he writes:

> The point he [Nishida] wants to make is that one does not first come into contact with specific colors and then abstract from these to form the abstract

notion of color in general. In order to see a specific color, e.g., red, as a color, it is already necessary to have the notion of color in general.[38]

Color is not merely a conceptual product of abstraction, i.e., an abstract universal, but is a system of distinctions of which "red" is a specific instance. The relationship between "red" and "color" is not one of degrees of abstraction, nor is it one of *two* independently existing things or entities which we must somehow struggle to unite. Rather, they are united from the beginning, for "red" and "color" are both parts of, or grounded in the color-system itself. Thus, the real subject of the sentence "red is a color" is not "red," nor even the grammatical predicate "color," but the system of colors itself. To have a concept of "red" is already to have a concept of color, and to have a concept of color is already to have something of a system of colors. Of course, the system, like "color" itself, has no color. Russell's logic of types and Frege's understanding of number make it clear that the class or system-concept (color, number) does not have the specific properties of any of the instances of the system. Thus, "number" is no specific number, and yet it makes possible *all* numbers insofar as it refers to the number-system. From the imagined vantage point of the individuals in the system, the existence of "number" itself is describable only as *"nothing"* (no-thing), i.e., it has no characteristics, for it is not "one," or "fifty," or any other specific number. "Number" has no specific number characteristics. "Color" has no color, and "number" is no number. From the vantage point of the encompassing *system* (Nishida's *basho,* or "place"), however, the instances are but determinations, articulations, expressions, particularizations of the system. Subject ("red") and predicate ("color") are not inexplicably brought together in a judgment, then, but are specific features of, and are carved out of, one and the same (whole) thing—the system of colors. They are intrinsically and inextricably related from the start. Indeed, what is difficult, given this analysis, is to imagine them apart, or unrelated. What would it mean to say that "red is not a color"?

As a look ahead, one sees here as well the influence of Hegel, for the universal is no longer abstract but rather *concrete,* in that it includes within itself the individual. The color system *includes* precise specification of the individual colors that make it up, and an account of the relations among the colors.

What is the source of the system of colors? Here Nishida is an Aristotelian *realist.* The world sorts itself out, just as the routed armies, first in total disarray, come back into "system" by first one taking a stand and then another.[39] The armies do it man by man, colors do it one after another, and the natural world is simply *organized* as it is. Color is a "field" in which specifications arise. Number is a "field" or "place" in which numbers come to focus, one after another. A field-theory takes the background as the real foreground, the real subject. So, in a field of energy, focuses or concentrations of energy are really specifications of the whole, just as in a Zen rock garden, a particular shape simply calls attention to the undifferentiated expanse on which it sits, or better, out of which it arises. A number only calls arithmetic and mathematics to mind, if one will but ponder the number deeply enough. The *field* itself, however, is not all colors, or all numbers, but that which supports, or even generates, colors and numbers. It is an *intuition,* a given of experience or conception of which individual instances are but partial articulations. Judgments are really about the nature and structure of the field itself,[40] and not only about the individual instances. The system or field is the grammatical predicate's predicate, the universal of universals. The system is the *real* universal, and the grammatical predicate but the proximate universal. To say what the "this" is of a judgment, then, is to go from grammatical-subject-as-universal ("red"), to grammatical-predicate-as-universal ("color"), to the universal of the grammatical universal (the entire system of colors). As will be seen later, this is far from the end of the matter, for there are yet further universals, or *bashos,* but the procedure is clear. One moves from the instance as verbally judged, to what such judgment *necessarily implies,* in increasing layers of *inclusiveness.*

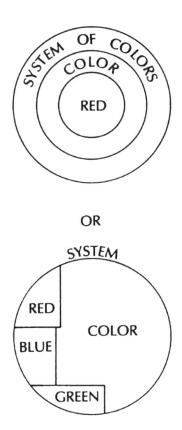

As illustrated by these two alternative diagrams, of the field/ subject/ predicate relationships, it is the "field" (system) that is closest to the original intuition, or given-in-experience-which-sorts-itself-out-as-colors, of which all of this is an articulation. The intuition is not itself part of a judgment, but is that which the judgment is about, namely, an experience. It is "neither predicated of a subject nor present in an object," for it is not itself explicitly a part of the judgment at all. As Wargo writes, "Judgment is the self determination of something which itself can never be the grammatical subject of a judgment—at least not within that specific domain of discourse."[41] Yet, for Aristotle, to be a being *(ens)* necessarily entails the possibility of being as actually becoming the grammatical subject of a judgment. So if Aristotle's first substance is never a predicate, Nishida's *basho* is never a subject. What Nishida actually claims is that nothingness, or *basho,* or the system/field, is always a predicate.[42] Yet this is confusing, in that it is not the actual grammatical predicate, but the predicate (system/field) of the grammatical predicate that defines the grammatical subject. He speaks of this as his logic of predicates, to contrast it with Aristotle's logic of the subject. It would be better to use his other designation, however—the *logic of place,* for, as the previous diagrams illustrate, the place/system/field houses or grounds both the grammatical subject and predicate. *Basho,* then, is that which is neither predicated of, nor present in, a subject, nor even the grammatical subject, but that which grounds both, and out of which both arise as specifications or determinations. In any case, it remains good Aristotelian logic that what can never become the subject of a judgment cannot be said to be a "being." It is nothing.

To review, then, Nishida's critique of Aristotle begins with the recognition (1) that knowledge is predicational judgment precisely because the world is logical, and lends itself to the grasp of language. To know is to say. Indeed, we can't really be said to know a thing until we can "state in precise language what that thing is, and why it is as it is. Knowledge and language are a flowering of the world."[43] (2) All knowledge is of the form that the subject of a judgment is subsumed by the wider, predicate term. (3) However, both the grammatical subject and predicate are abstract universals, rendering the true individual *qua* individual completely and forever beyond the grasp of the universals of so-called knowledge. "Red" and "wine" are not individual "thises," but universals pointing to the original intuition of the individual, which, by necessity, cannot be *said,* known, or defined. (4) A more probing analysis of the subsumptive judgment reveals that the epistemological glue of the subject/predicate relation is that they are moments, or modes, of a system of discourse, which itself is an articulation of an original intuition. Colors and numbers arise out of a "field" of color and numericalness. Specific colors and numbers are but articulations of a relationship of parts to field/system, given in an initial gestalt. (5) The field has absolutely none of the characteristics applying to the parts. If the parts have predicates that can be said of them, absolutely none of them can be applied to the field. It is literally nothing, if one means by something having any of the properties of the individual articulating the field. (6) It is not a being at all. The field is neither a particular individual, nor a grammatical subject (at least not in this sphere of discourse), not a predicate, and therefore not a grammatical predicate (i.e., as a concept). It is the ground or source of all judgments about the field as individuated (i.e., as determined). It is the place, given as an intuition, as a whole, a gestalt, which knowing, saying, analyzing, and defining try to specify. They all distort the original unity, take it apart, dissect it, re-structure it for specific purposes. So long as such partial and ripped-out-of-context specification is seen as having its place in its field, no damage is done, and indeed something is actually to be gained. Like a poet or painter looking at a familiar scene, to re-analyze the old and see it in new ways, e.g., by exaggerating, leaving out, streamlining, may yield a renewed experience of the seemingly inexhaustible experiential base. But such advantage is epistemologically sound if, and only if, one returns to the source intuition again and again to re-structure it anew. And even at that, the truly operative ground is not even all of these perspectives, but the intuition that we seem to have, but which, at the same time, we can never exhaustively speak of, or define, or analyze. Language itself is but a moment in the field of awareness. Basho *is the given-in-intuition prior to the analysis and expression of objectification.* The way out is to take two different perspectives at the same time the "double aperture" in knowing, as I prefer to call it—whereby one focuses on the part, the individual, and even the elements of a judgment (subject and predicate) on the one hand, and on the "field" or place on the other. It is the stance of the recognition of the *"contradictory self-identity"* of things, using Nishida's phrase. That is to say, a thing is an individual (or a grammatical subject), but only because it is a determination of a field which is presupposed in order for one to know that it is the kind of thing it is. In Plato's terms, one can't know that something is "red" unless one has a form of "redness," except that for Nishida the form is the field of color as a system of relations. The many particular colors express the color system, and the color system integrates the many. In order to know, we must take both perspectives at one and the same time. Hence, color is many, yet one. It is a contradictory entity.

THE FIRST UNIVERSAL

Color as a system (and not just as a concept) cannot be said to exist or not to exist. Judgmentally, the system (field) breaks up into the range of specific colors (functioning as the grammatical subjects), and the characteristics of colors in general (the predicates). Generalizing the example, we have Nishida's *universal of judgment*, which divides into subjects and predicates subsumptively related. The subject, however, in order to deal adequately with our actual experience of individuals, must be more than an *abstract* universal itself (e.g., "red"). It is a "this." The subject, then, cannot be an abstract universal, for our intuitions-in-experience are of individuals. No one wanted to stress the primacy of the individual more than Aristotle. However his analysis of knowing—which is of universals only—made this primary focus actually unknowable. For Nishida, what Aristotle's analysis of judgment reveals is that neither the system nor the predicate of the subsumptive relationship is adequately dealt with. The individual is not catchable as a subject universal, nor is the possible cluster of predicates able to capture the field/ *system/basho* (of color) itself. Thus, both the real subject (the individual) and the real predicate of predicates are beyond the scope and ken of the system of abstract universals. If all we had to rely on was the subject of abstract universals, then we could not account for the knowledge we actually seem to have. Indeed, even to frame the issue so as to make the problem appear as a problem, is to transcend the system of abstract universals. Our understanding is deeper than the system allows us to account for. In this sense, it is because of what Wargo calls "contradiction,"[44] and what we might term the "incomplete," that one must search for a more adequate account of human knowledge.

Charting Nishida's theory of knowledge as a theory of encompass-ing universals, there are three main universals, each of which is divided into three (lesser, or internal) stages, yielding nine universals in all.

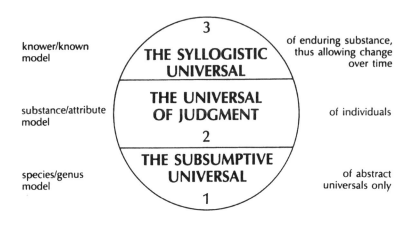

THE UNIVERSAL OF JUDGMENT
the first universal

The move from the purely abstract universals of the subsumptive model is necessitated by the need to account for the individual in knowledge. Aristotle's account of first substance achieves this, although it is less than clear how we *know* this. Still, what is at least recognized is that the true concept of the individual must somehow be concrete and not abstract or general. The concept or universal must somehow contain its own principle of individuation. Fixing on the actual "contradiction," or incompleteness, the subject cannot be an abstract universal, and the universal, therefore, cannot be an *abstract* universal. The true subject is now the *concrete* individual, which is the only thing that exists in the most fundamental sense. The individual, and not the universal, is the real for Aristotle. Substance *(hypokeimenon)* is a *compound* of universal and particular, such that the universal is *in* the particular. This is the concrete universal. What "in" turns out to imply, however, is that attributes of things cannot exist by themselves, but exist only in substances, as their characteristics, which together make up the individual thing. Abe calls this type of subsumptive judgment an "inherence judgment": "It is through an attribute inherent in a particular subject (e.g., the attribute of 'suckles' inherent in dog) that a subsumptive judgment is established."[45]

The addition of individuals, and the recognition of substance/attribute inherence is a step forward, but the "incompleteness" now is that while we have individuals, the individuals simply statically *have* attributes. Yet Aristotle wants to account for change, hence we need a dynamic substance which, while enduring, also undergoes change in time. We are forced to move to the syllogistic universal, the highest or deeper layer of the Universal of Judgment. The full Universal is of subsumptive attribution of predicates to substances which endure through change as individuals having general attributes.

Change requires time, such that time is the medium in which the before and after are related. But knowledge of individuals as changing in time requires consciousness of time by a subject. In the Universal of Judgment, the knowing self is viewed as an object-part of the world of nature, to be known analogously to the way any object is known. "It is essentially an ego, registering objects in time."[46] Yet the "I" as eye does not exhaust the "I" as that which actually watches the "eye" watching, and which enters into the framing and structuring of that which is seen. In short, the self, as self-activity, can never be caught via the Universal of Judgment, for to turn it into an object is to lose its distinctiveness as subjectivity. To make of the *pour soi* an *en soi* is to make it what it isn't. It is self consciousness as not conscious. But self consciousness is recursive or reflexive, and it infinitely doubles back on itself such that it always is precisely what it isn't at any moment of objectified "freezing," so to speak. The "contradiction" or "incompleteness" includes the recognition that in the Universal of Judgment, subject (the "eye") and object are both treated as objects, whereas more critical analysis reveals that the very having of the knowledge of the Universal of Judgment *includes* that which is self consciously having awareness of this relationship. Knowledge isn't the passive seem" of relationships; it is active consciousness of such relationships. Self consciousness cannot be accounted for without introducing new categories into our analysis, but that is just what we can't do from the perspective of the Universal of Judgment. Thus, unless self consciousness can be treated objectively, then it isn't knowledge at all. It is "subjective," or noumenal freedom, or just nothing. The self acts, and is aware of itself, and yet it can never be the subject of a judgment! It cannot be dealt with by object logic. Yet Nishida wants to take the form of self consciousness as the basic logical form,[47] for ultimately, all judgments are in self consciousness, or are judgments for and by a self.

DESCARTES

Nishida acknowledges his debt to Descartes as, it seems, all modern philosophers must. The *cogito* is recognition of the indubitability of the self as activity, and while Descartes overstressed the "I" of existence, Nishida, in tune with the thrust of the more phenomenological interpretation of Descartes, stresses not the "I" as *thought,* but the "I" as thinking. Even to view Descartes so crisply in this particular way creates a shift in logical perspective from emphasis on the grammatical subject--pole of judgment, to the predicate-pole. Graphically, Nishida's "predicate logic" may here be identified. The *sum* yields to the *cogito* such that to render a self an object is precisely to lose it, and to grasp it is to grasp it as an activity, a process, a flux, and an awareness of itself as aware, as aware, as aware, as aware.... The potential infinite regress isn't actually an infinite regress, for we stop the process by simply being aware of whatever object of consciousness we are aware of. But try to catch the "seen," and the regress begins. In any case, the direction of Nishida's new logic is to give preeminence to the predicate side of a judgment. Or, in different terms, the shift is from the major to the minor term of a judgment or syllogism.

What Descartes saw was that our actual understanding of our own selves demands that we not objectify the self, but instead come to understand it as having a logical place in our judgments. We know of the self in every act of knowing—thinking, sensing, feeling, willing, wondering. The self is not a thing for Descartes, in the ordinary sense of object. Nishida clarifies the status of the self by treating the self as the *basho*/field (of consciousness) in which all judgments and all knowledge arise. From the vantage point of this new *basho,* the *objects* of the Universal of Judgment are simply the *contents* of the field of consciousness, which now envelops them. The *basho* of consciousness is a deeper level of explanation, and it embraces, envelops, includes the earlier *basho* of the Universal of Judgment within it. Indeed, as the earlier Universal of Judgment enveloped the objects of the natural world, so now the Universal of Judgment, together with its objects, are enveloped *as content* by the new *basho*—the Universal of Self Consciousness. We do not simply posit it, however. It is required by the very knowledge of object logic.

THE SECOND UNIVERSAL *BASHO*

The universal of self consciousness, as with the universal of judgment, has within itself three layers, progressing from the most shallow to the deepest.

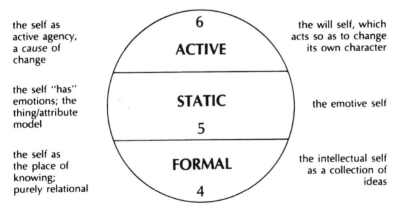

the self as active agency, a cause of change	**6** **ACTIVE**	the will self, which acts so as to change its own character
the self "has" emotions; the thing/attribute model	**STATIC** **5**	the emotive self
the self as the place of knowing; purely relational	**FORMAL** **4**	the intellectual self as a collection of ideas

UNIVERSAL OF SELF CONSCIOUSNESS
the second universal

We can conceive of the self as the passive place in which ideas arise, and which is ever at the background of objective knowing. At the very least, in order to be aware of objects changing in time, at the level of the syllogistic universal, there must be a self that is the unifier of boy/man/old man experience and observations. Time is an awareness of consciousness, and the aging of an individual, or the moving of a ship downstream, is made possible by a conscious self that links, or relates, several perceptions to a single object or era. The boy, man, and old man are not three different persons, but one person in change. Aristotle's *hypokeímenon,* which endures through change, must endure in time, and time is an awareness of some consciousness. Otherwise, the enduring of the *hypokeímenon* could not be known to be the enduring of "that" same substance/object. The Kantian "unity of apperception" is presupposed by the substance of object knowledge.

The self is not merely an intellect which ascertains relations among things in space and time, however. To assume so is not to have taken seriously the forced move from grammatical subject to grammatical predicate. Insofar as the focus of attention now resides with the predicate, and as the predicate is, in fact the *basho* of self consciousness in which objects and the systems of objects reside, then we are forced to analyze as completely as possible what this *basho* (self consciousness) of *basho* (judgment/objects in the natural world) consists of. It is no surprise that what the phenomenology of the self consciousness reveals is threefold: knowing, feeling, and willing, or the rational/intellectual, emotive or affective, and volitional aspects of consciousness. As the *individual* of the first level of the *basho* of self consciousness, the self is an intellectual self concerned with formal relations. The individual also has feeling, however, and these feelings are actual properties, predicates, or attributes of the self. As red is a color, so the self is angry. Emotion tends to be thought of as something that happens to us. We fall in love, or become angry, but we don't decide to fall in love, or to feel angry. We are overcome by them, in the sense of not choosing them. In Nishida's essay entitled "Affective Feeling," he observes that "the living personality is not a mere abstract concept,"[48] but a dynamic unity. More concretely, the living personality or self has feeling as its expression.[49] Joy, sadness, love, and hate "are the resonance of the larger and deeper self grounded in the union of acts."[50]

The move from formal to static self reveals a self which has emotions, but our observations of ourselves make it clear that we can and do reflect on the feelings that we have, and about the nature of the personality they express. We are not only passive; we are active—willfully active. "Will" is the deepest level of the Universal of Self Consciousness, and is manifested when we actually *do* determine our own nature, i.e., change it. In fact, it is only at this level that true reflexivity is apparent. We can reflect back upon our past, and ask if we want to be that way now. And in the future we can modify our selfhood. The willing, self reflective self is not limited by the past, nor by the perceptions of the present, for in order to be able to *act* for change, the willing self must have a goal to attain. Feelings are "had," but the having of goals actually *directs* activity. Only the willing self can establish and follow goals which it has itself set.

THE THIRD UNIVERSAL

To speak of goals, or ideals, is already to have moved to the realm of the intelligible. The move results from "forgetting the conscious self, by loving the object as oneself by becoming directly one with it."[51] Another *shift of focus* has taken place. The Universal of Self Consciousness arose as a result of shifting primary attention from the objects of the natural world, to the self as that which "lines" objective knowledge, for knowledge of things as substances *(hypokeimena)*, which endure change, necessarily implies some persisting consciousness that links various perceptions *in time* as pertaining to the same object. Now, the focus moves from self-consciousness to acts of consciousness in which the self is no longer the focus, but in which the self loses itself. We lose ourselves in our goals, aspirations, ideals. The third *basho* of course has three levels or layers.

Nishida thinks of the three levels of self consciousness as the focused nodules within the *basho* or field of intelligibility, just as the three levels of judgment are specific foci within the *basho*/field of consciousness.

The ideal of truth is given specific determination in the various intellectual accounts of self consciousness, which in turn serves as the field/ *basho* in which judgments about objects arise. The ideal of beauty is the *basho* of various feelings or sensitivities at the level of consciousness, which in turn is the *basho* for judgments about the attributes of things in the world of natural objects. The good or value as an ideal system is the *basho* of specific goals in the self of consciousness, which in turn is the *basho* for the "I" of judgment that has become aware of itself as changing in time. While it is still an "eye" of an "I," it can ask itself why and how it changes, and as it asks about the direction, it begins its change of focus from the "I" as object to the "I" as self conscious agent. A bit more needs to be said about these intelligible universals.

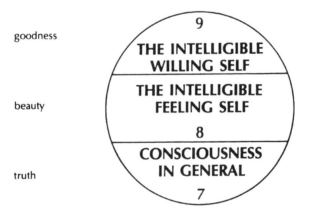

goodness

beauty

truth

9

THE INTELLIGIBLE
WILLING SELF

THE INTELLIGIBLE
FEELING SELF

8

CONSCIOUSNESS
IN GENERAL

7

THE INTELLIGIBLE UNIVERSAL
the third universal

TRUTH

The self is aware of its own *content* as "ideas"—hence the term "intelligible." Wargo succinctly says of these ideas that they "are the standards and the ideals that guide behavior and, as such, serve as the ground for the conception of goal-directed activity."[52] But while the ideal of Truth is now fully recognized as the goal of all intellectual activity, it is still a merely "formal" idea, Nishida tells us.[53] In other words, Truth itself is a formal idea from the outside, and one to which our intellectual activity ought to conform. The self does not yet see its own content *as its own,* but its focus of attention is on the ideal of Truth as an eternal standard to be achieved. Yet, in strictly Kantian terms, the ideal of truth is an ideal for each and every consciousness, i.e., for consciousness in general. And of course, the reason it is important to move to the *content* of the intelligible self itself is because we are now exploring the *basho* of the *basho* of self consciousness, and it will not do only to find ideals of intellect, feeling, and activity as merely external to the self The intelligible realm is the "lining" of the real self conscious self, and it must include the ground for objective knowledge, feeling, and the willed goal-setting of a fully reflective and self-conscious self.

BEAUTY

The intelligible feeling self *is* aware of its ideal—beauty—as its own content. Beauty is not merely something given from outside, but is an expression of the feeling self. Artistic expression is the expression of the nature of the self, at least in part. Artistic intuition is the actual content of our feelings. Nishida emphasizes the importance of this level when he observes that "we become free as we embrace and transcend the intellect on the feeling level."[54] It is worth asking what it is that feeling provides us with after all, since emotion is so often viewed as the internal frosting on the external cake of knowledge and understanding. Nishida flatly states to the contrary that:

> It is a common idea that feeling differs from knowledge, and that its content is less clear. To this I reply that the affective feeling of a sensitive artist is not necessarily less clear to him than the special knowledge of a scientist. The

> alleged unclarity of feeling means nothing more than that it cannot be expressed in conceptual knowledge. It is not that consciousness in feeling is unclear, but rather that feeling is a more subtle and delicate form of consciousness than conceptual knowledge.[55]

Insofar as artistic expression gives "clear shape" to our feelings it expresses a depth of self not accessible to the activity of intellect. Truth values arise in judgment, and aesthetic values arise in imagination. Of the two, imagination is the deeper level, and therefore the more fundamental. The life of the expression of beauty is expressed through various forms of art. The artistic consciousness appears "when it is focused into one activity—when the self is one with its world."[56] This total identification may also be expressed as losing one's self, and becoming the object. One has become the bamboo that one is sketching. There is, in awareness, only bamboo-ness. Sympathetic union, identification, empathy, compenetration, all are terms in our language that seek to express the act of artistic intuition. Feeling includes or envelops truth, and its grasp of a more concrete reality, based on an enlarged expression of self. "is a more profound consciousness than cognitive knowledge."[57] Feeling is the content of imagination. Feeling disappears when we turn our attention to it (whereas knowledge becomes clearer the more we reflect on it). Yet if feeling is unclear to knowledge, it must become clear when viewed as the content or determination of the layer/*basho* which envelops it, and of which it is the expression. This necessitates the move to the third and deepest layer of the Intelligible Universal.

VALUE, OR THE GOOD

A work of art is not created to change the character of the self. Feelings do reveal the full content of the self, but the self of self-determination, of goal orientation, is the intelligible willing self "The purer the [will]…, the clearer the content of feeling becomes."[58] The *transparent* will sees what its feeling content is, but rather than merely expressing this content as the artist does, the intelligible willing self deliberately acts so as to modify, re-direct, re-form, or transform that content. This is the self of Kant's practical reason, which acts so as to determine its own nature. This is the teleological dimension front and center. The idea of the good is a pattern, form, or ideal which one adopts as the goal towards which the molding of the actual (feeling) self moves. As an ideal, it transcends the self nature as it is, and is that standard with which the self seeks to be in harmony. Here *conscience* appears for the first time, for there is now a clear distinction between the "is" of the self as revealed in feeling (and intellect), and the "ought to be" of the self as aspiring. Note that "the good" has no specific content, just as beauty and truth were also variables in terms of the specific content which they housed. But to the contrary, of the various "truths," "beauties," and "goods or values," none of them alone, nor even all of them together, completely captures the intelligible "idea" itself. One continually reaches back to the ideal, to give content to it. It is in this sense that Nishida speaks of the *will* as infinitely deep. Any and all content is but coagulation in a portion of a field which itself can never be exhausted by, or entrapped by, the specifications of content. This will become clearer shortly.

At the level of intelligible willing self, the goal is to modify or re-create the self, i.e., to determine its own nature. Conscience has a primarily negative note to play as the manifestation of an awareness of the gap between one's present self nature and one's ideals. Yet conscience no more has the goal in mind in any final sense, than any conception of goodness or system of values can be said to be the ultimate system.

Even at this deepest level of the Intelligible Universal, a contradiction, or an incompleteness in the story told, becomes apparent. For to view the willing, self determining, moral self as a being (object) is to conflict with a most basic requirement of morality—free will. To view the willing self from the perspective of its content-plane, is to view it as determined by its ideals of truth, beauty, and goodness. To give content even to goodness is already to think of the self as an object within the deterministic chains of cause and effect. This is an old Kantian story again. Morality, however, requires that we be free agents, and so the regulative ideas of God, Freedom, and Morality must be introduced, and while we cannot *know* that we are noumenally *anything*, let alone *free*, we must act as though we were free. Nishida agrees totally with the gist of the analysis, except that he cannot accept the "unknowability" of the noumenal. His strategy is simply to show that the self as object, even as intelligible object, is itself enveloped by that *basho* which is beyond the subject/object, *nóēsis/nóema* distinctions. Obviously, to "know" it will be to lose it, precisely by focusing on the determination as a congealed objectification, and losing the field/basho in which the objectification occurs. On the other hand, to focus on this *last* field, is not to be able to say anything at all. To say is to know, as Aristotle stated so well, so that which can't be said can't be known, as Kant agreed, but from the later vantage-point of his own categorical analysis, and the forms of intuition.

Nevertheless, Nishida's final move must be one to the unspoken and unspeakable, for to introduce yet another set of categories would simply set in motion the analysis of a still deeper universal—no doubt divisible into three layers and so on to infinity. There would be a difference of focus, a change of categories and in terminology, but no end to the process would be possible.

THE FINAL *BASHO*
the *Basho* of Absolute Nothingness

The move must be to a final *basho* that removes the final contradiction, and which yields the ultimate completion of the project, yet about which we can say nothing. From the vantage point of the notion of self, the move is from the willing self to the *behaving* self. The behaving self is a self that can never, in any way, be viewed as an object. The self as activity is never objectifiable, and, hence, forever eludes us. It is ever at the background of any foreground of consciousness, which means, of course, that it is the real or implicit foreground to the seeming or explicit. It is the subject of our thinking, except that it can never be the subject of awareness, nor can it be the predicate either. It is that out of which subject and predicate, subject and object, *nóēsis,* and *nóema,* knower and known are carved. It is prior to any and all of these distinctions. The Intelligible Universal is the deepest universal, and as such it enfolds the other two—or put differently, the ninth level of distinction enfolds the other eight, which together are its determination. Yet these still remain within the Intelligible Universal. The distinction of subject and object, *nóēsis* and *nóema,* even if at the level of transcendental intelligibility, remains. In Nishida's words, "In the case of the intelligible world, which has its place in the intelligible Universal, *nóēsis* and *nóema* still confront each other."[59] Now, taking all of the universals and their levels together, they form the expression or determination of the behaving self.

Recall that Nishida is not positing an unknown, as Kant posits a noumenal realm. What Nishida has attempted is a radical analysis of what is given in experience. His starting point, that the subject/object dichotomy is not ultimate, is now his logical conclusion. When asking of this final *basho* of absolute nothingness, what is its structure, and what can be said of it, Nishida replies that its structure is precisely the whole system of universals and their levels, for this system is an articulation of the precise way in which nothingness determines itself. The system itself is the characterization of absolute nothingness. Absolute nothingness actually expresses itself in terms of the subject/object distinction at every level, and yet it is not thereby caught, nor completely exhausted by such categories, nor adequately dealt with.

The various universals and their levels are the *nóēsis/nóema* of the ultimate *basho* which is potentially both of these, and actually neither. The ultimate *basho is* the ground of the self which sees but cannot itself be seen. It is as no-self, an ultimate intuition out of which and on which all distinctions are based.

An "experience" in which no conceptual distinctions are made is one which allows of no conceptualization, and to which logic applies not at all, or only with contradictory results. To speak the unspoken, or to label the unlabeled or to conceptualize the unconceptualized is to miss that which contains or is the ground of all distinctions.

> There must be something that transcends even that [intelligible] world. That which serves as "place" for one true Self, may be called the "place of absolute Nothingness." It is the religious consciousness.[60]

The necessity of there being this final level is not a conceptual one, but remains rooted in the experiential. Nishida asserts that "the content of religious consciousness," about which nothing can be said (for to "say" is to become conceptual, and to reintroduce dichotomous distinctions), is "experience."[61] God is the transcendent subject of the intelligible world, and the ultimate unity and unifier of truth, goodness, and beauty.[62] Truth, goodness, and beauty are the highest values noematically discerned, as Wilhelm Windelband notes, and for which Nishida praises him.[63] But even these noematic absolutes are further "'lined' with the Universal of Absolute Nothingness, the 'last Self' becomes visible, and there remains only the proceeding in the direction of *nóēsis.*"[64] Religious value is, however, the losing or negating of the Self, and so religious intuition pushes beyond intellectual intuition until it "has completely transcended the standpoint of knowledge, and may perhaps be called 'world of mystic intuition,' unapproachable by word or thinking."[65] The relation of God to religious consciousness ("mystic intuition") will be picked up again in chapter 4, but in anticipation, the following summarizing passage from *The Intelligible World* points the direction for the remainder of Nishida's philosophic/religious life-project.

[An understanding of God as the absolute unity of truth, goodness and beauty] is, in my opinion, not deep enough.... It is still bound to be the intelligible world where it has its origin. If one is really overwhelmed by the consciousness of absolute Nothingness, there is neither "Me" nor "God"; but just because there is absolute Nothingness, the mountain is mountain, and the water is water, and the being is as it is.[66]

The religious standpoint transcends concepts, and therefore knowledge, yet it is the ground of both, and both arise out of it. Conceptual knowledge is not foreign to nothingness, but as much a manifestation or expression of it as are mountains, water, and individual consciousness.

SPEAKING THE UNSPEAKABLE

While Nishida makes plain that he rejects the label "mystic," this is so because he observes that mystics the world over tend to announce their experiences, rather than give them a philosophical ground. It is not that Nishida is not writing of the mystical experience, but that he is a philosopher to the marrow. Nishida's genius is that he steadfastly refuses simply to announce the fact of *satori* (absolute nothingness), but insists on demonstrating in technical, philosophical terms, and by means of an analysis of ordinary experience and our knowledge of it, exactly why the foundation of nothingness is necessitated. Nishida adeptly distinguishes Zen from what is more commonly taken as mysticism as follows:

... Zen has nothing to do with mysticism, as many think. *Kenshō,* seeing one's nature, means to penetrate to the roots of one's own self.... What has been called mysticism in Western philosophy since Plotinus is something extremely close to Zen, but I think that Western mysticism has not in essence the standpoint of object logic. Indeed, the One of Plotinus stands at an opposite pole to the Zen experience of nothingness. Neo-Platonism did not in fact attain to a religious celebration of the ordinary and everyday as we find in the Zen tradition.[67]

The initial problem of this sub-chapter seems insuperable, nevertheless: How can one speak of the unspoken and unspeakable? In the purest sense, one cannot speak of absolute nothingness because it is beneath or beyond all distinctions, conceptual categories, or any other means of differentiation. In the language of much Western mysticism, this must be so because the experience is of an undifferentiated *unity*, and not of Zen's "form[s] of the formless." All *multiplicity* has been eliminated, and both language and logic presuppose there being a differentiated manifold whose essential and accidental structures can be discerned and articulated. W. T. Stace, in his provocative *Mysticism and Philosophy* makes this point first at the conceptual level:

> You cannot have a concept of anything *within* the undifferentiated unity because there are no separate items to be conceptualized. Concepts are only possible where there is a multiplicity or at least a duality.[68]

Without multiplicity there can be no distinctions, and therefore no groupings or classes, no concepts, and hence no words. There can be only silence. Stace is quite emphatic, however, in observing that this is so only *during* the mystical experience of *oneness*.[69] Afterwards, when we are back "in our ordinary sensory-intellectual consciousness," "we can contrast the two kinds of consciousness."[70] Nishida, however, as can be seen from the above quotation, does not presuppose that nothingness is an undifferentiated unity, or indeed that the mystical vision is an experience at all. It is the place, the openness, the emptiness in which all particular occurrences are to be found, and yet is known only through their very occurrence. For Zen, the multiplicity does not disappear, but is actually heightened, while at the same time pointing to the emptiness beneath.

A word of caution needs to be introduced here in order to be certain not to conflate the positions of Stace and Nishida on this issue. Whereas Nishida, as we will see in chapter 3, proposes a detailed account of the precise *structure* of paradoxicality that he has in mind (as the identity of self-contradiction), Stace has been criticized because he has not done so, but leaves "paradoxicality" empty of structure and content. Steven Katz queries Stace's "claim that mystical language is defined by its 'ineffability' and its 'paradoxicality,'" noting that these two features are standard in phenomenological accounts of mystical experience.[71] In fact, they cloak or hide mystical experience from the scrutiny required to help us understand what characterizes mystical experience. If such experiences are baldly ineffable and paradoxical, then there is no reason to conclude that the various authors and traditions are actually dealing with the same experience at all.[72] There is no way to get "behind" the expression, to compare, or even to understand. Nishida, too, wishes to go "behind" appearances, even mystical experience, to provide a logical-philosophical account of both the paradoxicality of the everyday, and of the unspeakable and formless that lies beneath it, but is ultimately exhausted in or by the everyday. And he wishes to point out that such speculation rests on direct experience, i.e., religious intuition.

ZEN KOANS

The influence of Zen on Nishida might be brought to focus by attending to the final *basho,* absolute nothingness, or by comparing the logical structure of Nishida's concentric universals (the deeper enveloping or "lining" the more shallow) with the function of the koan. To be sure, Nishida does not himself make such a comparison, for his aim is to bypass the techniques of religion, including Zen, in order to focus on the metaphysics and epistemology of the varieties of human experience. Nevertheless, in *The Intelligible World* he is quoted by Schinzinger as interpreting the following poem by the Japanese Zen Buddhist Kanemitzu Kōgun as a problem for meditation:

> From the cliff,
> Eight times ten thousand feet high,
> Withdrawing your hand,—
> Flames spring from the plough,
> World burns,
> Body becomes ashes and dirt,
> And resurrects.
> The rice-rows
> Are as ever,
> And the rice-ears
> Stand high.[73]

Schinzinger glosses the poem "according to Nishida's personal interpretation":

> The master has given a problem for Zen meditation, and you are laboring to solve the problems of being, as the farmer over there, on top of the high cliff, is laboring to plough his field. You are hanging on the usual way of thinking like somebody who is hanging on an infinitely high cliff, afraid of falling into the abyss. Withdraw your hand! And see: From the farmer's plough spring sparks,—and you, while the experience [I would add a word of caution here, substituting the word "awareness" for "experience"] of Nothingness springs from your laboring thinking, find "satori," enlightenment. But in the same spark of Nothingness, you regain the world and yourself in wonderful self identity. In the experience of Nothingness, everything is as it is: the rice-rows are as ever, arid rice-ears stand high.[74]

A koan is a seeming puzzle, or problem (e.g., "What is the sound of one hand clapping?") the solution of which will forever evade the intellect. In part, study of the koan is meant to reveal the inadequacy of all merely intellectual accounts of ultimate reality. The expectation is that by demonstrating the futility of reason, one will force the genuine searcher to seek other ways of "understanding," i.e., to go beyond the intellect. Isshu Miura crisply aserts that "koan study is a unique method of religious practice which has as its aim the bringing of the student to direct, intuitive realization of Reality without recourse to the mediation of words or concepts."[75] Nevertheless, the koan is itself made of words. What it teaches is that the words are but tools, pointers which serve their purpose if, and only if, they force us to look through or past them at that which they head us towards, but cannot utter. To understand a koan is precisely not to understand its surface meaning—or to understand that you can't arrive at a solution to the puzzle by means of logic and reason—but, rather, to look by means of it, past it to its deeper meaning. Zen maintains that no rational or intellectual doctrine or belief is necessary for the achieving of ultimate truth, i.e., to attain Buddhahood, precisely because *all* such intellectualizations miss the point of that which cannot be objectified, spoken, conceptualized, or otherwise grasped by reason. The koan is a tool, and as such has a purpose and a rationale. That purpose is to point one in the right direction, *viz.* away from ordinary surface meaning, to that which lies behind or beneath ordinary understanding and experience, and even beneath any and all intellectual theories and systems. The surface logic of the koan is p is q only if p is not q.[76] Cheng remarks that such paradoxes are only "paradoxical to those who are not enlightened in Zen. Once a person has Enlightenment, the paradoxes are no longer paradoxical to him even though they remain the same in their linguistic appearance."[77] As though speaking of Nishida's ultimate *basho* of absolute nothingness, Cheng urges that the paradoxes of Zen are designed to sever the supposed link between semantic structures at their surfaces, and the "standard framework or reference," whatever one takes that to be. One discovers that it is inappropriate and misleading to attach "any reference to the given semantic structure, and for that matter, to any semantic structure, and thus should directly look into an uncategorizable ontological structure of no specific reference which has been referred to as the ultimate reality of self-nature or mind."[78] The realization sought arises just because one has been brought to forego *"all* ontological commitments to *all* semantic structures or semantic categories of language."[79]

Perhaps this puts us into position to fruitfully reflect on what tradition holds out as "correct" solutions or answers to the koan puzzles. If one says of the "sound of one hand" koan, "listen," or "hear the rain," or "the geese fly south," or stamps one's foot, it is all the same. No semantically literal answer is correct, and therefore, every semantically literal answer is as good or as ineffective as any other. The effectiveness will be determined, pragmatically and contextually, by whether the answer moves the attention to or away from the literal surface meaning, and to or away from the deep meaning. However irrelevant the answer may seem (and semantically, actually is!), at the deeper level it "will be justified on the ground that it will have the same ultimate reality as its referent and therefore is logically equivalent to any other."[80] The resulting recognition is profoundly Nishidan: all signification, for one who "understands," refers "to the ultimate reality in which all experiences become incomplete portions or representations."[81] It is no more complete to say that knowledge is of universals, than to say that it is of individuals (p is q and p is not q); that the world is ultimately many or one; that ultimate reality can be spoken of, or can't be. It is closer to the truth to say both of these at once, letting neither collapse into the other, but recognizing that (1) the unspoken ultimate is the ground or place of both opposites, and that (2) the best that we can speak of it is to speak of a reality that transcends ordinary classification insofar as it is beyond all such partial or limited categories.

To return to W. T. Stace, "the language is only paradoxical because the experience is paradoxical,"[82] although, strictly speaking, only statements or propositions are paradoxical. Stace's "experience" should be thought of as unclear, ambivalent, as seemingly self-contradictory or in conflict with common sense, although when one probes beneath the surface, sense is restored, and given the new interpretive context, it can be seen to be essentially true. It is closer to the truth of the experience to speak paradoxically, and closer yet to say nothing at all directly. Instead, one can point. All that language can do, on this theory, is to point, which in itself may be a step towards a new interpretive context, and a step away from the old. This is real non-attachment to things! With an open mind, one looks through names and words, to that which language, however precisely it may be employed, merely hints at by pointing to. For Cheng, non-attachment *is* the principle of ontic non-commitment.[83] On the one hand, all language misses the mark, since the ultimate is beyond all possible semantic descriptions; on the other hand, all language, even the most far-fetched, hits the mark because all things *are* it, and "all sounds are the profound and exquisitely subtle voice of *Dharma*."[84] All semantic utterances, gestures, acts, ultimately refer to the same ultimate reality, and hence each is an incomplete portion or account of the whole, of which it is an expression. Everything uttered falls within the universals of judgment, self consciousness and intelligibility, which, in turn are enveloped by the unutterable, of which they are precise and partial expressions. All utterance, if genuinely purposeful, must be a pointer to judgments and/or their objects, or consciousness, or the ideal and acts of consciousness, or to the formless.

Outside of mystical literature, some religious writing, and the bold "indefinite" *(ápeiron)* of Anaximander, it is uncommon to find writers taking seriously this alleged experience of the undifferentiated, i.e., the formless. Usually, the rebuttal takes the form of "Ah, but you couldn't know it, if it was seamless and beyond concepts," or "All knowledge must bear the *nóēsis/nóema* mark in order for it to be knowledge and knowable." "Exactly!" both Nishida and Zennist would reply. But beyond this knowledge lies a deeper realization. *Meditation* is the mainstay of Zen Buddhism, coming before, along with, and after practice with the koan. "Only the student who has achieved some competency in Zazen practice is permitted to undertake the study of a koan."[85] The goal is *kenshō*, a "seeing into one's own real nature."[86] It is said that a Zen monk without *kenshō is* worthless. One who has *kenshō* has seen that everything is as nothing, even one's own self. Everything is "lined" with absolute nothingness; to attain Buddhahood is to be one with nothingness, with that which is beneath relational knowledge.

> The attitude is achieved only when one looks upon all things as beyond every form of expression and demonstration, and by transcending knowledge and argument.[87]

As Kim describes it, in the apparent violation of the law of noncontradiction, the aim is to illuminate the law of ultimate identity. Paradox actually affirms the law of noncontradiction, and probes the seeming contradiction in an attempt to resolve or understand its implications. Satori, or enlightenment, or seeing in a transformed manner, does not point us away from this world to a different world. Rather, it is simply seeing the background as well as the foreground of things. It is the knowledge of individual objects *and* of the reality at the back of them. Zen aims at gaining that "pure experience" in which the subject/object, *nóēsis/nóema* poles have not yet been separated, and, because of which, the mountains are mountains again, and the rice-ears stand high.

NISHIDAN DIALECTIC

The deep self, which forever eludes our conceptual grasp, is yet somehow known, nevertheless, as that at the background of our experience. It is never known but is ever present as a background "lining." Absolute nothingness forever eludes our conceptual grasp, yet it is the "lining" of everything known and knowable. Because I am the I of the *cogito,* and because objects are objects, the deep I is revealed and nothingness has become graspable. All forms are forms of the formless. It is like seeing the faces hidden in the gnarled trees of a cartoon sketch, or seeing both perspectives in a psychological drawing, or grasping both Wittgenstein's duck *and* rabbit—once you see what you didn't see at first, you now no longer see only what you once saw. The transformation of perspective leads one to a double aperture—one now sees first the one, then the other. But unlike the duck and rabbit, the double aperture is binocular. One eventually sees both dimensions at once, and the binocular vision adds depth to both. A double aperture is now in place. It would seem that the growth and maturation of satori itself, or in Western mystical terms the "unitive life," is to be able to "see" through both lenses of reality always, and at the same time.

Things are the absolute, and the absolute is things. Nirvana is samsara and samsara is nirvana. I am I, things are things, and so the unknown is known; I am nothingness, things are nothingness, and I and things are for the first time truly what they are. In Nishida's words "things stand out vividly against the background of nothingness. Indeed, they are the *background's foreground.* The art of satori and of philosophy is to see both the background and foreground at once, and the paradox of one and many as resolved, but not by doing away with either term of the opposition of one and many, speakable and unspeakable, good and bad, life and death, or by creating a synthesis which is other than these two poles in tension. The Zen and the Nishidan solution is to ignore, or to go beyond the law of noncontradiction as a binding force, and to leave in place the elements in tension. In Nishida's words, we have an *identity of contradiction,* or an *identity of self-contradiction.*[88] Hegel, too, argues that truth is the whole, but the difference "is that the universal of universals in Hegel is the Absolute, while in Zen it is Nothing, which is a sort of absolute itself."[89] Furthermore,

> What really distinguishes Zen from the dialectic of Hegel may be found in its thoroughgoing contradiction included in the antinomy. In Hegel, the antinomy is sublated in the synthesis, as canceling and preserving the original antinomy, thus progressing toward an endless realization of the possibilities of the original term. But Zen simply asserts the identity of the antinomy, without following the three-way dialectical process of Hegel. The antithesis, instead of developing into a synthesis, reverts to the thesis, and Zen simply declares that thesis is antithesis and antithesis is thesis. In this process, the unitive power is assumed, and it is Nothing.[90]

The "twist" can best be caught if one sees that it is correct to say, not that there is unity *in* multiplicity, or that there is living *in* dying, but that unity *is* multiplicity, and multiplicity *is* unity; that to live *is* to die, and to die *is* to live. The truth is not *beyond* these, but is the identity of these seeming contradictories. The natural world itself is the contradictory self-identity of space and time. Things stand as separate, and sometimes in opposition to each other in space, and in time. Things, whether in opposition to one another or not, are united.

THE STANDING OF UNIVERSALS

Insofar as all philosophical theories legislate that a certain way of looking at the world is the "correct" or preferred way, it is inappropriate to attempt to say which position is the right one. It is possible, of course, to give one's own reasons for finding another more justified, or more in accord with the evidence from one's own perspective. It thus becomes impossible to say whether Aristotle or Nishida is "correct" in the analysis of the logic of the individual. Every scholar of Aristotle whom I have encountered on this issue has observed that the problem would not even arise for Aristotle. Aristotle took the reality of the individual as a given, and the purpose of logic-as-predication was to precisely specify the status and nature of the individual as a member of a collection of universal classes, and to elaborate upon how the interrelationships of those classes define the individual. Of course the individual is primary! But the individual *qua* individual is not available to Aristotelean logic, which is exclusively of the general.

Nishida's critique of Aristotle arises because he challenges us to take hold of a differing perspective in which the individual as object of knowledge has a firm place. In addition, he wishes to show that just as an epistemology of the general is incomplete without an equivalent epistemology of the individual, so the opposite holds as well. In fact, the point of the insight is to lay bare the contradictory identity of individual and class, class and individual, in order to communicate his central insight that a more complete account of the given-in-experience maintains the tension between individual and class memberships, and all other dichotomies. To this extent Nishida did push beyond Aristotle, not by showing Aristotle to have been in error, but by expanding the declared content of experience to include considerations not present in Aristotle's account. What might be concluded from this is not that earlier philosophers err and are to be discarded, but that the very richness of experience itself far exceeds the grasp of any logic or system of understanding. James and Nishida together urged, and likely for this very reason, that it is "pure experience" that represents this richer content of experience, even though it, too, may forever exceed our intellectual grasp. Pure experience is selected from and carved up for practical purposes, and in accordance with the requirements of a specific perspective. Such experiences are all, at best, partial glimpses of the "aboriginal sensible muchness" which Nishida contends is best captured in concepts and words as a unity or identity which itself is absolutely contradictory.

Perhaps it should also be remarked that Nishida abandoned the highly ornate and perhaps unnecessarily intricate analysis of universals, the systematization of which has been the focus of this chapter. It stands in sharp contrast both with his inaugural *A Study of Good* and with his final "The Logic of the Place of Nothingness and the Religious Worldview." As Joseph S. O'Leary has aptly written, Nishida spent "a lifetime rummaging among untried linguistic and conceptual possibilities,"[91] and among the wide range of Western philosophical and religious systems with which he had familiarized himself. His aims did not greatly change over the course of trial-and-error which led him through numerous complex attempts to state his own position. He may have abandoned the "gothic architectonic" of the universals, and the Neo-Kantianism of *Intuition and Reflection in Self-Consciousness*, in specific detail, but throughout he continued to affirm and elucidate the notions of pure experience, the unobjectifiability of self-consciousness, and the logical and metaphysical priority of nothingness. The various ways of utilizing Western philosophical traditions which Nishida explored in order to explicate his own views on these central themes can only assist us in grasping the difficulties standing in the way of the magnificent partial successes that he achieved all along the way. It is difficult to imagine his final writings being nearly as well comprehended without approaching them via at least a few of his earlier trackings of those insights which, for most of us, are so difficult to take hold of precisely because we were not brought up within cultures of meditation and nothingness.

THREE

Self-Contradictory Identity

In a telling encapsulation, which Yusa translates, Nishida summarizes his years of work:

> This world of historical reality, wherein we are born, act and die, must be, when logically seen, something like the contradictory self-identity of the many and the one. I have come to this point after many years of pondering.[1]

All identity, i.e., all consciousnesses and objects of consciousness in the natural world are self-contradictory unities. But as the elucidation of the levels of universals examined earlier has made amply plain, two things cannot be self contradictory unless they are related by an enveloping matrix which, at the same time, unites them. For things to be in opposition implies thereby a deeper, underlying and grounding unity/system/*basho*. In Nishida's words,

> To think of one thing is to distinguish it from the other. In order for the distinction to be possible, it must originally have something in common with the other.[2]

To emphasize the contradiction is to plunge into the world as many; to emphasize the matrix or ground is to plunge into the world as one. The one is self-contradictorily composed of the many, and the many are self contradictorily one. The world can be viewed in two directions—the double aperture—and its unity is not the unity of oneness, as the mystic would likely express it, but the unity of self contradiction. It is *both* one and many; changing *and* unchanging; past and future in the present. Nishida's dialectic has as its aim the preservation of the contradictory terms, yet as a unity. An individual, as an expression of the universal, negates its individuality, and yet, by negating its individuality by becoming the universal, the universal negates itself as an individual. This is the logic of *soku,* or *sokuhi*—the absolute identification of the is, and the is not. In symbolic representation: A is A; A is not-A; therefore A is A. I see the mountains. I see that there are no mountains. Therefore, I see the mountains again, but as transformed. And the transformation is that the mountains both are and are not mountains. That is their reality. The world of contradictory self-identities, or of the "unity of opposites," as Schinzinger translates the phrase, is not some other distant world, but the actual phenomenologically experienced world in which we find ourselves. The identity of the one points not to oneness, but to the allpervasive presence of self contradictions. Everything is change, or impermanence, says the Buddhist, and yet it is precisely as change that persons and things are what they are. As with Aristotle's *hypokeimenon,* there is that which endures change, but it is not as unchanging. Rather, it is that that which is changes, yet changes not but remains what it is; it is many, yet is not many but one, and so forth. It is not that Aristotle did not know this to be so, for he is the philosopher of change who welds Parmenides and Heraclitus together, as Plato tried to do but with less success. Yet in trying to say all of this logically, Aristotle provided a logic which gave primacy to the grammatical subject, and thus to the unchanging substratum. Nishida wants to right this by placing full emphasis on the grammatical predicate, or to the underlying matrix of place out of which the subject arises, and which actually gives it its proper shape-as-contextualized. Still, it seems to this author that Nishida would have done better to have spoken not of his "logic of place," but to have stressed his logic of subject *and* predicate, or of object and place. It is not exactly a logic of place, but a logic of place as the matrix or context out of which all differentiations or determinations arise, and in which they and their mutual relationships are grounded. Nishida's logic of subject and predicate allows one to see exactly how the individual and the universal relate, and how they may be said to belong together inescapably. In Nishida's words, as found in a letter to a friend, we read:

> In the logic of *basho* the correspondence must be counter-correspondence. The correspondence of the world and self, namely, of whole and one in the logic of *basho* is linked up with the self-identity of contradiction because if we keep saying "One becomes the many, and the many becomes One" they will be forever opposed to each other.... The Absolute is what embraces both of these opposite directions as the Self-identity of contradiction.[3]

The conclusion reached is that absolute nothingness, the final *basho*, is nowhere else but the place where you are. It is not something to be looked at objectively, but rather is that place where your self consciousness and all of its objects of consciousness arise. Still, to see it objectively, that is, to see the form of the formless, is to see the world of dialectical contradiction. The dialectical universal as the form of the ultimately formless is nothing else than the actual world of contradictory self-identity, while the world and its formless base together may be said to be *absolutely contradictory and a self identity*. It is simultaneously being and nothingness. It is transcendent of its form, yet everywhere immanent in each of its forms or instantiations.

Absolute nothingness expresses itself by means of forms in accordance with the subject/object dichotomy. Or, at least, that is how human consciousness deals with all form, all knowledge and all ordinary experience. Husserl was quite right in insisting that all knowledge and all experience is intentional. The only exception to this caveat is, for Nishida, "pure experience." Pure experience is prior to (ontologically), or subsequent to (psychologically) the subject/object split. We experience this way when we move increasingly towards the infinitely bottomless self, or when we experience the nothingness at the base of every object in the world. In other words, when we focus on the manifold of forms of the absolutely formless, we always do so within the logical context of subject/object, *nóēsis/nóema*. But when we look through these forms to the formless basis of them all, we realize that the forms are but expressions of the formless, which is not itself thereby caught. The formless is inescapably nondeterminate, just as the self that is prior to objectification is really a no-self; it sees things but it does not see itself as an object of its seeing. It is prior to, or at the base of, both objectivity *and* subjectivity, and itself is both of these and neither of these. This is the paradoxical formulation of Nishida's identity of opposites, or the self-identity of absolute contradiction, or self-contradictory identity.

SELF-CONTRADICTORY IDENTITY

Translators have offered various alternative renderings of *Zettai mujunteki jikodōitsu:* the "unity of opposites,"[4] "contradictory self-identity,"[5] "self-identity of contradiction,"[6] "identity of contradiction,"[7] and "contradictory identity."[8] What a successful translation of this phrase must communicate to the reader is (1) the paradoxicality inherent in Nishida's perspective on reality, (2) the dynamism of a philosophic perspective which in principle allows no epistemic resting place (i.e., "now I understand" must immediately give way to "and, so, I do not understand"), and (3) a deeper understanding of the dynamism of paradoxicality which allows the seeing of each as both different from each other, and yet the same as each other. I am inclined to de-emphasize *identity,* for the temptation to emphasize sameness at the expense of difference is too great. This temptation is not only to be found in Western thinkers (cf. Plato's attempt to ascertain the common form which was the intelligible reality underlying the less-intelligible sensible instances), but may be found in Eastern traditions as well (cf. the assumption in some Indian traditions that multiplicity is illusory—maya—while Brahman, the underlying identity or oneness, is real). For Nishida, the real is no less one than it is many, no less different than it is identical. The differences must be fully retained and re-affirmed in the face of the realization of the sameness of things, and vice versa. Additionally, emphasis on the sameness or oneness of things tends to suggest the eternal, immutable, unchanging, and static—all characteristics that Nishida is at pains to reject in his account of a reality that is (Buddhistically) impermanent, and ever in process.

THE DYNAMIC OF PARADOX

Nishida's "logic of *soku hi*" (the "is" and the "is not" of a thing, or the oneness or identity of the is and is-not) can be expressed as follows: A is A, and *yet* A is not-A, therefore A is A.[9] What the is *and* the is-not of the *soku hi* formulation protects is the dynamical tension of affirmative and negative "without synthesis."[10] The only reality that Nishida seeks to analyze, then, is the everyday world of dynamic activity, which manifests itself to ordinary consciousness as logically paradoxical. As Nakamura Hajime has emphasized, for the Japanese who is influenced by Zen thought, it is this world, the everyday world of common-sense, that is *absolute*.[11] It *is* the ultimate, even though it is not known ultimately, absolutely, or completely. "Complete knowing" is surface knowing, and it is inevitably either one-sided, or hopelessly inconclusive because paradoxical. Kant's antinomies forever dwarf claims to know fully, while scientific discovery warns that yesterday's "proof" incessantly yields to "reformulation" in accordance with a new paradigm. More to the point, the Japanese and the Buddhist recognition of the indeterminate which lies behind the determinate, necessitates the view that whatever can be said or conceptually known is neither complete nor ultimate. But it is no less real for that. Rather, it is but one side of, or one perspective of, reality. It is one aperture of reality-awareness, and even at that, it is an aperture of unrelenting paradox—of incessant contradictoriness. The real is, in itself (as we know it) contradictory. In order to apprehend things as they are "means to seek contradictions."[12] Through the aperture of consciousness which is the logical, conceptual, subject/object, *noetic/noematic* mode, reality appears as a contradiction, and not as a synthesis. What made coming to this insight so arduous is the fact that Nishida had to reject both the perspective of ordinary logic, which seeks to eliminate paradox—i.e., which takes the law of non-contradiction as its emblem *(either* a thing is, or is not)—and the perspective of dialectic, which eliminates paradox and contradiction in a series of syntheses, and ultimately rests on a final synthesis of all into a single whole or oneness. What Nishida struggled for was a different perspective which could embrace both the thesis and the antithesis, the subject and the object, without suppressing either.[13] The real, phenomenal world *is* both one and many, subjective and objective, changing and unchanging. Reality is self-contradictory.

NĀGĀRJUNA'S INFLUENCE

Nishida's logic was undoubtedly influenced by the Middle Path logic of Nāgārjuna (c. 100-200). To what extent was Nishida's use of Nāgārjuna's logical analysis consistent with the more standard interpretations of Nāgārjuna's purposes and point? If divergent, what might be revealed is a purpose and point quite distinct from, if not distortive of, the orthodox understanding. Yet even the well-studied texts of Nāgārjuna lend themselves to quite different interpretations. In a recent volume by David Kalupahana, a brief summary of what is perhaps the major modern view is offered:

> Modern scholars, favoring an interpretation by Candrakīti made known to them by T.R.V. Murti, insist that Nāgārjuna had no thesis of his own *(svapaka)* to present. This Vedantic interpretation presents Nāgārjuna as a critical or analytical philosopher whose sole function was to criticize or analyse *(vigraha)* views presented by others without having to recognize or uphold a view of his own.[14]

Kalupahana takes Nāgārjuna to be close to original or early Buddhism in that "the middle way" is a rejection of all closed dogmatisms, and advocates that one remain nonattached to each and every one of them. Thus, "non-attachment to views does not necessarily mean having 'no views.'"[15] What the Buddha and Nāgārjuna were attacking was a dogmatic arrogance which, in its quest for absolute certainty and security, caused thinkers to cling "like leeches to an objective world as an ultimate reality."[16] Each and every position is but a half-truth adopted for a purpose, and wrenched from a richer whole actually available (in degree) in the original experiences.

> The "middle position" as the right view *(sammā-ditthi)*, whether it be dependent arising *(paticcasumuppāda)* or non substantiality *(anatta)*, or as Nāgārjuna puts it, "absence of self-nature" *(nihsvabhāva)* or emptiness

(*sūnyatā*), leads to worldly fruits as well as the ultimate fruit. However, if that right view were to become another dogma, it would certainly contribute to conflict and suffering, thereby losing its pragmatic value.[17]

Even the middle view can be held dogmatically, and such closure is everywhere to miss the point of the openness of genuine nondogmatic understanding and discovery. The point seems to be that all philosophical distinctions ought to be seen as "empty," i.e., as inadequate, relative, and distortive if taken absolutely. As Kasulis observes,

> [Nāgārjuna,] after drawing up a list of the major distinctions assumed by the various philosophical systems of his time . . . demonstrated, one by one, that if these distinctions are *considered to be absolute*, they lead to ineluctable absurdities.[18]

Nāgārjuna's insight is that each and every philosophical position and claim can be shown to be untenable because any assertion, or the making of *primary* any conception (the *cogito*, cause, or Buddha-nature) is achieved at the risk of downplaying one or more related concepts. Kasulis cites the example of one's Buddha-nature (personal essence) which, if understood restrictedly, would no longer have the possibility of real discovery or change, but would rigidity as a fixed essence. But to reject the even tentative limits of human nature is also to make change impossible, except in a single moment, for there would be no center of experience to undergo continuous change.[19]

Lived experience seems to require both antithetical models—we are free, and yet we are free only within the limits of our nature. An open-system of thought grasps and accepts the paradoxical demands of more adequate accounting, and also knows that even these ingredients are but partial and even temporary. To deny perfection in analytic thinking is not, however, to deny all order or epistemic gain. Just because you are unable to sweep the kitchen floor clean once and for all does not mean that sweeping is hopeless, worthless, and ought to be abandoned. One sweeps, and the result is a more livable environment, even though the sweeping is but one of many positions, and will be done yet again, likely differently. Sweeping is necessary, but absolute or "final" sweeping is a delusion. Quoting Kasulis again,

> The philosophical distinction between personal essence and no essence, for example, merely presents two alternative models. For Zen, completeness and consistency are not as critical as the intended use and appropriateness of the model. Therefore, when it furthers his aims, the Zen Master may speak as if there is a personal essence; when it is more helpful to deny this essence, he will do so with as much aplomb as the campaign manager shifting his attention from one map to the other.[20]

If we push far enough and hard enough, we see the co-existence of all utterances with their opposites: existence alone needs an essence, and essence requires the freedom of mere existence-as-becoming; waves and particles, while antithetical, are together necessary ingredients in the explanation of any quantum phenomenon; the *a priori* seems to be somehow experientially derived, and the *a posteriori*, is already a category of purely conceptual understanding, else we could not explain why we initially attended to just this aspect or dimension of experience. No conceptual distinction has an absolute grounding, and so "any assertion of one side of a distinction over the other is, at its foundation, self-contradictory."[21] Indeed, "any assertion or distinction only highlights one aspect of a situation and, in so doing, casts into shadows an equally important, though incompatible, aspect."[22] Concepts filter out much of the richer manifold given in immediate experience, yet it might be that *the more adequate* view is a middle one which salvages the paradoxicality of the necessary tension between the opposed contenders. The logic is a *both-and,* and not an *either-or* one. It is also a logic of relative approximation conceptually, pointing towards the richer source and, I think, maintaining that both dimensions need to be held, and held in tension. The nature of that tension is that one never "gets it right," for as soon as one comes down firmly, and once and for all on the side of an issue, one must return again to the indefinite no-distinction-no-thing of pure experience, in order to drink again from the richer source. Like an artist at a favorite painting spot, one sees the vista anew each time, and one could paint a thousand paintings from the same spot, each quite different from the others. One must paint, and then un-paint by looking again, "without prejudice." It is far easier to be open in this way if one does not begin by assuming that there is a "definitive" painting to be done. It is better to capture a facet of the whole in a fresh or unique way, and to recognize it as only a facet or a portion of the scene, than to hold out for the "right" depiction which, we now see, may be logically impossible to achieve. Indeed, it would be to look in the wrong direction for understanding and insight.

Standing on the shoulders of Nāgārjuna, Nishida's great insight is that, even while recognizing the limitedness of all conceptual systems and their parts, it is still possible to recognize that a system of philosophic understanding can be truer than another because it points us through and beyond itself toward its (and our) ground of origin, which as a result is experienced more richly, immediately, or directly (if not more definitively). At the same time it is analyzable into concepts that are more fruitful to the original richness and which more approximately represent the depth and complexity of the pure experience itself. In fact, no apprehension of the immediately experienced ground (nothingness, śūnyatā, nirvana) is complete without this fuller account of the forms-of-nothingness in the space-time-world-of-human-conceptual-consciousness (samsara). The two are aspects of the same identity—distinct, yet unified. They form an identity, yet are different. This is the self-contradictoriness of the world of experience itself, as an absolute identity of self-contradiction. It is not that only pure experience is to be attended to, nor that "nothingness" or "emptiness" must be elevated to take the place of "God" or "Being." Even empti*ness* must be emptied, leaving only *the empty,* and then the empty must be emptied, leaving things as relatively full and distinct. Then, one empties things, and one returns to indefinite no-thing-ness again, and all is empty. The process of emptying, based on the premise that all conceptualization is relativistically limited by its own necessarily arbitrary ontology, must itself be emptied by the reality of another way of knowing, *viz. prajñā,* by means of which a synthetic or holistic direct apprehension of reality-as-immediate-experience is afforded. These two, together, as form and as perpetually interactive process, yield as much as we can know about reality. Even then, as a noted Zen scholar did in the midst of a four-hour conversation at his home in Japan, we must chuckle and perhaps guffaw at the vision of reality we have gained. Laughing at the array of propositions and diagrams we had together worked out in order to convey the Zen understanding, my colleague laughed until the tears literally ran down his cheeks. I, too, had caught his gist, and the all too human had similarly reduced me to tears as well. "I'm terribly sorry," he said while the laughter continued to force itself on us both, "but this always happens to me when I try to talk about ultimate reality!"

If Nāgārjuna had no position at all, then Nishida parts company with him. If, however, as Kalupahana contends, his position is that all conceptual thinking is relativistically limited, and that the enemy is the one who does not see this but who grasps at the straws of dogmatic and absolute certainty, then Nishida and Nāgārjuna share a common perspective. Both use analysis to point beyond itself to a deeper reality which can only be apprehended directly and lived directly. Perhaps it can't be said to be "known" at all, for knowing is linguistic and conceptual. As Kasulis remarks, "Remember that the master not only perceives *mu* ('nothingness'); he *is* it."[23] It is here, in the individual as the place *(basho)* of paradox, where contradictories meet, that identity is achieved as well. But we don't only live, we also think. The fullest picture of reality, or of reality-for-beings-like-us, includes both the seamless emptiness or immediacy without form, and the forms of material and conceptual life, both in mutual determination of each other. All is in process, even the world of thought.

THE WORLD AS CONTRADICTORY IDENTITY

In his 1939 essay, "The World as Identity of Absolute Contradiction," Nishida applies his notion of contradictory identity to the historical world. As centers of self-consciousness, we encounter a vast array of things which constitute our environment. We, as self-conscious determiners, interact with our environment such that we have influence on it—transform it—and are transformed by it. It sets limits, and we overcome those limits. It resists, and we change course, or alter the resistance directly. Either way, the interaction is *mutual*. And, therefore, the contradiction is also mutual: the individual is (partially) negated (changed) as an individual through its encounter with the environment; the environment is (partially) altered (negated) by the individual acting on it. *Mutual contradiction is* the shape of Nishida's self-contradiction, thus emphasizing the dynamic and never-ceasing character of it. Self-contradiction appears again in the individual/species dichtomy. The species is only to be found in the individuals comprising it, and the individuals comprising the species are the kinds of individuals they are precisely because they are members of just that species.[24] The contradiction lies in the mutual effect which one member of a pair of opposites has on the other, and vice versa. The *identity* in "self-contradictory identity" is always presupposed, in that for a thing to "resist or conflict with one another presupposes the same underlying generic concept."[25] Just as the colors presuppose the system of colors, which is the source of identity and contact among them, so individual and species, self and environment, the one and the many must be taken in pairs, and as mutually interacting, in order for the dynamic of the world-as-process to be approximated conceptually.

The world is also the contradictory self-identity of space and time:

> In the standpoint of abstract thinking time and space never join. And yet actuality is precisely their contradictory coincidence. I do not say that actuality is merely a compound wherein these irreconcilables are reconciled; it is their contradictory identity.[26]

Time is not space, space not time, and yet the world we live in is an identity of space-time. So it is with time itself. It is in the identity of the present that past and future meet. The past negates itself by already containing within itself the present and the future, while the future is negated by carrying within itself the past, and arising out of the present moment. Even the present "contains its self-negation and is always transcending itself—but it transcends itself from present to present."[27]

Time is itself the contradictory unity of the present.[28] The eternal present is itself a self-contradictory unity or identity.

IDENTITY

"At the base of the world," writes Nishida "there are neither the many nor the one; it is a world of absolute unity, of opposites, where the many and the one deny each other."[29] The present is the temporal place, or *basho* where the self contradictory past and future mutually interact. As well, "this contradictory identity," in any and all of its forms, "is the very place where we find our self."[30] Thus it is that the place where one is, is always *basho*—not something one can look at objectively, but the place where contradictions mutually interact. This is the unity, field, or matrix in which contradictions arise, for "if there were no point of contact anywhere, neither would there be any contradiction."[31] While the contradiction is not resolvable (since it is descriptive of how things actually are), it is a contradiction that is embraced by, or arises out of, an identity/field/place/*basho* which expresses itself in precisely this self-contradictory way. As Nishida wrote in a 1943 letter to a friend, "The Absolute is what embraces both of these opposite directions by the self-identity of contradiction."[32] All being is an expression of, or "a self-unfolding of the eternal, formless nothingness; all finite forms are shadows of the formless."[33] Nothingness, the enveloper of all things, is the unifier of opposites, the identity of its own self-contradictory expressions. It is the lining that is common to everything. Nothingness *is* the world as contradictory identity. The countless and unceasing contradictions of the world are expressions of a unity or an identity. Thus, it is quite right to say that these contradictions are only contradictory from the perspective of objectifying logic,[34] which steadfastly maintains the law of noncontradiction. But object logic, which Nishida takes as but one perspective on the real world, is itself grounded on the logic of *basho* or place, which understands contradictions as themselves related in a unifying matrix that is "beyond," or not completely characterizable by, either of the conflicting characteristics. This unresolved contradiction, or paradox, is itself grounded in the identity of contradiction. The unresolved contradiction remains a fact, but the underlying unity of which they are expressions is the second aperture, and the two apertures taken together constitute the fullest and best account available. Everything is self-contradictory and, therefore, all things are at bottom identical, i.e., arise out of an ultimately common matrix or field, *viz.* absolute nothingness. The identity of things can be grasped, at least initially, by ignoring the peculiarities of things, and concentrating on their common ground. As Schinzinger writes,

> The Buddhists use the word *"soku"* which means "namely," and say: the world is one, namely many.[35]

Similarly, the fact that all is ultimately one means that it is, therefore, many. The double aperture is now in place: the paradoxicality of the world of ordinary experience is now overlaid with a grasp of the identity of things, yielding the ultimate paradox. The one is self-contradictorily composed of the many, while each of the many are self-contradictorily one with all of the others, forming a unity. The world can be viewed in these two directions, and wisdom requires both *in tension*. The tension must be maintained, as the two ends of a guitar string must be firmly held in a stretched condition for musical tones to be emitted when the string is struck. Understanding requires both apertures to be maintained in mind simultaneously, thereby leaving the paradoxical self-contradictory-in-identity in place. Nishida's strength is that he did not attempt to resolve the contradictions of experience, but saw them as inescapable as descriptions of the way the world is, as it is known by us. The result is not a synthesis, but a unity-in-contradiction, an identity-of-opposites. At the same time, absolute nothingness as the ultimate and final universal (the universal of universals) is itself beyond all characterization, and therefore beyond all contradictoriness. It is, by the same token, also beyond identity.

NOTHINGNESS AND THE OX HERDER

Ueda Shizuteru, a member of the Nishida-inspired Kyoto School, describes the eighth, ninth, and tenth drawings from the twelfth-century Chinese Zen text *The Ox and His Herdsman,*[36] as depicting "the dynamic correlatedness of negation and affirmation."[37] The earlier stages, in text and drawings, describe the journey from ordinary-mindedness to enlightenment. The first seven stages lead the reader to join in the search for a deeper understanding of self. The progression illustrated in the ten drawings is spiritual progress, and the ox is "whitened,"[38] or perhaps better, held increasingly lightly (or "emptily") until it disappears. The first picture shows no trace of the ox, with which we are totally out of touch … except, perhaps, for the still small voice which is barely audible, and at that only when we are silent and meditative. "Desire for gain and fear of loss burn like fire, ideas of right and wrong shoot up like a phalanx."[39] The noise of the world deludes us into thinking that the noisy alone is the real. Sutras, and whatever else occasionally calls one to reflection, reveal *traces* of one's deeper, true nature, one's Buddha-nature, in spite of the constant clatter.

Discovering the traces is the theme of the second frame, and still there is no sighting of the ox, only scant traces. Perhaps it is a myth, a legend to keep us humbled and in line. The traces could be explained away.... In spite of the confusion in mind and emotions, the traces become increasingly undeniable.

The quest continues, and the third stage is that of actually *seeing* the ox. "He finds the way through the sound; he sees into the origin of things...."[40] His self is now present, in the background, in every act of consciousness: "It is like the salt in water and the glue in color."[41]

Yet in the everyday world, the ox remains in the background, and has not actually been caught, harnessed, and brought to the surface of control. He is unruly and ungovernable. The herder's senses are not yet in harmonious order: his empirical self is disordered and runs wild. The taming of the deep self requires focused concentration and diligent training. Practice and discipline alone will lead to success. This, the fourth stage, requires severe self-discipline, else the ox will recede or return to the quiet pasture from which it came. It is frightened by the noise and stress of the everyday world.

The fifth frame, "Herding the Ox," is the stage of discipline. One is now free of conceptual distinctions which serve to filter out of experience the unexpected. Now, "When a thought moves, another follows, and then another—there is thus awakened an endless train of thoughts."[42] For the enlightened person, the person in touch with his deep nature, "all this turns into truth." We can still give in to wrong thinking, however, and find ourselves estranged from the flow, somehow separate from it. But the ox is now nearly under control.

The sixth picture shows the herder on the ox's back, riding home. "The struggle is over," and he is no longer distracted by the noise of the world, and he and his ox have become as one.[43] The herder is no longer distracted or enticed by the world of everyday appearance, no longer grasping and hoarding, but is joyful in the flow of things, awestruck by the exquisiteness of each unique moment that announces the background of the whole of things along with its shimmering foreground. In the seventh stage, the realization occurs that one is already one's own deep self (symbolized by the ox). All has always already been one, united, and the ox is only separate symbolically: "Lo! there is no more cow [ox], and how serenely...[the herder] sits all alone." [44] He has let the ox go; there never was an ox, only one's enlightened self, one's Buddha-nature.

The eighth stage includes no reference to the herdsman, the ox, the world, or anything at all. It is depicted by an empty circle, a "zero." It is a negation of all that went before. One negates who one thought one once was, and thereby the chains of the empirical ego are broken. All things have collapsed, and with them, all substance thinking. Things are, at bottom, one in their nothingness. In Nishida's terms, they are expressions of this field, which itself is inexpressible. It is neither being, nor non-being, nor both, nor neither. The ox herder's mind is completely clear, tranquil, mirror-like. Not even the trappings of holiness remain. Spirituality is not a separate event, an ox. It includes the herder, for he too has *merged* with the whole of things. All distinctions have vanished into the fullness of nothingness.

In the ninth drawing one finds the world of nature—trees, blossoms, a stream—again present. In Ueda's account:

> In the movement from the eighth to the ninth it is no longer, as in the preceding stages, a matter of gradual progression but of the correlatedness, or an oscillating back and forth. Nothingness in the eighth stage and simplicity in the ninth belong together, metaphorically speaking, like two sides of a single sheet of paper, a paper without thickness. The two sides are neither two nor one. It is rather a matter of a correlated double perspective each of which penetrates the other.[45]

This double aperture is both the same as it once was, and yet different (transformed) as well. As the Zen epigram makes abundantly clear, the mountains that one once saw in a straightforward and ordinary way were then lost in the identity of nothingness in which all differentiation gives way to the undifferentiated sameness, only to be recast *(emptied)* such that the mountains again seen are now seen differently because they are (1) freed from old habits of understanding, (2) seen in and for themselves, and (3) *lined* with the depths of nothingness. One sees the same world of nature in the ninth stage as one did in the earlier stages, but now one sees it "as-it-is-by-itself," in its "thusness."[46] One's "no-mindedness" has allowed nature to "nature."[47] The resulting mutuality of stages eight and nine is, I think, exactly the self-contradictory identity that Nishida struggled to capture in more precise philosophical terms. Stages eight and nine are not two sides of one stage, nor does one swallow the other. Each infiltrates the other, while each maintains its "otherness" as separate and utterly distinct. The two are "reversible," for the world of nature *is* nothingness, and nothingness *is* the world of nature: "form is emptiness, emptiness is form"; nirvana is samsara, samsara is nirvana.[48] The two are not one, but remain two. They are not somehow identical, but are interrelated, complementary, mutually interactive, and therein is their "identity" or oneness. It is an identity of non-identity, a oneness of twoness (hence of multiplicity). The self-contradictions now multiply, but not as the earlier stages (1-7), as contradictions of the nothingness of stage 8, but as 1-7 transformed so as to become 9, contrasting with 8. The self-contradiction is at an even deeper level. As Ueda states, nature as transformed (stage 9) may be viewed from the perspective or focus of nothingness (stage 8), or nothingness (stage 8) may be viewed from the perspective or focus of nature as transformed (stage 9):

> The direction of seeing through form as nothingness is designated Great Understanding, while the direction of seeing nothingness immediately concretized as form is designated Great Compassion.[49]

One's focus not only does, but actually ought to shift back and forth from the formed to the forming, the created to the creating, the cup to its empty space, the form to the formless, nirvana to samsara, but each time keeping the other perspective or aperture *open* wide so that from whichever focus one is looking, one is still able to see the other as well.

Form as formless, or the formless as form, are two distinct and distinctive perspectives on the world, but both are required if one is to climb towards an adequate epistemological grasp of the world. The seeing prescribed is a sort of double-vision, but the two images are, taken separately, each far, far clearer than they have ever been before.

Ueda urges that the tenth stage, which depicts an old man meeting a youth on the road, announces that one's selfless-self has now expanded to include both "I and Thou."[50] One now encounters others in the world, but "without forsaking absolute nothingness."[51] He catches the double aperture perfectly with these words:

> On the roads of the world as in nothingness, in nothingness *as* on the roads of the world. Untiring and serious efforts made on behalf of another is thus, at the same time, in virtue of nothingness, play for oneself, though not in the sense of a play that entails the loss of effort and compassion.[52]

10

The *identity* in self-contradiction must not be clung to. The oneness implies multiplicity, and multiplicity implies the oneness of identity. Nishida's insight is that it is both that must be said, and that both are related by virtue of nothingness. Nothingness is an identity, and therefore, it is not an identity, but a multiplicity, and vice versa. What then is nothingness or, for that matter, anything? It is X, *yet* not X, therefore both X *and* not-X, *thus* neither X nor not-X. To say all of this about any one, any thing, any event or any relation, is to speak in the context provided by the schema of self-contradictory identity.

MIRRORING

> The most fundamental and inclusive universal from which everything comes and to which everything returns must be the universal of expression.[53]

Everything may be viewed as an expression of its field, or *basho*, and every *basho* is eventually embraced by the ultimate *basho*, absolute nothingness.* Thus, everything is, ultimately, an expression or manifestation of absolute nothingness. Even in his earliest work, Nishida is steadfast in warning against a conception of God, or the ultimate reality, as a creator of a universe separate from him: "The universe is not a thing created by God, but a 'manifestation' of God."[54] There is nothing that is not such a manifestation, and, hence, it will be Nishida's task to explain how evil can be, and be a part of the ultimate. His early answer to the problem of evil is that while not absolute (i.e., without granting it the alienated individuality of Satan), it arises from the ultimate itself as part of the very process of individuation. Our own individuality is not a "phantasm," but one of God's "differentiating functions."[55] Therefore,

> if we ask from what arises this thing which is conflict, we can say that it is something which is based in the differentiating function of reality, and is one necessary condition of the development of reality, and that reality develops according to contradiction and conflict.[56]

While Nishida only hints at a solution in *A Study of Good*, he already anticipates his "final essay," which forms the latter part of the present study. "Love is the zenith of intelligence," he states, and instantiates this claim with an example:

---

*The universal of expression is the *medium* in which self-contradictories oppose one another. It is *basho*, the place where mutual interaction arises. Every space-time being manifests or *expresses* itself as it does because of its own nature, and because of the other determinants impinging upon it. Things self-determine themselves, i.e., express themselves, and they do this in the *basho* where all expression as the identity of self-contradiction arises.

> ...love is the union of subject and object. Our loving a thing means our
> casting aside the self and merging with the other.... When a parent merges
> with his child and a child merges with his parent, here for the first time the
> love of parent and child arises. Since the parent has merged with the child,
> each advantage and disadvantage of the child is felt as if it were the
> advantage and disadvantage of the self, and since the child has merged with
> the parent, each joy and sadness of the parent is felt as if it were the joy and
> sadness of the self.[57]

Buddha's love, as we would expect from this analysis, "extended even to
birds and beasts, grasses and trees."[58] The overcoming of evil is to
identify with the all, to merge with it, and the Zen model of such
merging is to enter the realm of nothingness, of "zero," where because
all distinctions disappear, when they reappear to individual consciousness, they are now lined with the never-to-be-forgotten field of
non-differentiation. One overcomes evil by loving the whole as oneself.
This, and only this, is to know reality, for love is "the deepest knowledge of a thing" insofar as love "is the power to seize the basic substance
of reality."[59] Love is the culmination of intelligence.

Absolute nothingness, as has been said, expresses itself as a
self-contradictory identity. It is neither a many, nor a one, nor even
both. Still less is it neither, for both identity and difference, oneness and
multiplicity arise out of it, as self-expressions. One can only approxi-
mate the truth of things by recognizing the interplay of the contradictions, which everywhere imply each other and mutually interact or
interpenetrate in their identity, as well.

A constant image in Nishida's expression of the notion of absolute
nothingness is that of *mirroring:*

> That we mirror the world means we become one perspective [of the many].
> From the viewpoint of the world, what is meant by it reflects itself within
> itself in that we, as self-contradictory, countless individuals, reflect the
> world.[60]

In commenting on this passage, Yusa emphasizes that here too, the
self-contradictoriness is at work, for while, on the one hand, each

individual reflects or mirrors the whole in a unique and distinctive way, on the other hand, each individual mirrors the entire world, and even expresses absolute nothingness in and by its own nature.[61] As with the hologram, each part of the projection includes the pattern of the whole, in its entirety, even though it only overtly expresses itself as a distinctive part of the whole. At the same time, "that I mirror the world is that I am mirrored by the world,"[62] thus switching the activity to the whole, to absolute nothingness which actively expresses itself as a unique and distinctive thing or self.

Jikaku, self-awakening or self-consciousness, is the awareness of myself as independent of others, and of the whole that is the world, of which I am a part. The double aperture here operates as always, for one can view one's own self from the perspective of the whole which is mirrored, and the individual which mirrors the whole. As Nishida describes it, "What is meant by 'I have my existence in the contradictory self-identity' is that what is expressed and what expresses are one and the same thing."[63] The self, as the place, or *basho* where nothingness arises in this world, is itself an expression of absolute nothingness, and as such is a continuity of the discontinuous moments of time (where past and future interact). But just as the individual self is conscious of its individuality, and of the discontinuity of the discrete moments of its history, so each self is an aspect of the self-consciousness of the whole, which without such difference would be without the differentiated perspective necessary for self-consciousness to exist anywhere. Thus God, or absolute nothingness, or ultimate reality in its/His absolute self-negation faces Himself/itself *in an inverse correspondence (gyakutaiō-teki)* "Because He contains absolute self-negation within Himself, He is that which exists by itself. Being absolutely Nothing, He is absolute Being."[64] It is both transcendent and immanent and, as Schinzinger observes, may be likened to "the one and undivided moon [which] is reflected in water, in the ocean as well as in millions of dewdrops, or even in dirty puddles. In each reflection the moon is whole and un-divided,"[65] and yet each reflection is distinctively unique. The two apertures by means of which we apprehend the moon exist side by side, with the one encircling the other in the consciousness of the individual who can grasp them both. Stages 8 and 9 of the ox-herding sequence must interact with one another, in our consciousness, of course. While at bottom, the individual is identical with the enveloping nothingness of the totality, each is also a unique aperture of and on the whole which is available nowhere else.

— FOUR —

God and Nothingness

Another central image in modern Japanese philosophy, in particular that of the Kyoto School, is that of *the form of the formless*. It is also one of the most difficult notions to comprehend. Within it, however, are the seeds of understanding and comparative contrast which may help those of us brought up in the West to make sense of, and even to learn from, the Eastern emphasis on the epistemological and metaphysical priority of nothingness over being.

The fundamental question is, of course, what does nothingness add to human understanding? For if it has no clear referent, then we may be able to cut it off with Occam's razor, much as science has eliminated ungrounded additions such as phlogiston and animating spirits in the blood. Indeed, it is generally assumed in the West that *being is* the primary category of understanding, and that "nothingness" is simply a term which refers to the negating, denial, or removal of being. There is being and there is non-being. Non-being isn't anything that has an existence of its own, but is a dependent notion referring to the no-longer-beingness of a thing, situation or property of a being. Thus, being precedes non-being, both in ontological validity and in epistemic significance. Non-being is dependent on whatever being it negates, as is evidenced by the awkwardness of trying to have it the other way around, i.e., referring to being as non-nothingness.

While who is right is an academic question at this point, the going gets much more difficult when the issue is raised in a specifically religious context. While few would volunteer for active service in the fight of being over nothingness in epistemic priority, the issue is different when "God" is substituted for "being." Paul Tillich comes to mind as the modern Protestant Christian advocate of such a substitution, for he tells us that God is being itself, or the ground of being, or the "unconditioned."[1] Tillich is careful to point out that all of these locutions are terms which, for religious purposes, are used symbolically, i.e., they refer to God as knowable and partially revealed by the world of the finite which is his creation, and in which we share, and yet they also refer to God's transcendence, to his being wholly other and beyond all finite understanding.[2] To take the term "God" literally is to miss its major purpose, to point us away from the finite. Religious language is always "self-transcendent,"[3] and so Tillich must call attention to the "God above the God of theism."[4] To hold any conception of God is, by necessity, to focus on the finite, and to let go of the "ecstatically transcendent" which is religious language's main focus.[5] But to emphasize the transcendent at the expense of the finite and conceptualizable is to fall into conceptual emptiness or linguistic meaninglessness. Thus Tillich cannot emphasize the unknowability of God as primary, but only as a procedure for callmg attention to the limitedness of the finite, concrete images which must remain in the forefront of meaning. In a way, one could say that our ideas of God are the forms of the formless, and that while the formless can never be captured by finite forms, it can be pointed to.

For modern Japanese philosophers, however, there are problems with such a view. Abe Masao observes that it is odd to speak of the ground of being as itself being, and as embracive of non-being. While it is now commonplace to follow Heidegger in speaking of that nothingness that lurks at the heart of being, the logic of the claim, as Tillich interpreted it, is that being, or God, embraces both non-being and itself. Abe asks how being can be its own ground,[6] and while this point has force, it is surely no more clear that nothingness demands our quick agreement as the correct alternative. The substitution of a monistic position for a dualistic one is an old solution and represents an old battle in philosophy. Abe's operant thesis is that behind the dualism of being and non-being there is a monistic principle that is not Tillich's ground-of-being. Whether or not Tillich's insight is also monistic is, however, only secondary to Abe's main concern, namely, that Tillich is an advocate of being, whether ground-of-being or otherwise, whereas the Japanese tend to emphasize a monism of nothingness. Abe does not settle the issue. He simply suggests that what is able to embrace both being and non-being must itself be neither of these, or, at least, both of these, although such recognition would be but a stage along the path to non-dualism. This is, in fact, the form of the formless: because it is neither being nor non-being, both can arise out of it. The dualism of being and non-being is the form, and both require the "ground" which is neither, and therefore can give birth to both. Nothingness, or the formless, is non-dualistic because it is *prior* to any dualism. Nothingness is the non-dualistic whole which is as it is, and before it is sliced up by the dualistic logic of being and non-being. It is not simply the negation of being, but includes both being and non-being. It is not simply the negation of being, but includes both being and its negation. It is not *any thing*, but is beyond all predication, or any sort of description, since all description is already to be on this side of dualism.

What is one to do with all of this? By denying the adequacy of the dualistic perspective—creation/creator, self/other, subjective/objective, matter/mind—have we not skewed Tillich's formula such that the transcendent meaning of ultimate reality has collapsed into vacuousness and meaninglessness? The answer would be an unqualified "yes" if the only approach to the matter was verbal and intellectual. But the East has long viewed language and reason as but inadequate tools for the partial revelation of that which is neither verbal nor intellectual, but *experiential*. More precisely still, the nature of the experiences here identified is usually described as being like "feeling." To come face to face with the formless, then, is to cultivate feeling in direct experience. As Nishida expressed it:

> It is a common idea that feeling differs from knowledge, and that its content is less clear.... The alleged unclarity of feeling means nothing more than that it cannot be expressed in conceptual knowledge. It is not that consciousness in feeling is unclear, but rather that feeling is a more subtle and delicate form of consciousness than conceptual knowledge.[7]

THE FORM OF THE FORMLESS

For Nishida, feeling is what is left when we imaginatively *remove* all content from consciousness, for when we do so we are left with "personal unity, the content of which is precisely that of feeling."[8] It is revealed when the self is merged with its activity, and all qualities disappear in one undifferentiated awareness itself.[9] It is awareness that is aware, and that is all there is. It is perfectly lucid and clear, for it is everything, without being a distinguishable anything. It is not an awareness *of* something, nor is it someone's being aware. There is just *awareness*. The East typically teaches that the most efficient way of reaching such feeling is through the paths of *meditation*. The methods of the koan, or the chanting of sutras, or silence and stillness, are all meant to lead one to the depths of self where all subject/object distinctions vanish into the lucidity of *pure* experience. Thus it is that the Buddha is your own mind, and your mind gives way to your self as the place or focus of all things/experiences. Your self, as pure experience, is an undifferentiated place (Nishida's *basho*) or arena where all things arise, except that it is not a place or arena, but an aperture or opening. It, too, is characterized as impermanent. To try to characterize it as anything more than an aperture or dynamic place is to lose it. It is nothing. And because it has no characteristics of its own, it is able to experience an indefinite number of forms as characteristics. Yet in doing so it reveals its own form: it is formless. And the only route to an understanding of this formlessness is by the direct experience of its grasping of the myriad of forms. The awareness of forms reveals beneath these forms the formless which makes the awareness of forms possible, in the same way analogously that the seeing of things presuppose an unseen seer, *viz.* the eye. In the very act of experiencing, out of the corner of one's eye, one catches sight of that self that is the unknown knower, the unconscious or non-conscious consciousness, the inexperienced experiencer. This self can never become a subject of consciousness, i.e., an object, but is forever an uncatchable subjectivity which is, nevertheless, glimpsed as an awareness, as a feeling, that is, as a unity of discrete acts of awareness, or as awareness itself. It is not a thing that has freedom, but the *freedom* itself. It is self revealing. All unity of consciousness, whether God's or that of an individual, "cannot become the object of knowledge, and transcends all categories; we are unable to give it any fixed form, and all things are established according to it."[10]

The path to an understanding of nothingness, then, is the nothingness of pure experience, i.e., the self as pure awareness. Is this nothingness of self the same as the nothingness beyond God, or absolute nothingness? If we see the principle of emptiness as the formlessness behind or beneath all things as formed, must it not then be beyond or beneath even God who is said to be the ultimate "form" of being? The answer is not only complex but varied, depending on the tradition that one adheres to, as the extremes in Buddhism, from Pure Land to Zen, make amply evident. Still, Abe may be taken to speak for Mahāyāna Buddhists as a whole in trying to distinguish Nothingness from the Christian conception of God: "If Ultimate Reality, while being taken as Nothingness or Emptiness, should be called 'Him' or 'Thou,' it is, from the Zen point of view, no longer ultimate."[11] In any case, within the Zen tradition, Abe states unambiguously that "True Emptiness is never an object found outside of oneself. It is what is really *unobjectifiable*. Precisely for this reason, it is the ground of true objectivity."[12] Some Buddhists will speak of Buddha, or even of God, in seemingly Christian terms. Nevertheless, the self-corrective background of Buddhism forces one to use such words symbolically, and thereby analogically. A creed, an image, a sacred work, even the actual Buddha himself are but pointers, "hundred-foot poles" to be used as finite springboards into the depths of nothingness itself. Thus, as D. T. Suzuki remarks, "What we must grasp is that in which God and man have not yet assumed their places."[13] This "undivided something" out of which even God arises is the nothingness beyond God, which is the ground of God, being, and non-being. It is the ultimate ground of everything.

TRANSCENDENCE AND IMMANENCE

Nothingness is not just transcendent. It is immanent *and* transcedent. While it is true that "in Judaism and Christianity, God is unquestionably transcendent," it is also true that "according to the main tradition[s] of Christian thought, God is also immanent."[14] St. Augustine maintained that the light of God's presence in human reason made it possible for us to apprehend the truth; St. Thomas saw God in all things as an efficient cause; numerous mystics argued that we have a "spark" of God within us. Nishida was correct to urge that he was comparing a transcendent-immanence with an immanent-transcendence, for the issue is one of degree. Nevertheless, it remains true to say that Christianity and Judaism *emphasize* God's transcendence, his ultimate distinctness from the world (e.g., his essence is distinct and separate from all else), and the separation of the creator from the created. This concern proved a focus in deciding whether the mystical teachings of Meister Eckhart were heretical or not. Since they did not show a clear distinction between creator and creation, several of Eckhart's sermons were deemed heretical. By contrast, Nishida writes of the world (samsara) as nirvana (the holy). It does seem that the "secular" is rendered "sacred," and the sacred this-worldly. More precisely still, nothingness, unlike the Judeo-Christian God, is neither transcendent nor immanent in the Western sense of these terms. At the least, nothingness is *both* transcendent *and* immanent, and at most *neither*, because it is beyond (or different from) these categories. If one must choose one of these terms as best capturing nothingness, however, then "immanent" must get the nod.

Nothingness is found underfoot, as it were, as the ground of everything in the everyday world. Nirvana is samsara, samsara is nirvana: indeed, nothingness, using Kantian language, is the condition of the possibility of everything. But not only is it the condition of the possibility of *everything*, it is only knowable in the phenomenal world of experience *as* every *thing*. Each and every *thing* is an expression of (a manifestation of, a self-determination of) nothingness itself. The phenomenally real is not a creation separate from the creator, nor is it simply made in the image of the absolute. Rather, it *is* the absolute, expressed as the absolute expresses itself, phenomenally. Everything "is" the forms of the undivided, the formless. Transcendence is other, but nothingness is given at the base of one's own everyday experiences.

Borrowing a schema from Kant, the regulative ideas of *Freedom, God,* and *Immortality* are transformed when applied to nothingness. (1) Kantian freedom gives way to what Nishida calls "Affective Feeling,"[15] i.e., the self which is ever free because it is unobjectifiable, undeterminable, without characteristics or distinctions, but which is at the ground of all determinations. The self as directly given in feeling is absolutely free and is the ground of even such categories as causality itself. (2) For Nishida, the notion of God no longer refers to a being-as-substance, and therefore as objective, nor as a symbolic concept with the characteristics of finiteness and infinity, or immanence and transcendence, but God is, in the form of nothingness, the pure experience of the formless and undifferentiated *whole* from which, or on which, the ripples and waves of the temporary and differentiated are registered. Nothingness is revealed in experience, but only when one is able to look through the forms at the formless of which the forms are expressions. To view a Zen garden of sand, and to see the mounds and ripples as things-in-themselves, rather than as temporary forms of the underlying oneness of sand, is to miss the point. The finite world can become transparent in the same way as the self can. In either case, one must learn to look through the specific acts of consciousness or substantial shapes, to the undifferentiated awareness or ground on which such differentiations float.

Kantian freedom and the Kantian God have given way to an immanence that transcends differentiation, as the inside "transcends" the outside of a thing. (3) The outward must now be recognized as the self-expression of the inward. Kantian immortality gives way to the ever-recurring and eternal *Now.* Everything that occurs in time is also outside of time. Insofar as time is a form of the timeless, a differentiation of that out of which time is a specific awareness or focus, Nishitani Keiji writes, "The self is in every instant of time, [wholly] outside of time. In that sense ... everyone's self is originally anterior to the world and things."[16] According to the Buddhist theory of "interdependent origination,"[17] we know that all is intertwined causally, such that every event and every moment is inextricably interconnected with every other thing and every other moment. Thus, a moment drags with it all other moments, both past and future and, therefore, all time enters into each and every moment. All pure experience is then, quite literally, eternity. On the other hand, each distinct jewel of time as a fresh and unique moment is as it is in its *suchness,* and thereby may be seen as a fresh form of the formless. Every moment is a fresh and sacred revelation of the absolute, because it is a self-expression of the absolute. All being and all non-being are a self-unfolding of nothingness.

Whereas the Christian God creates the world, and through a special or particular revelation makes evident his wishes for men, nothingness does not create the world as forms, but *is* the world of forms, for forms are the self-expressions of, and thereby the self-revelations of, the formless. Furthermore, no special revelation or moment is privileged, for "every single moment of infinite time has the solemn gravity that these privileged moments possess in Christianity."[18] The secular has taken on the fabric of the sacred, and to use that fruitful image of Nishida's once more, it is like the deep and precious pure silk lining of a Japanese kimono: It is the unseen and rarely glimpsed which gives shape and ultimate meaning to the whole.[19] The connoisseur alone realizes the importance of the lining, while also recognizing that the value of the lining is best revealed by paying attention to the shape and color of the outer form of the kimono. Rich linings are best evidenced by attending to the shape and texture of the outer cloth. As Abe remarks, "Ultimate Reality is not something far away, over there, it is right here, right now. *Everything starts from the here-and-now.* Otherwise everything loses its reality."[20] You, me, rocks, and the seeming emptiness of outer space itself are all forms of the formless, and as such, they are particular revelations of that which is prior to both the finite and the infinite, the secular and the divine. Any attempt to define it in words will fail, but one can catch it in the marrow of direct experience, of pure experience. It is the place, itself without characteristics, out of which all things with characteristics arise. Nothingness is God's face, your face, and my face before any of us were born—that is, before we were individuated.

THE POETRY OF SELF-TRANSFORMATION

An additional comment is perhaps in order here. It may appear to some that the final thrust of the analysis of nothingness is to make philosophy into *poetry*. To talk of genuine "kinship" among men and rocks, trees and rivers, is to blush philosophically because of the richness of literary metaphor. Yet nothingness demands nothing less. If we are all selfmanifestations of the whole, then each of us is sacred, divine, godly. The very act of losing our ego and finding the self is the clearing of a place—again, Nishida's *basho*—where the suchness of everything as it is, luxurious in its lining, may appear. Indeed, it is one's own nothingness of place that is "a field of love of fellow man," and even more strikingly, "a field of love toward all living things and even toward all things."[21] It is an authentic capacity that has arisen, and it is not metaphor when it is termed the "Great Compassion." Compassion is the capacity to empathize, to treat the other not as one would oneself, and not merely as he, she, or it may view himself, herself, or itself. To truly empathize is to enter into the deep self of the other, the Buddha-nature of the other, such that he, she, or it arises as a *self* within one's own place of appearance. Nishitani calls this "circuminsessional interpenetration,"[22] and Robert S. Hartman writes of "compenetration."[23] Whatever one calls it, note well that in losing my ego I have cleared a place where all things may appear in their suchness, my *self* included. The nothingness as clearing makes evident that all that appears is lined with precious infinity, and clothed in the self-expressive garments of the self-revelation of impermanence, of Buddha, of the nothingness that embraces and yet is beyond God.

All is one, and the great kinship of the universe is revealed. Ethically, one acts in love, compassionately, not because one must, but because now one is unable to act in any other way. Just as a healthy ego serves as the standard of the Golden Rule, it is the non-ego of the deep self of nothingness that allows all things to present themselves in their suchness. The non-duality of self and others is realized. Love is now spontaneous, an outpouring from the depths of the self where it is understood not as meaning that I am my brother's keeper, but that my brother and I are cut from the same cloth. We share, with everything else, an identical parentage. The love that is, ideally, expressed within a family is now the standard of ethics. Poetry has become a way of living, of acting, of viewing all things in the cosmos, and even a preparation for the final impermanence—death itself. If attitudinal changes are the proof of the vitality and reality of religion, then the religion of nothingness must be classed as among the most powerful and noble of transformative paths. Once the *enlightenment* of nothingness is grasped, one will never see oneself, others, the world, or God the same way again.

EAST/WEST

I remarked earlier that it is not my point to say who is right—the advocates of being who are the dominant thinkers of the West, or the advocates of nothingness who are the dominant thinkers of the East. Not only would trying to decide the issue be a gesture unworthy of serious academic inquiry, but it would also miss the point of what has been described. East and West have very different contributions to make to human understanding, and there is nothing in what I have said to suggest that the two approaches are not complementary. One can either look at religious questions from the perspective of dualism, or one can seek to find a perspective prior to the dualistic split, i.e., some sort of monism or "mono-dualism." One can find salvation both within or beyond this world through either of the approaches. It is far easier to dismiss the more abstract and unexpected ultimate principle of the East as mere vacuous assertion, a legacy of unethical times past, than it is to dismiss the Western theorizings about God, being, and being's ground. I suspect, however, that Nishida is closer to the truth and to the point of this essay, when he writes:

> Reality is both being and non-being; it is being-*qua*-non-being and non-being-*qua*-being. It is both subjective and objective, both *nóēsis* and

nóema. Subjectivity and objectivity are absolutely opposed, but reality is the unity of subjectivity and objectivity, i.e., the self-identity of this absolute opposition.[24]

It would, of course, be too much to hope that the *yang* of the West and the *yin* of the East could simply be viewed as two perfect halves of an ultimate whole. There is too much to be considered in the many traditions that will not fit, and likely will not blend without force or compromise. Nevertheless, it would be an even greater mistake to suppose that the highest religious and philosophical achievements of East and West are necessarily in opposition, making the clashes to come inevitable. Instead, it would be wiser to struggle to see whether, as Nishida suggests, the greatest insights about the most important matters come from a yoking of perspectives, Eastern and Western, in an attempt to glimpse whatever can be glimpsed of the infinite and inexpressible. Being and nothingness may *together* add up to a total which yields a more complete, though still only a partial, understanding of the "shadow of the Eternal."[25]

FROM PHILOSOPHY TO THE PHILOSOPHY OF RELIGION

Absolute nothingness cannot be conceptualized, nor can its structure be indicated since any attempt to do so would result in an abstraction, or partial objectification, of that which is other. But the transformative act of enlightenment makes possible a direct experience of that which is prior to the subject/object split that is inherent in the conceptual. Pure experience is intrinsically non-dualistic while at the same time intrinsically dualistic insofar as it is expressed in form. It is for this reason that truly religious experience is ineffable, for it has no specific content, no form. Insofar as it is a state in which there are no distinctions, description is impossible in principle and in fact. Description, speaking, and ordinary object logic are based on and themselves are tools that make distinctions and account for their relationships. Direct or pure experience is not conceptual thought, but spontaneous life itself. It is "the flow of internal life,"[26] and the flow of absolute nothingness itself as it gives expression to the 10,000 things of form. To label the "flow" is to determine it, to stop it in mid-flight by objectifying it, or rendering it abstract. In speaking of the unspeakable, one must use words to point to the pre-words, of which words are but an expression and an abstraction. At the level of the pre-verbal awareness there is just the flow. Everything is just as it is. The self "drops off," is negated, and there is just seeing (without a seer). Still, it is at the depths of our bottomless self that we come to see in this way, and so it is necessary to speak of religious experience as "an event of the soul" as Nishida does in his final essay.[27] Religion arises in the *basho* of the self, i.e., in the place of conscious acts arising.

RELIGION AND GOD

Nishida affirms that religion is about God, and that "God is fundamental to religion in any form."[28] Yet it is not a distant God of which he speaks, a transcendent God who is wholly other, for "God appears to the self as an event of one's own soul."[29] At the same time, God is beyond conception (or nonconception), Nishida warns, which points us in the direction of "pure experience," i.e., awareness prior to the distinctions of conception. Indeed, even God is but a final gasp, a fixing point, prior to the letting-go that is the recognition of absolute nothingness. God, in other words, is not a conception, an idea, a creed, a logical truth or necessity; God is experience, but only a "pure experience," undifferentiated and concrete, rather than abstract. Kant is taken by Nishida as someone who completely missed the authentic religious dimension, for Kant made God, the immortality of the soul, and freedom *postulates*. They are not given in experience, and hence are not truly knowable. God is an intellectual assumption. And this assumption is not even able to stand on its own, but is subsidiary to morality. It is not that religion and God are somehow required because of our nature, or as a final step in the completion of our understanding of the world, but that the completion of morality requires that there be a God to attend to the just desserts owing to the worthy and unworthy alike. For Kant, religion is not an event of the soul, but a supplement to moral understanding. For Nishida, religion "arises with a consideration of our own consciously active self,"[30] the form of which is "a dialectic of mutual negation and affirmation of self and other."[31] We are living contradictions. We represent the species, the "formed" which makes us recognizable as an Aristotelian this-somewhat. But we are also unique, individual, and constantly pushing beyond our past, our "formedness," to our future, our creative "forming." We represent the "one" of the species, and yet we are one of the many. We interact with our environment, becoming it through eating, drinking, being influenced by climate, danger, and delight, and we make it us by digesting it, transforming it, making evident that we have passed this way. Thus, our very individuality is an absolutely contradictory identity of the many and the one, of individual and species, self and other, individual and environment. Indeed, "each individual conscious act is a contradictory identity";[32] we are, through and through, nothing but such a self-contradictory identity. Again, Nishida emphasizes that we are the place, the *basho* where even absolute nothingness arises—at least as pure awareness, for its seat of possibility is the self-contradictory identity that constitutes the bottomless self, which is a no-self:

> Our conscious worlds are the places in which we express the world in ourselves in the form of the contradictory identity of transcendent and immanent, of space and time, that is constitutive of the act of consciousness itself; and we are only active as formative positions in the world's own calculus of self expression.[33]

Each and every act of consciousness occurs in the absolute present, which itself is a self-contradictory identity of past and future. Thus it is that "each moment of time both arises and perishes in eternity."[34]

Wherever you strike at the act of consciousness in an attempt to understand it, it unfolds as a contradictory identity. Indeed, this is the logical form of understanding necessary if one is to gain a glimmering of how to conceive of the inconceivable self: "in the form of a contradictory identity."[35]

A conscious act is an act of expression, and the formula for expressive acts is that by negating itself, i.e., by becoming other than what it is, an act expresses itself. Life itself is continual self-expression as self-transformation, i.e., of self-identity by means of self-negation. Returning to Kant, Nishida concludes that "the *Ding-an-sich* is nothing other than the transformational matrix in which the self finds itself."[36] The self finds itself not just in the *physical world* of action and reaction, nor in the *biological world* of organism and environment (individual and species mutually interacting), but in the *historical world* as the culminating form of the identity of self contradiction. In the historical world, the activity is from the formed to the forming, from past to future via the eternal present, the only experiential aperture that consciousness has. The self negates itself in self-expression, yet, at the same time, this negation is creative positivity or assertion, for by negating what it was, the self is now able to affirm what it has become in the eternal present. It lives by dying. Kant saw the antinomies as results which made evident that the understanding was beyond its powers and devoid of the necessary data. Nishida accepts this but, by switching to another level of understanding, takes the fact of the paradoxical as indicative of the real, on at least a deeper level of that which cannot be reduced to the either/or non-contradictoriness of object logic. The logic of paradox takes the fact of an either/or dichotomy, and preserves it by seeing both as constitutive of an identity. Not that the identity is a Hegelian synthesis, which resolves the thesis and antithesis, but an identity which embraces and preserves the thesis and antithesis without any possibility of synthesis. The self is such an identity.

Religious experience is a direct result of recognizing that the very existence of the self is problematic. In other words, religious experience arises when one becomes aware of "a profound existential contradiction in the depth of his own self."[37] The foreground of this existential awareness is the fact of our own mortality. We live by dying. This is a biological fact. The human fact includes more than this, however, for the existential death of which the religious individual is aware arises from our looking directly at the nothingness at the roots of our bottomless self. We not only die a biological death, but we die an eternal death at each moment. At the depths of our awareness of self is the recognition that we are a no-self. The point could be elaborated by retracing the path of Gautama Buddha himself, and his denial of the substantive nature of the self in his doctrine of *anātman*. It is enough here to assume this Buddhist background that makes easy the conclusion that the self is not a self in any lasting or essential sense. We face our own depths, and we find our individuality slipping away into "absolute infinity, the absolute other."[38] This is absolute negation, for we are the impermanent reflection of the whole. Essentially, we are absolute nothingness; temporarily, we are a form, an expression of this infinity. We are a self-determination of the absolute. It is thus that "the self truly realizes its own temporal uniqueness as it faces its own eternal negation."[39] But eternal negation it is, nevertheless. My very existence is, therefore, an absolute contradiction, and it is this realization that enables me to become truly self conscious. My individuality is my mortality, and my true nothingness is my immortality. I am a contradictory self, and my awareness of this is the ground of my religious awareness. Indeed, "the self-contradiction" is "in the absolute itself," for I am, as individual, an expression of the absolute. The absolute is my ground. I am the absolute's self-negation of itself. The absolute relates itself to itself in the form of self-contradiction. Herein arises the sense of sorrow in human life. Again, a Buddhist would emphasize that all life is suffering and sorrowful, for it is the first Noble Truth taught by the Buddha. Nishida simply observes that sorrow is the recognition of one's own mortality, at least at its foundation, and thus we know that our biological death-in-time will also be an existentially eternal death. We will slide back into the nothingness, from which we sprang. We are, at our bottomless depth, empty.

The absolute contradiction is ever present, layer after layer, and so Nishida turns what appears to be mere anguish into anguish *and* the realization of meaning and joy—another contradictory pair: "For to realize one's own death is simultaneously to realize the fundamental meaning of one's own existence."[40] It is by dying, by leaving the self behind, and confronting the nothingness that is at the core of our being, that we actually come to encounter the divine at all. Thus, our loss is our gain; our death is the giver of eternal life. The dying is not washed away, however, for the antinomy of paradox remains. Immortality arises only at the price of mortality. The divine is immanent, for it is our own bottomless self. At the same time, this divinity is, "in itself" absolute nothingness. Hence, "God is 'nowhere and yet everywhere in the world.'"[41]

THE LOGIC OF RELIGION

Nishida utilizes Western philosophical traditions, by and large, in his work, and while it is apparent even in his premier *A Study of Good* that he was Buddhist and Zen Buddhist influenced, it is nearly impossible to find any explicit reference to this background in his writings. In his final essay, however, he is quite explicit about his Buddhist influences, and he actually emphasizes that his paradoxical logic of *soku hi,* of the simultaneous assertion of "is" and "is not," is Mahāyāna Buddhist through and through. This assertion reaches all the way back to Nāgārjuna's brilliant logical display, which itself is claimed to be scripturally based on the teachings and traditions of the Buddha, as has already been noted. Nishida's quotation from the *Diamond Sutra* is a clear example of the "is" *and yet* "is" not" logic:

> Because all Dharmas are not all Dharmas,
> Therefore they are called all Dharmas.
> Because there is no Buddha, there is Buddha.
> Because there are no sentient beings, there are sentient beings.[42]

What the paradox comes to in terms of what religion terms "God," is that God is absolutely self-contradictory. God is one, and yet God "returns to itself in the form of the infinite many."[43] The "and yet" formula requires self-negation. It is this that Nishida refers to as the necessity of God's *emptying* himself.[44] If God is thought of as a unity, then the unity must also express itself as a plurality. The plurality, of course, must "empty" itself such that the many are the many of a unity. God is immanent, and yet is transcendent; transcendent, and therefore immanent.[45] This is the paradox of the absolutely contradictory identity of God. Because God is immanent in all things, God is absolutely nothing. Absolute nothingness, however, must "empty" itself and express itself as absolute being. Absolute nothingness negates itself and is immanent in all beings, and because it is immanent in all beings, it empties itself by self-contradiction, and all beings transcend their being and are, at base, absolutely nothing. Even the dualistic conceptions listed above should be overcome, and so it may be more correct to say that it is precisely because God is a unity and a plurality, he is both of these, and therefore *neither* of these.

It is perhaps acceptable to end an analysis of the self-contradictoriness of the identity of the absolute with the neither X, nor not-X formula, which, of course, is the precise articulation (or non-articulation) of absolute nothingness. It is no determinate anything. It is that which lies at the ground of such distinctions, at the very ground of logic and reasoning itself. But no sooner has one come to rest for long enough to seem to catch one's logical and conceptual breath, than one is cast back on the paradoxical wheel of activity, for absolute nothingness is not the resolution of paradoxical tension, but its actual cause. If absolute nothingness is neither X, nor not-X, then for this very reason, and in order to empty the empty, it must be X and not-X, and so is *both X* and not-X. The wheel turns incessantly. As with the Buddhist notion of the wheel of rebirth, which I have here loosely adapted as a metaphor for the logical procedure of emptying, one can only stop the wheel, or get off it, by an act of transformation of perspective. To focus on the paradoxical tension will require that the emptying go on as long as we attend to the polar opposites. The solution is not to fixate on these, beyond recognizing their factuality and inescapability in the conceptual mode, but to switch one's attention enough to include the *identity* of this antinomial flow. The arising of the double aperture makes possible the seeing of the identity of the parts, and of any and all contradictory pairs. "Active" [or 'acting'] intuition," a term that Nishida uses to apply to our historical be-ing/acting as contradictory identities, is itself twofold in that the direct seeing of sensuous intuition, and the various cultural and historical acts of human beings are one in that there can be no intuition without action, and no action without intuition. Seeing and acting are inextricably interdependent.

In a passage reminiscent of the "ascent" in Plato's *Symposium*,[46] Nishida remarks that love becomes increasingly embracive, and deepens; as one moves "from the love of parent and child, and husband and wife, one advances to the love of friends, and from the love of friends one advances to the love of mankind."[47] Finally, and taking the love of the realized Buddha himself as the example and norm, he concludes that "the love of the Buddha extended even to birds and beasts, grasses and trees."[48] One abandons the "self-power" *(jiriki)* of independent egohood, and one lives in accordance with the "other-power" *(tariki)* of faith. One lives in God by leaving behind the boundaried self, and immersing oneself in the whole. Religious value "means absolute negation of the Self."[49] When one is fully realized, i.e., when one's self is truly left behind, "there is a seeing without a seeing one, and a hearing without a hearing one. This is salvation."[50] Our "soul" has become "a pure mirror," and this pure mirror is "the 'place' of absolute Nothingness."[51] As noted earlier, in Schinzinger's paraphrase of Nishida's interpretation of this point, "In the same spark of Nothingness, you regain the world and yourself in wonderful self-identity,"[52] precisely as frames nine and ten of the oxherding pictures illustrated. One participates in the fundamental unity of the cosmos by realizing that at the base of all things there is the indeterminate, unutterable nothingness of ultimate reality. It is not seen, heard, or touched except insofar as we look towards it through things in the everyday world that we can see, hear, and touch. Indeed, it is precisely *because* there are touchable, visible, and audible things in the world, that we can come to know that of which they are determinate expressions. Even more significantly, it is because we see, hear, and touch that we can come to grasp that there is a seer seeing, a hearer hearing, and a toucher touching. Paradoxically, we can never touch the toucher as an *object* of consciousness, but we are ever aware of the untouchable toucher through the very conscious awareness of touching, and so on. Nothingness is the lining of the kimono, known only by the very way in which the kimono hangs, and holds its shape. One sees the lining by not seeing it, but by reading its nature from the hang of the formed kimono. This is the form of formless. The double aperture consists in the ability to read the nature of the lining from the shape or hang of the kimono; one reads the nature of the formless from the formed. To see both is to have penetrated to the identity of the lining of all that exists, as it is manifested in the uniquely individualized manifold of being. Beings are enveloped by nothingness—the universal of universals. Here religion and philosophy meet as two perspectives, both of which seek the same understanding, but in radically different ways. The religious standpoint is that in which "the conscious Self disappears," and with it all conscious content (i.e., all discrimination). It is the awareness of the primary form ('Urform') of knowledge."[53] The standpoint of philosophy, "which is [awareness of] Nothing as well as Being, can become evident for the theoretical Self, only in self-reflection of knowledge as such."[54] Throughout his career, Nishida maintained his emphasis on the ultimate as nothingness, and while he does speak of "God," it is clear that

the truly divine is not to be construed as the usual idea of God, but rather as *die Gottheit* spoken of by the Western mystics, or as the "emptiness" (*śūnyatā*) concept of the *Prajñāpāramitā-sūtra* literature.[55]

FIVE

The Dialectical World of "Action Intuition"

Nishida's analysis of the three universals—the universal of judgment, of self-consciousness, and the intelligible universal—provides three distinct stages (or spheres) of knowledge: knowledge of the physical world, of the human world, and of ideal value. And the background to this analysis of knowing is Nishida's agreement and disagreement with Aristotle on the issue of individual substance. Aristotle held that the *real* was individual substance (that which is always a logical subject and never a predicate), but as such, was ultimately logically indefinable. In Noda Matao's words, "no matter how far we might pursue the individual by specifying the universal, the individual would always remain beyond our reach. Over against this difficulty, Nishida always seeks the principle of individuation in the universal itself."[1] This demands a different sort of universal, one which manifests the individual in its concreteness, and yet remains a universal, as with Hegel's "concrete universal." Hegel's concrete universal was not the result of abstraction, as in selecting red as a common color among many different individual things. Such a universal is abstract because it *leaves behind* all of the other differences and distinguishing characteristics of the multitude of individual things which are red. Hegel's concrete universal gathers up, or retains the flesh and blood differences and the fullness of each and every singular thing. The Latin word, *concrescere*, from which "concrete" derives means to merge, to pull together, to fuse, to gather up, rather than to abstract from something. Thus, the concrete universal pulls together all of the properties of all of the individuals and things which together make up the full sense of the universal notion. For example, both Hans and Toshi are citizens of a State, and yet as "citizens" they are fully Hans and Toshi. By contrast, abstract universals like "farmer" or "businessman" are generalizations which do not carry the fullness of the unique lives and physical, psychological, emotional and spiritual qualities of the individuals who constitute these classes. Hegel sought to show that the universal need not always be abstract, but could be concrete as a gathering up of singulars. The State and the Church, thus conceived, would be examples of this. Both are constituted by real people. Yet Hegel is seen by Nishida "as still following Aristotle in the notion of *hypokeimenon* [substratum], that is, a 'substance that becomes subject', and which leads to a 'logic of the subject'."[2] Thus, Aristotle and Hegel advocate a subject logic, and share the belief that reality consists of in*form*ed "being." Nishida, by contrast, proposes a predicate logic, and is steadfastly Eastern in taking reality to be formless, empty, and to be characterized as "nothing" rather than as "being," or at the very least (and perhaps more accurately), as *both* being *and* nothingness, the formed and the formless.[3] Nishida's concrete universal was the *basho* of nothingness, which Noda refers to as his "field of nothingness."[4] Noda recalls that the scholastic tradition understood Aristotle (and Plato) to have posited *matter* as the principle of individuation, and in a similar vein Nishida conceived of his concrete universal "as a sort of material field wherein forms emerge, so to speak."[5] This analogy is helpful, except that it does not make clear that what emerges from the "field" is both form and matter, the subjective and the objective, the conscious and the non-conscious, the animate and the inanimate. Nothingness is a plenum, chock full of all that has been, is now and will become. The strictly materialistic understanding of "field" and "plenum" as ordinarily used must be taken to include, for Nishida, the material, the ideal, and the spiritual. It is the source of all, and yet it has none of the characteristics of that which is determined, i.e. expressed or given existence and form, by it. That is why it is advisable to refer to it as "nothingness": it is, from the point of view of all that which emerges from it, without any of those familiar and essential characteristics. It is beyond being and non-being, and yet, in a sense, is potentially both of them.

Given the Buddhist background to Nishida's thought, it is to be expected that he would not accept the view that each of us is a unique ego, a permanent substance, but instead presupposes the ground of nothingness—a predicate which cannot become a subject—as the genuine concrete universal, which generates and preserves each and every individual thing in their just-so individuality. As Dilworth reminds us, nothingness "guarantees that sensible forms or beings are precisely as they are."[6] Furthermore, nothingness not only determines the individuals which it expresses, but it then is determined by the individuals which it contains (to use a spatial metaphor). In this dialectical world, the individual things are so central that they are expressive of reality as individuals, and yet, they are also subsumed in the universal of nothingness, the final *basho* or place of unification. Nirvana is samsara, samsara is nirvana: nothingness is all individuals, and all individuals are nothingness. And the mutuality of influence, the incessant change in both the universal and the singular individuals, is not to be found in either Aristotelean or Hegelian thought. There is change in both, to be sure, but the substratum is unchanging, else fixity would be lost. Nishida, however, needs no such guarantee, for Buddhism offers no fixed substance, but only an interconnected flow of "dependent origination," which sustains itself in a web-like fashion of mutual determination, and then collapses back into the nothingness from which it came. All is empty of substance, and the flow of individuals can only be understood against the background of nothingness which is both the source, and the destination. All the while, the play of forces as interconnected and mutually determining individuals, may be taken to be the historical face of the faceless, the forms of the formless.

One additional contrast needs to be drawn. Hegel's conceptualism dominated even his concrete universal, for it was the *notion* of "citizen" or "businessman" which continued to serve as the focus of his understanding. Logic does not take you to the things themselves, but to linguistic formulations of a unity of perspective and characteristics of a thing by means of which we are then able to designate and helpfully, but not completely comprehend the nature of a thing. For Nishida, not only is the concrete universal itself beyond language, it is also grasped, at least in part, through action, and not simply through intellectual, conceptual and logical expression, analysis, and synthesis.

In referring specifically to Nishida's second stage of knowledge, that of the universal of self-consciousness, Noda observes that Nishida's thinking at this stage gives primacy to intuition over action: "The whole volitional process in the historical world of man has its true end in man's complete vision of himself. Man acts in order to see."[7] Self-awareness, self-consciousness and self-realization form the focus of Nishida's concern. The real world is the world of self-consciousness, and not the historical world, i.e. the world of culture and of social and political involvement. It is this lack of historical (cultural, social and political) emphasis that serves as the catalyst for the "turn" in thinking which is characterized as Nishida's "later" philosophical phase.[8]

A MORE POWERFUL METAPHYSICS

It was in 1927 that Nishida introduced what David Dilworth calls "a more powerful metaphysical base" through his concept of the *topos* or *basho* of nothingness.[9] His approach was to develop a concrete logic, a systematic approach to knowledge-as-action in the everyday world of social and historical encounter, and it took him beyond a focus on self-consciousness, to the dialectical world of action. We have already looked at his "predicate logic" in which both the grammatical subject, and that which is predicated of it are engulfed by, and in another sense arise out of that place within which they are related. Thus, you will recall, red and color can be related in a logical judgment affirming that "red is a color" only because of the *basho* of the system of colors, which itself is without color but yet is the ground or matrix out of which color in general, and red in particular arise. It is in a relative sense only, given this particular example, that the system of colors is an empty place in which all determinations arise: but the ultimate or absolute *basho* of arising is emptiness itself, i.e. nothingness.

Basho as the empty place of arising, a *concrete* predicate logic, and the discerning of the world and all that is in it (including ourselves) as identities of self-contradiction constitute the foundation pieces in Nishida's later interest in the philosophy of history, and in *action intuition*. The term, "action intuition" serves as epistemological notice that seeing, intuiting, perceiving and sensing are not to be conceived of in purely intellectual terms, trapping us within our philosophical heads with no internal guarantees that the way we see the world is actually the way it is. There is no Cartesian God to certify that what we see and sense is descriptive of the world as it really is. The phenomenal world is also the noumenal world in that the one is to be discerned within the other, and vice versa. Nirvana is samsara, samsara is nirvana once again. Except this time the equation is not meant to send us to the meditation room to encounter the noumenal depths in the everyday world of experience, but out into the everyday world where we will encounter and engage the world in a mutuality of being affected by it, and affecting it directly ourselves through our actions. We need to "intuit" the world, to sense it in its contradictory flow, but our intuiting it or knowing it serves to inform us how to *act* upon it, thereby changing it, however slightly, in our knowing of it and acting in it and upon it. We encounter immediately an identity of self-contradiction. In knowing the world, we act upon it and change it. In affecting us, the world opens itself to being affected or determined by us. The mutuality, which is essential to true self-contradictory identity is present. Further contradictions emerge: in the very act of affecting the world, we change who it is that we are, as well as the world. Thus, in order to act, we must become what we were not previously. We are changed in the very process of acting. And the world changes us, too, for in order to act effectively we must be open to what the world is like, we must see it acutely and effectively, but in so doing the world changes us. And we do all of this in time, bringing the past to bear upon the present, with some future aim or expectation. The past is gone, yet still affects the present and the future: the future is not yet, but nonetheless alters the present and conceivably our understanding of the past. The present, the eternal *now* as the self-contradictory moment of past and future in the right-here-now, is what it is by not being what it is. We are caught up in a whirl of self-contradictory motion, and yet there is an identity through it all which enables us to know that time is a continuity within this discontinuity, that we are continuous albeit ever-changing selves as well, and that the flux of the world remains the world in which we act and live. Time, and, it would seem, life itself is a continuity of discontinuities.[10] We live by dying, Nishida tells us, in that what was is forever giving way to what will be, while our own selves die each minute in order to become what we previously had not been, whether by learning or knowing what we previously did not know, or by acting in the social-historical world of everyday reality.

YUASA YASUO AND ACTING INTUITION.

The above is a simplification of a very technical analysis which Nishida provides in such places as his *Fundamental Problems of Philosophy*. Nonetheless, it is offered in aid of attempting to explain what is involved in the varieties of human experience. Yuasa Yasuo maintains that Nishida's theory of "acting intuition," as he prefers to call it, helps to clarify "the mechanism at the base of the lived experience in Zen. Yuasa praises Nishida for having observed that acting intuition has both a surface and a base structure (a "dual" structure). At the surface level of ordinary experience, self-consciousness actively relates itself to the phenomenal world through passive sense intuition (perception), and then "actively directs itself toward the target object."[12] Information is taken in, and on the basis of that information some activity is entered into. At the base level, the self of self-consciousness (the surface level) recedes, and forgets itself in the descent into the nothingness of the authentic self, or the deep Self. Dōgen charted just this path when he counseled that to study the self is to forget the self. And it is only by forgetting the surface or ordinary self that the deep Self is enabled to emerge at all. Recall the ten ox-herding pictures of Chapter 3, where at first there was no trace whatsoever of the deep Self (the ox), but eventually, after sustained meditative practice which stilled the ordinary self, the deep Self is caught sight of and merges with the ox-herder, only for both to disappear into nothingness. Yuasa observes that at this base layer level, it is out of the unconscious itself that a creative intuition springs forth, propelling the ordinary body-mind self into motion in the phenomenal world. Thus, "the self becomes an instrument or empty vessel receiving this intuition, that is, it simply acts as no-ego. The intuition potentially takes hold of a targeted action, and the bodily behavior, guided by this intuition, simply follows the path made visible."[13] Here there is no need to work out what it is that is being perceived, or to reconcile and confirm the information gained through the sensory organs, for intuition has already "reached the act in a single stroke."[14] Yuasa cites Mozart as an example of acting intuition at this base level, for Mozart sometimes became aware of an entire musical piece all at once, from beginning to end. The creative intuition was complete, and the action was utterly spontaneous, joyful, and in some sense spiritual. He further observes that such creative intuition is not a common occurrence, but that "by training the body-mind continuously, it is possible for even an ordinary person to have a glimpse of this dimension."[15] One may recall any of the countless instances of the Japanese swordsman, or martial artist being so aware of his opponent that he instinctively anticipates his every intention, and in an intuitive instant knows exactly what is happening and how to act in order to fell the enemy and to preserve his own life. All of this is accomplished in an instant, without calculation or analysis, and without a decision taken which is at all separate from the initial intuition. The surface consciousness is not engaged, nor are its tools of deliberation and calculation involved. There simply would not be time, for what is required is instant recognition of the circumstances, and an intuitively instantaneous response (which, nonetheless, has been honed by years or even decades of preparatory practice). Eugen Herrigel's *Zen in the Art of Archery* speaks the same theme.[16] Herrigal, a Westerner studying the Zen of archery, has to learn that only when the archer reaches the stage where the arrow shoots itself, spontaneously and without calculation or decision, has one begun to experience the depths of the acting intuition of the deep Self. All is mere preparation for this transfer from the bright consciousness of the surface self, to the intuitively instant recognition and reaction of the deep Self, the Unconscious. Indeed, the goal of all of the Japanese "ways" or "*dō(s)*" is the same: the way of tea is a journey towards spontaneity via disciplined cultivation; sumie brush and ink painting is necessarily spontaneous in that quickly absorbent rice paper forgives no mistakes or second thoughts; and a seventeen syllable haiku poem is meant to capture the instant of pure experience in the *nikon* of the right-here-now. Haiku is short enough to be read "all at once," and is intended to exhibit no reflective gloss on the snapshot of the moment of pure experience. Such spontaneity as intuition which is already acting, is evident in genius, in the work of masters, yet by training even the ordinary person can catch a glimpse of this dimension. Thus, there is only the smallest gap between the movements of the body and mind on such occasions as a gymnast's performing his or her best techniques in a state of no-mind, or a master pianist's performing in total absorption, or an experienced actor's acting out his role on a stage, becoming the role itself. These people are, so to speak, in a state of 'the oneness of body-mind' (*shinjin ichinyo*)."[17] In the training of the martial artist, it is essential to reach the disciplined point where "intuition and action ... spring forth at the same time. In the practice of *Būdo* [the martial arts] there can be no conscious thought. There is no time for thinking, not even an instant. When a person acts, intention and action must be simultaneous."[18] Roshi Deshimaru further explains that "the action takes place of itself before any conscious thought."[19] He refers to such spontaneous action as "pure action," echoing Nishida's originary notion of "pure experience" of which it is no doubt an instance.

It remains true that a genius is somehow already predisposed to such depth response, Yuasa muses, and yet even the genius requires practice in order for this predisposition of character to become realized. But what is instructive about this analysis of "the authentic dimension by which the intuition guides action," is the fact that this authentic dimension may well lurk as "a possibility at the base of each person's body-mind."[20] The Canadian pianist Glenn Gould is said to have gone to the piano at the age of three, in an attempt to play the piece that he had just heard on the radio. He heard what he needed to hear in order to reenact the musical sounds, and his body responded by making the required sounds (more or less) without previous exposure or practice.[21] Genetically, the pathway between the surface consciousness and the base unconsciousness was somehow already present, and the infant Gould "just knew" how to play what he heard. Intuition and action were both one, and all-at-once. Such deep level intuition is "like a flash of light, breaking the darkness and issuing out of the nebulous region of the unconscious at the base of the bright [surface] consciousness."[22]

Whether at the surface or the deep level, it is action intuition which is our engagement with, and our making of history. As human beings we are all *embodied,* and as such our seeing, learning and creativity are all expressed in action in the historical world. Nishida tells us that our "task" in the world is "to form," and that this "task is put before us by the historical nature through the fact that we are born with a body."[23] Yusa Michiko summarizes Nishida's position when she paraphrases Nishida as follows: "Not only is my existence inconceivable without my body, but it is by virtue of it that I gain knowledge. I grasp things 'physically' upon seeing them."[24] We encounter the historical world, and to some extent we alter it. All the while, of course, it continues to affect us. Here we encounter the familiar self-contradiction which Nishida utilizes to explain the mutuality of influence of environment on the individual, and individual on the environment: we are determined (the world), and yet we determine (the world). But human reality, that is, the world as experienced by human beings, is not only material and mechanical, it is historical, and so the mutuality described is not a mere mechanical interaction, but is self-consciously intentional. Schinzinger writes that "man, formed by his environment under the spell of the past, is looking towards the future, trying to be creative, 'forming,' and free. This contradiction of past and future, or the struggle between environment and individual, takes place in man's mind and heart."[25] The world is a struggle of individual and world, of part and whole, and therefore "is equivalent to a struggle of the world with itself."[26] Thus, "the subject forms the environment. But the environment, though formed by the subject, is more than a part of the subject; it opposes and denies it."[27] In this sense the world, as active process, is both formed and forming, created and creating, process and product. Here we encounter the world as an identity of self-contradiction once again. The identity of self-contradiction mirrors reality, and yet reality in its depth, as absolute nothingness, is neither one nor many, or any of the other contradictories. In Nishida's words, "at the base of the world, there are neither the many nor the one."[28] This is precisely why it is incorrect to conclude that "the expanded field of awareness is more valuable."[29] R.P. Peerenboom adds that "there seems to be no *a priori* reason for privileging experience of the whole over a more focused experience of particular details,"[30] and he is correct in this. However, rather than being a critique of Nishida on this point, it actually seems to reinforce Nishida's express purpose. Nishida does not claim that either "religious experience," or the awareness of the whole is more valuable, but only that such experience is based on or arises out of a heretofore non-differentiated primal experience—pure experience as he first termed it. He is, to be sure, offering an alternative metaphysics to that of the empiricisms of the particular, but it is grounded in direct experience itself. If one will simply attend to what is given in direct experience, not in refined or highly interpreted experience, one will come to an experience of the undifferentiated out of which will arise both a oneness and a differentiated manyness. This is the realm of the identity of self-contradiction, which is the closest that we can come to apprehending nothingness itself in our conscious, and intellectually active awareness. The world is intrinsically self-contradictory, as given, and it rests on an *absolute* identity of self-contradiction, namely nothingness, which can only be given in a pure experience of a distinctly religious sort. But Nishida is not claiming that this *absolute* Oneness is privileged, epistemologically, but that it serves as a foundational starting-point for the East, as Being does for the West. In this sense both East and West do privilege a specific metaphysical starting-point, but starting-points of this sort must be argued for by presenting the entire viewpoints, and then contrasting and comparing various aspects of each in order to ascertain which positions are the stronger, and which are more in accord with experience and the world as we encounter them. Each existent, and particularly each self-consciously aware existent is a unique perspective on the world, and yet the world as a whole is mirrored in each and every self-consciously aware existent: "The monad mirrors the world, and is, at the same time, a viewpoint or perspective."[31] In the identity of self-contradiction, neither position is privileged, or perhaps better, both are. To the extent to which the whole, even nothingness or God negates itself in order to express and manifest individuality and differentiatedness, then to precisely this extent is individuality as real as the Absolute itself. And yet, as individual and differentiated, each and every thing manifests, is "lined' with the whole, the One, which it and every other individual *mirrors* within. The One is many, and the many are One. The self-contradiction is unqualifiedly *Absolute*.

DIALECTICAL LOGIC AND REALITY

At the base of all that is, of the myriad individuals that have been, are, and will be is that *One* which absolutely negates itself in order to create, or give form to the many. It is the ultimate negation, because it is the negation of the ultimate, and that which it formed as a result of this negation of oneness, are the many. In Nishida's words, "The self-determination of the dialectical universal means that the universal negates itself. That it negates itself to become an absolute other is the very process of the one becoming many. In this process the world of independent individuals is established."[32] This dialectical universal is so-called because it manifests or expresses itself as the self-identity of absolute contradictories, or unity of opposites. Nishida elaborates on this, stating that "reality is both being and non-being; it is being-qua-non-being and non-being-qua-being. It is both subjective and objective, both *nóēma* and *nóesis*. Subjectivity and objectivity are absolutely opposed, but reality is the unity of subjectivity and objectivity, i.e. the self-identity of this absolute opposition."[33] A dialectical universal is one which, while contradicting itself, is yet identical with itself: it is both one, and not-one or many, neither subjective nor objective, and yet both at once and contradictorily. And this identity of self-contradiction, in terms of our experience of the world, is not a mere logical postulate on Nishida's part, but is based on direct experience —this is how the world presents itself to us, if we will but attend to our own experience without prejudice. We actually experience the world, and our own lives as identities of self-contradiction.

In a recent and telling essay by G.S. Axtell exploring dialectical thought comparatively, Axtell observes that throughout most of Western philosophical thought, paradoxicality and the "logic" of opposites has been "pushed to the side as a concern only for those studying 'deviant' logic and 'archaic' thought."[34] The reason commonly given for this is that such thinking does not conform to Aristotle's definitive work on logic, and his sense of the relationship between logic and language on the one hand, and reality on the other. Yet Aristotle's own logical axioms are themselves expressive of a definitive metaphysical stance and outlook. As Axtell writes,

> Aristotle was first among the Greeks to call into question the license of his predecessors to 'adopt opposites as principles.'... For all his foundational work on the principles of identity, contradiction, and excluded middle, and for all his revision of earlier abuses of language and logic, Aristotle's theory of enantion [contrariety] remains in many ways at least as wrapped up in metaphysics as those of his predecessors. His own metaphysics is found in the suggestion that discursive thought is a reflection of reality, and that the dependence of intelligible discourse upon basic rules of consistency is a reflection of the essential and self-identical character of the real.[35]

And while Nishida follows Hegel in affirming a *concrete universal*, both Hegel and Aristotle affirm a "reality as form" rather than an Eastern emphasis on the "formless." Thus, Nishida's logic is not that of a substance as subject, but a logic of the predicate that must not become subject. The concrete universal for Nishida is *mu*, or absolute nothingness, or the place in which opposites confront one another. It is also the ground or basis of their identity. Individuals, and the absolute one stand in a paradoxically non-dual relationship with one another.[36] This opposition is not to be resolved, or synthesized, but persists as an unreconcilable tension. It is in this sense that his dialectical logic is negative.[37]

What is it that Nishida thinks he has gained by the development of such a logic? Nishida tells us in his *Fundamental Problems* that "things that resist or conflict with one another presuppose the same underlying generic concept. For they oppose one another in the determination of the same universal concept."[38] This idea is at least as old, and as culturally basic to the East Asian milieu, as the writings of Chuang Tzu, where we read that in order for two things to be different, they must already be significantly the same.[39] Nishida's predicate logic allegedly brings us closer to the "real world" of lived, historical experience, by demanding that it be made an explicit part of one's logical understanding of opposition, to see that opposites are ultimately connected: "From the standpoint of abstract logic, it is impossible to say that things which contradict each other are connected; they contradict each other just because they can not be connected."[40] Red and blue are connected by the system of colors, while wine and convex are not obviously connected (unless some system is provided). It is dialectical logic which has the capacity to both affirm contradiction, while at the same time negating it at a deeper level by showing that "there would be no contradiction if they did not touch each other somewhere. Facing each other is already a synthesis."[41] Following the synthesis back, from universal to universal, we eventually come to the ultimate universal, the place as absolute nothingness. There is "always identity at the root of mutual contradictories,"[42] and it is an "identity-in-difference of the permanent flow—or of the infinite whole of the process."[43] What is gained, then, is entry into a world of impermanence, where everything is what it is, and yet is at the same time connected to everything else as a manifestation or expression of that undifferentiated ground which negates itself in order to give expression to individuality. Axtell sums up Nishida's position well in the following:

> For Nishida, an Aristotelian "logic of the subject that cannot become predicate" would be a reflection of a world of essential kinds. But in a world

characterized by *engi*, mutual interdependence and codependent arising, such Aristotelian logic is a vehicle to partial understanding at best. Nishida's predicate logic is based upon the transcendental predicate as a kind of universal that alone can give knowledge of things.

For Nishida, the real is a dialectical whole which expresses itself by negating itself. Expression is a creating of that which is not itself, and so is individual, and yet which nonetheless *is* itself, and so remains one. The particular and the universal are interconnected, and interfuse in this complete way, while at the same time maintaining their own qualities as both one and many. This is the logic of *soku hi*, which draws out and casts into relationship the *is*, and yet the *is not* of experience. Nishida's logic is not an intellectual and abstract logic, but a logic of experience, as displayed against the background of East Asian metaphysics. It would be too grand to claim that while Aristotle had metaphysical assumptions, Nishida did not. It is more helpful to note that they both rested their logical reflections on metaphysical outlooks. For Nishida, language does not adequately or accurately slice the metaphysical pie, nor does intellect and conceptualization. Not only is contradiction to be affirmed as descriptive of reality, whether conceptually neat or not, but that which is beyond all conceptualization, *nothingness*, is to be viewed as the foundation of all that is, including the self and its thinking capacity. Aristotelian logic, which rigidly separates things, and renders them fixed and unchanging, is less likely to be able to describe the East Asian world of impermanence, emptiness, and flow. This requires a logic of dialectical contradiction, and yet dialectical unity at one and the same time. Such a logic brings us at least closer to lived experience. It brings us closer to history.

THE HISTORICAL WORLD

It is commonly recognized that Nishida in his writings prior to 1931 placed his emphasis on the forms of self-awareness (often translated as "self-consciousness") (*jikaku*): "Nishida finally arrived at a full grasp of these forms only in his mature theory of self-consciousness, around 1929 or 1930."[44] Hans Waldenfels demurs from translating *jikaku* as "self-consciousness," and substitutes "self-realization," because it has both an ontological and a cognitive component. Waldenfels' rendering of the term is helpful because it makes evident that Nishida was not simply undertaking a philosophic task of conceptual clarification, but was attempting to understand the transformative aspect of self-understanding. Self-realization is a potentially progressive journey from dim awareness of one's individuality, to the loss of the everyday self and the robust appearance of that deep Self which understands its own self-contradiction, and at the same time its identity with the all of nothingness, to some sort of *self-awareness*. Thomas P. Kasulis points out that the term *jikaku* literally means self + awakening. He notes that the *kaku* of *jikaku* is a common synonym for enlightenment, and the *ji* component does not necessarily refer to the self as the seat of personal identity. "It can also mean 'automatically' or 'spontaneously,' that is, it can refer to something occuring without external help or agency."[46] Thus, the emphasis may be less on realizing one's "self," and more on awakening to one's selflessness, or spontaneously forgetting one's self, rather than realizing or becoming conscious of it. To forget the self, as Dōgen reminds us, is to become aware of all that is, but is not necessarily to become aware of the self all over again. Self-consciousness is precisely what blocks this wider and more profound sense of "awareness."

Ueda Shizuteru calls to our attention that pure experience refers to that which is prior to language ("it is not possible to talk about pure experience"),[47] is not an object of inquiry ("rather than being a concept, pure experience is a term which expresses the primordial *Ereignis* at 'the moment of seeing a form or hearing a sound, before there is a subject and an object"),[48] and as such it is a non-propositional awareness. It is "an originary event that cuts off all words."[49] In expressing this philosophic foundation of Nishida's paradoxically and provocatively, Ueda asserts that pure experience is a principle of Nishida's philosophy which "negates the principle itself."[50] Thus, "in the saying of what cannot be said (indeed, the true saying), the negation of what is said is included simultaneously in what is said."[51] The principle which results from this direct and immediate encounter with pure experience is philosophically expressed, and yet this expression is not at all what it pretends to be: an adequate expression of that which in fact cannot be expressed at all. Therefore, the fundamental principle and starting-point of Nishida's philosophy is self-contradictory. Yet it is the formulation of that which cannot be put into words that leads the careful reader and thinker to that which underlies the spoken, the philosophically expressed, namely to pure experience itself, to the pre-reflective on which the reflective is established and of which it is an attempted articulation. Pure experience does not exist as an object of inquiry: "it is only possible to speak of pure experience in terms of the self-awareness of pure experience itself."[52] Nishida's doctrine of pure experience is not a doctrine at all, but a directly given, or intuited plenum of awareness, itself prior to all distinctions including conceptual, propositional and logical, and the goal of writing about it is to *awaken us, to self-awaken us to pure experience itself.*[53] Ueda takes us beyond the question whether self-consciousness or self-realization is the better translation of the middle course of Nishida's thinking—from pure experience, to self-awareness, to *basho* and the dialectical world—by placing us within Nishida's apparent philosophical purpose: self-awareness is the self's awareness that pure experience is the "absolute *arche*" of thought, where there is yet no language and no philosophy. Ueda writes, "'the philosophy of pure experience' is concerned with the self-awakening of pure experience, or in other words, the unfolding of the awareness whereby pure experience awakens to itself."[54] Again in a stereoscopic manner, self-awareness informs us of the impossibility of a philosophical accounting of pure experience, and yet at the same time, becomes a thinking which offers a foundational starting-point for all subsequent philosophizing.

Ueda insists, as does Kasulis, that "self-awakening" is the preferred term, and he passionately draws out the reasons why he thinks this:

I want to name the event of pure experience thus awakening to itself "awakening" (*kaku*). Awakening is the event of the mode of being enclosed within some kind of framework (the so-called self-consciousness) being sundered and stepping out into a bright opening. Pure experience is the event of coming out into an unlimited openness, as the framework of subject and object is sundered instantly in "the moment of seeing a color or hearing a sound." If there is no opening up in this manner, "the self facing the self" comes to a halt in self-consciousness and does not reach self-awareness.[55]

This "bright opening" is the *basho* of the later period of Nishida's thought, wherein the self dwells as a not-self. At all events, for Ueda, "the tendency of the idea of pure experience to develop first in the direction of self-awareness and then from self-awareness toward *basho* was at work from the very beginning."[56] There is an evident and consistent development from the earlier to the later Nishida, with each stage being a further working out of what pure experience itself entails philosophically and in terms of personal transformation.

Against accounts of this sort, Woo-sung Huh argues that Nishida's philosophy takes a "turn" about 1931, and the emphasis is no longer on self-consciousness (or self-awareness as Ueda insists), but on the philosophy of history and politics.[57] Huh ably chronicles the turn towards history, but he is sharply critical of Nishida for thinking that a philosophy of self-consciousness could be applied to the philosophy of history and its epochs and cultures, without a second thought. Huh writes,

> ...the deeper problem is whether it is possible to apply forms of self-consciousness, which originate in the discussion of acts of self-conscious-ness, to nonconscious phenomena. If one believes that these are categorically different entities, then Nishida clearly makes a category mistake. ... I would call this ... a category mistake, since acts of self-consciousness and a historical epoch are not similar enough to be treated by similar forms of self-con-sciousness. Hence, Nishida's turn to the philosophy of history is a wrong turn.[58]

Whether it is a wrong turn or not cannot be decided here, if only because so few of the central essays by Nishida have yet been translated. Yet it seems to me that there is reason to think that Nishida was not attempting a full-blown philosophy of history, but was attempting to include *homo exterior* (and not mere *homo interior*) in his account of who we are. Heidegger has made the enterprise of philosophy acutely self-critical through his warning that to reveal is to simultaneously conceal—that emphasis on one issue, is inevitably to conceal others precisely as a result of the desired emphasis. Nishida's earlier emphasis on the self had indeed down played, or even ignored the importance of society, culture, history and politics. It was this lack that he sought to address.

Just how radical a "turn" is this redressing of Nishida's philosophy? When we read such reformulations as "the historical world is the only real world,"[59] the change of focus seems extreme. Nonetheless, such a claim is exactly what one would expect from Zen Buddhism. This world is the real and only world, and enlightenment is the realization of this within oneself. Even a more general account of Japanese cultural traits, such as that provided by Nakamura Hajime, also emphasizes the Japanese belief and insight that this phenomenal world is the absolutely real world.[60] But Nishida's historical turn does more than reaffirm that this world is the real world—that nirvana is samsara—it also gives center stage to history, culture and politics, which is not something that Zen Buddhism does, or does very well. No, the new claim is that true reality is historical, that the social and political world is the central reality and the central focus of philosophy. It must be noted as well that part of the impetus for Nishida's reconsideration of his philosophical position in such a way as to include history and politics came from the inner dynamic of the intellectual and political climate of his times. Nationalism was on the rise, and Marxism had become both an intellectual and a political force. The concerns of several of Nishida's fellow philosophers such as Watsuji Tetsurō and Miki Kiyoshi no doubt also pushed him to deal with ethical, political and social issues. Able philosophers speak to the issues of their own day and culture, and Nishida was clearly drawn into and spoke to the intellectual and political issues of his time and place in history.

THE HISTORICAL WORLD AS DIALECTICAL

The historical world is a dialectical world. It is a world of contradictories, and yet these contradictions are at the same time unified. Recall that the contradictories include the universal and the individual, the one and the many, time and space, individual and environment, living and dying, past and present (past and future, present and future), etc. The tension which exists between opposites fuels creative generation and expression. Nishida tells us that the historical/dialectical world is a world in motion, and that this movement is from *creatus* to *creans:* that is, it is from the created to the creative, from the formed to the forming, from being to becoming, from one's past to one's future via the present. The historical world is not a static world, but is a dialectical tension or interplay between opposing or contradictory forces: we inherit our bodies, and our culture, our language and our thought patterns, *and yet* as creative beings we condition or wreck our bodies, learn from yet reject portions of our cultural tradition, use yet reform our language(s), and restructure our thought patterns throughout. By introducing the historical significance of his philosophy, Nishida is himself moving from the formed to the forming, from *creatus* to *creans:* he is building on what he has said up until now, but he is also radically revising and significantly going beyond the "earlier" Nishida. Human beings "make" things. We make ideas, tools, languages, art forms, agricultural enterprises, cities, constitutions, medical correctives, and all manner of theories which supposedly serve to explain the world in which we live. All of these are instances of "tool making," of humankind as *homo faber:* "the fact that man is 'homo faber' means: the world is 'historical.' On the other hand, the historical character of the world means: man is 'homo faber'."[61] We encounter an environment which shapes or determines us, *and yet* we ourselves break from and give a new shape to the environment, thereby determining it. The matter is more complex still, however, for not only do we determine in part that which determines us, in part, but by giving *form* to a creative expression (such as a new law, or new legislation, or a new art form, or a new philosophical insight or position), we not only to some degree determine or shape the environment into which it is sent, but we ourselves are determined or reshaped by the very creation that has come from us. The dialectic is that we are shaped, and yet shape that which shapes us by creating, which creation in turn shapes us, as we have shaped it (in part because of who we have become, and in part by that tradition in us which has also shaped us). And this dialectical energy keeps churning, in a creative, independent, thoughtful person such that being again generates becoming, and yet gives way to it. Thus, who we were "dies," and makes way for who we "become." In this sense we live by dying, which is another way of saying that we move from the created to the creative, from the formed to the forming, from *creatus* to *creans*. We not only express a fresh viewpoint or perspective of the world, but at the same time we mirror the world. This creative contradiction pulsates with possibilities, for we mirror what is, yet and at the same time we create a new outlook on the world. And insofar as we mirror the world, we mirror the one, and as such are ourselves an expression of the one. And yet, as unique perspectives on the world, we are original and distinctive creators of the world. We are ourselves identities of self-contradiction: we are one and yet many,[62] just as nothingness is one, and yet by its own negation, gives expression to the many. It, too, is one and many. It, too, is an identity of self-contradiction.

This dynamic, dialectical, pulsating, self-contradictory world is the world of history, moving from what was to what is, and from what is to what will be. That is what history is about. Nishida writes,

> ...in the historical-social world subject and environment confront each other and form each other. This means that past and future oppose each other in the present, as unity of opposites, and move from the formed towards the forming....The subject forms the environment. But the environment, though formed by the subject, is more than a part of the subject; it opposes and denies it. Our life is being poisoned by that which it has produced itself, and must die. In order to survive, the subject must, again and again, begin a new life. It must, as a species of the historical world of unity of opposites, become historically productive. It must become a spiritual forming force of the historical world.[63]

This pulsating, identity of self-contradiction characterizes the *expressive* nature of all creation and all existence. If the true basic and fundamental "stuff" of the universe, the true *hypokeímenon*, is "an absolute self-identity as the unity of absolute contradictories,"[64] then nothingness characteristically and by self-necessity expresses itself in just this manner. We ourselves are expressions of this nothingness, and so we must live in such a contradictory fashion: "Truly lived reality must be a contradiction in itself which is grasped through action."[65] Action-intuition means that we see the world in order to act in it, even if that action is just an attempt to understand the world: and action is not just blind action, but is action informed by intuition, by seeing the world as it is presented to us. Here, too, dialectic is at work: we act by seeing, and we see by acting. Action must be informed, and seeing must be practical or action oriented. My seeing is determined by what is "out there," by the physical, biological and historical world, and my action in those worlds also determines or shapes them. Action-intuition is Nishida's attempt to point out that we don't just contemplate the world, or ourselves, but that we act in the world. We are tool makers, shapers of our own destiny, at least in part, and of our own environment. His earlier emphasis on self-consciousness, therefore, does naturally lead to a self-conscious awareness of our freedom to shape not only ourselves, but our external environment. We are actors, not just thinkers, practical, not just theoretical. In a powerful account of the historical as human activity, Nishida states that

> ...the historical world is complete unity of opposites, as moving from the formed towards the forming, and so it is on [an] evolution of the world of living beings to the world of man. So historical life makes itself "concrete"; the world becomes something that truly moves by itself. I do not want to say that this evolution is merely a continuity of biological life, nor that it is merely negation of biological life. It means that the historical world is through and though unity of opposites. Biological life already contained the contradiction; but biological life is still in accordance with the environment, and not yet truly "from the formed to the forming." At the extreme limit of the contradiction, the evolution leads to the life of man. Of course, this is the result of the world of the historical life for many millions of years. At the

extreme limit of acting life from the formed towards the forming, a stage is reached where the subject lives by submerging into the environment, and the environment is environment by negating itself, and becoming subjective. Past and future, contradicting each other, join in the present, and the world, as unity of opposites, progresses from present to present, forming itself; i.e. the world is productive and creative. The body is no longer a mere biological body, but a historical one.[66]

To see things through action-intuition, then, means to see them productively, as an opportunity for action which will shape, or give new form to that which is seen. Seeing is not passive, but demands expression. In fact, "intuition, separated from action, is either merely an abstract idea, or mere illusion."[67] Whatever action ensues is inescapably self-contradictory, for it reflects the given of the seen, while encompassing the creative and deviant: "But if we would act only according to the tradition, only in the way of the species, it would mean a mechanization of the Self, and the death of the species. We must be creative, from hour to hour."[68]

THE ONE AND THE MANY

All is one, and yet all is not one but many. The identity of the one and the many is a foundational instance of the absolute identity of self-contradiction. "'All is one' does not mean that all are one without differentiation. It is, as unity of opposites, essentially that One by which all that is, is. Here is the principle of the origin of the historical world as the absolute present."[69] All that is, is because the One had within itself its own negation, i.e. its own capacity for differentiation, and expressed itself as a One which emptied itself of its oneness, expressing or manifesting manyness, while at the same time remaining one. In Nishida's *Final Writings*, he gives to this process of negation a theological flavor, indeed one that is surprisingly Christian:

The fall of Adam who ate of the fruit of the tree of knowledge of good and evil, in disobedience to God, is nothing other than an expression of the existence of mankind as God's own negation. The paradox of God's own negation is also behind the phrase of *The Awakening of Faith in the*

Mahāyāna: "A thought suddenly arises." Humankind is bottomlessly self-contradictory. The more that humankind is rational and volitional, the more is this true. Humankind is born in original sin.[70]

Original sin is our original separation from God, from the One, from nothingness. It is the centripetal direction of our lives, the force that moves us increasingly away from God, and towards our own separate individuality. The thought which suddenly arises is negation expressing itself as that which is differentiated from the One. Hence there exists a contradictory identity of the One, or God with the self:

On the one hand, there is that which transcends the self and yet establishes it in being—that is, what is transcendent and yet the fundamental ground of the self—and, on the other hand, there is the unique, sheerly individual, volitional self. Religion consists in this contradictory identity of transcendence and immanence. It cannot be conceived of in merely objective or in merely subjective terms. It must be grasped from the perspective of the creative historical world which exists as the self-determination of the absolute present.[71]

In this sense it is legitimate to offer that the One loves the individual, even at the sacrifice of the One itself, for by negation, by emptying itself, it gives rise to the many, to the differentiated "ten-thousand things" of the world. As self-sacrificial, it is the ultimate *agape*, for it is unconditional creative expression. Our sin is our separation, for our very existence as individuals betrays the fact that we have lost our oneness, our relation with God, with the One. And yet, the religious act is to become aware of our bottomlessly self-contradictory Self, which reveals that while we are separate, we are also, at one and the same time, one with the One. Religious consciousness rekindles our awareness of our own divine ancestry, and allows us to be who we are as individuals, while at the same time recognizing who we are at our depths. We are one with the One, while we are also not one with the One. And that is our freedom, while at the same time it is our destiny. For when we have lived by dying for the final time in this world, we re-enter that Oneness from which we originated: "Death is an entering into absolute nothingness; life is an appearing out of absolute nothingness."[72] Death is the absolute negation of the Self, as differentiated, and religious awareness is likewise the "absolute negation of the Self. The religious ideal consists in becoming a being which denies itself. There is a seeing without a seeing one, and a hearing without a hearing one."[73] Yet while we are alive, our consciousness is a self-contradictory consciousness, religiously aware of the importance of the negation of the self in understanding who we are from the perspective of our oneness, and historically aware of the importance of the affirmation of the self as creative expression in a world where such expression is life itself. Historically and actively we are differentiated, and expressive of this differentiation. Religiously we realize our oneness with the oneness of nothingness from which we originated, and to which we shall return in death. In the meantime, we create and express, and self-realize in the midst of a ceaselessly changing environment of physical, biological, and historical action-understanding. We act and thereby come to understand whether our understanding was adequate: we understand and thereby are able to decide how to act most appropriately. Humility and long experience reminds us that understanding is constantly revised in the light of the results of actions taken, and actions taken are re-considered in the light of further refined understanding. Action-understanding is itself a self-contradictory enterprise, and it is we ourselves who constitute the identity of that self-contradiction. In a sense, and from the perspective of human knowledge and action, it is we who are the *hypokeimenon* of action and intuition, of action and understanding, for it is we who continue to be able to act in revised ways, and to understand in quite different ways over the years. And yet, we are additionally changed by our environment, including the opinions and actions of others, and by our own creations and theories. And so in a broader sense, it is that which underlies both the individual, and the greater environment that is the true *hypokeimenon*, the absolute rather than the relative *hypokeimenon*. Nothingness, or the One is the final and foundational *hypokeimenon*.

CONCLUSION

The real world resists us, "stands opposed to us."[74] At the same time, everything which opposes us, which serves to negate us, at the same time affirms us, for "even the mountains, rivers, trees, and stones—is a Thou. In such a sense, the concrete world becomes a metaphysical society."[75] In opposing one another, we, and others (persons and things) affirm each other through action, as history, and, therefore, as creators of a common world. That historical world is also spiritually lined with our common kinship of oneness, which unites us affirmatively, and which leads us to realize the absolute kinship in our own, and in all else's depths. This last step is a religious one, to nothingness, and is the end-point and the origin of our understanding and of our existence.

Does Nishida claim to have reached "absolute truth?" Interpretations do vary on this point, but it does not seem to me that he either does, or needs to. He does not need to, although Zen is often excessive in its claims here as it is with nearly all of its claims generally, because it is enough to maintain that one sees more clearly, more fundamentally, more holistically than ever before. He does not appear to have made that claim, for even when he states that each individual "becomes an Archimedean point," mirroring nothingness, nonetheless Nishida carefully observes that "the more one is an individual, the more one stands in the truth," which suggests that "truth" is ongoing, and that realization is a practice, a process.[76] In any case, he explicitly denies that he is drawing on, or referring to "mystical" experience here, for he thinks he is applying his new dialectical logic of the predicate to call our attention to the given at the base of both ordinary and extraordinary experience: to the identity of contradiction within our experience itself. Even more important, insofar as Nishida points us towards pure experience as his non-propositional starting-point, we are at the philosophical, conceptual and logical beginning not only of what can be said, but of what cannot be said. Pure experience is true reality in that we simply can't push back any farther, beyond that which is the root and ground of all that can be thought and said, to our very existential foundation. Ueda argues that if we take that which is neither the one nor the many, neither subjective nor objective as the foundation, what we end up with is neither monism nor dualism nor pluralism, "but what could be called a dynamic non-foundationalist multi-dimensionalism."[77] It is as though Nishida were challenging each of us directly: if you can go beyond this archic intuition, then do so. Otherwise, at least take seriously where it is that I have reached in my thinking about the real and the absolutely ultimate.

However, an issue remains to be dealt with which seems to me to have not been completely cleared up by Nishida. It appears that action-intuition refers both to the oneness of intuition, and to direct and immediate action achieved by masters of the various contemplative and martial arts of the East, *and* to the ordinary everyday historical acts of common people. Yet how can it be both, or if both, can it be both in the very same sense? The incredible spontaneity of a swordsman, who is so well trained as to no longer have to think about his sword skills, is fully attentive to the complexities of the moment and acts without thinking, without hesitating, without anticipation, without conscious goal-direction: he is no-minded. Such examples make abundantly clear how intuition in the instant is needed for appropriate action, and how the appropriate action in the same instant arises out of the information gained through intuition. The one, in a flash, implies the other. But as I type these words, am I akin to a samurai master? I struggle with my thoughts, attempt to be as clear as I can, backspace on my computer to "erase" a word or a phrase, and wonder whether future readers will share my perplexity. The texts strewn around me are my intuition, as is the fact that I have worked on Nishida and related texts for decades. Clearly this is not yet the immanence and spontaneity of the samurai—the kindest thing that can be said about my scholarship is that I am still in training. My acting does advance, perhaps, for I think I can express myself more clearly, and more accurately than a decade ago. Nishida has also influenced me at some depth, and I live in the world differently than I might have had I not entered into this journey with him. And the whole is inescapably self-contradictory in the best Nishidan sense, for as he has decidedly influenced me, I have inescapably interpreted him in ways which either distort his philosophy, or in ways which expand and develop his philosophy along new lines. The identity of this self-contradiction is the obvious academic on-going quality of scholarship and textual interpretation (hermeneutics, and the inevitable "fusion of horizons" wherein both the interpreted and the interpreter are altered due to their interactive contact with one another). The book is about Nishida, and the reactions to the book will also be about Nishida and his interpretation. Yet is all of this action-intuition? Is the point that everything is action-intuition? Is it impossible that there be any awareness, or any action in the world which is not an instance of action-intuition? Has Nishida simply made a concession to the Marxists that all knowledge is *for* some action, is praxis?

My understanding of Nishida on this is that the action-intuition of the samurai or master in any field exemplifies what he wants to say about the spontaneous identity of the self-contradiction of knowing and acting. All other actions do, to some extent at least, display a trace of this masterful excellence. It is a matter of degree: one usually does not act without being somewhat informed (although it would not be difficult to dream up instances in which a reflex response, or an impaired response was not well-informed, and possibly not informed at all), and information is inescapably action-oriented, even if the action is only thinking, or realizing something. The model of action intuition is that of the master painter, or master swordsman, or archer, or poet whose integration is such that there is no intervening moment discernible between seeing and acting—all calculation is absent, all goal-oriented desire, all concern about the future, or about the nature of the results to be achieved—there is only the smooth and seamless seeing-as-acting, action-as-correct in the here-and-now of this moment. The resulting self-awareness is the seeing of the self without a self, seeing that our surface self faces our deep Self within an "openness without a self. To the extent that this openness is an openness wherein the self opens up without a self, the self belongs to the openness and the openness belongs to the self."[78] The opening up is itself self-awareness, and the opening to the openness of the openness is the awareness of *basho*. So it is that nirvana is samsara, for our encounter with the everyday "reaches all the way to 'beholding the glory of God'."[79] The "I" of self-consciousness gives way to the "Thou" of self-awareness, and both give way to pure experience where both "I" and "Thou" disappear. And yet, precisely because they have opened to the openness, to nothingness, "I am I without an I" is now who we are.[80] Our ego-attachment is gone, our various conceptualizations of self and world are no longer present, and we are free to intuit things "as they are" and to act spontaneously. Placed squarely in the eternal now, in the moment of openness, we see as though for the first time, and we are utterly and totally "there." Uncluttered and unmediated by language, logic, and deliberation, we act with effortless freedom upon a "world" which is not separate from us. We are, we see and we act from the center of the world, as though from the center of an empty circle, as though an expression of the self-determination of nothingness itself. We are fully in the world, the world of pure experience.

Nishida's later philosophical stage stakes a claim for the centrality of the *ordinary*. All seeing and all acting *is action intuition*, and it is not necessary to become a master of some practice to realize or achieve this integration of seeing and doing. As creators, as embodied creators, as embodied creators who dwell in a world of historical dialectical interaction and interconnection, we are inescapably thrown into a world where we must see and at the same time must act in order to survive, to learn, and hopefully, to flourish. Nishitani Keiji remarks, in aid of his interpretation of Nishida's position, that "even everyday things like eating and dressing originally include an element of no-mind."[81] Action- intuition is "nothing other than all our ordinary thinking and acting. In this sense it is even referred to as 'eschatological ordinariness'."[82] Yet the creative and ever developing path which the masters teach leads us—if we walk long enough and far enough—to a way of being in the world where distinctions give way to a direct immersion into the very flow of being and becoming, and then into the primal creativity of sheer distinctionless nothingness. Ultimately, for Nishida, even then we apply that distinctionless realization to the historical world once more, as embodied "masters" of living who walk in the world like the old teacher depicted in the tenth and final ox-herding picture (p. 76 *above*). The master walks along dusty, worldly paths, teaching those who wish to hear that realization is not an otherworldly act, but a renewed and deliciously self-contradictory plunging into the world of everyday experience. Because reality is ultimately without distinction, all distinctions have now become ultimately real in and of themselves.

SIX

Religion and Morality

Every religious tradition seems to have its "scandal," or sticking point when viewed from another tradition or perspective. The scandal of Buddhism has been its seeming amorality. If all is an expression of the whole, then all is divine. The distinction between good and bad is but relative, and so from a higher perspective they would be equal, or at least the one would collapse into the other. Nishida seems to accept such a view, for he is firm in his systematic overcoming of the realm of morality and values by the final universal of absolute nothingness. His critique of Kant hinges on Kant's making the moral ultimate, with religion becoming a kind of intellectual afterthought or corollary of morality. Instead, Nishida believes that the religious overshadows the moral. Religious consciousness is a higher consciousness, and so takes precedence over the moral which preceded it. Clearly, the ultimate goal of Buddhism, and of Zen, is not morality, but spirituality. One does not have to look very far in Zen literature to find Zen masters performing or recommending acts which are at least morally controversial. Cutting off an initiate's finger or chopping a live cat in two are not exactly imaginable as indications of the message of Christ, for example. It is not that the Judeo-Christian tradition is immune to such interpretation, of course, for the story of Abraham and Isaac, or God's slaying of the Egyptian firstborn, do raise ethical issues of a mind-boggling sort. Nevertheless, the Jewish and Christian traditions are throughout steeped in ethical analysis, and attempted resolutions of moral issues. Buddhism certainly has its eightfold path, and this may be enough to indicate that one must first be moral before one can proceed along the path of religion. But Zen is less evidently concerned with the doctrines and forms of Buddhism, and has often flaunted its doctrineless break with any and all tradition, including the moral. One must kill the Buddha (i.e., eliminate all threats of closure) if only to keep one's own religiosity free of the dogma of (any final) determination, since the ultimate richness given in pure experience is never exhausted by any system or conceptual grasp, but is only appropriated-in-part via some specific perspective. To think one knows is evidence that one does not know. The truth of Zen is not doctrine, but no-doctrine. To have a dogma is not to have Zen understanding. All morality, however, is notoriously specific, if not rigid. To be moral is to have universal rules or criteria by means of which one must act. Good must be clearly and sharply distinguished from bad, and the valuable from the non-valuable.

GOD AND EVIL

Early despair is likely to set in when one reads in the final essay that "God as the true absolute must be Satan, too."[1] The all-embracing perspective is not meant to blur distinctions, however, but only to impress one with the fact that distinctions must be balanced by another aperture of understanding that embraces *all* distinctions as the partial working out of the whole of things. But the world is no less a world of objects *because* it is a world which appears only to subjects (to state the relationship of the first two universals), nor does the world of intelligible universals (the third universal) negate the first two. It embraces them, transcends them, but does not negate or abandon them. While Nishida nowhere explicitly states this, his enveloping universals can be taken to mean that we are talking about stages of the development of understanding, and that just as one must crawl before one can walk, so one must be moral before one can move to the religious.[2] Perhaps this is a bit overstated, however, for whereas true religiosity is a way of being (or not-being) for Nishida (although much religiosity is mere belief or assent), more typically morality *can be* a way of thinking only. One can understand the requirements of morality without living them, or live them by following the rules, even grudgingly. Presumably, to *be* moral would be to spontaneously instantiate the requirements of morality in one's everyday living. Such a moral stance would be radically un-Kantian, for spontaneity smacks too heavily of the dreaded inclination, rather than of action performed strictly in accordance with the demands of duty. It seems that Nishida here, too, is unable to follow Kant, as will be argued shortly. It should be said, however, that had he concentrated on the Middle Ages, for example, instead of on the Kantian ethical tradition, he would have found a very different ethical understanding that quite literally advocated instantiating the Christian virtues in one's everyday life. It is also evident, of course, that in contemporary ethical debate not all Western thinkers are either Kantian, or, for that matter, universalistic consequentialists (utilitarians).

Even though Nishida can assert that "the creative world is a world of absolute evil,"[3] for the world of physical nature "is an atheistic, a God-absent, world,"[4] this should not be taken to mean literally that the world is estranged from God and therefore Godless and evil, but only that part of the meaning of God's self-negation is that the many are absent from (or unaware or forgetful of) the one. But the identity of opposites also requires one to realize, religiously, that the many are also God-filled at their bottomless depths. Again we encounter the ultimate selfcontradiction: what is Godful is so because it is God-less, and what is Godless (the world of Satan)[5] is for that reason Godful. The world is not just the objective world, but the subjective, historical, and religious world as well. Nishida's God is not a relative God "who merely opposes, and struggles with"[6] evil. To conquer evil, to be a supremely good God, "is a mere abstraction."[7] The true absolute is not at war with negation, but "includes absolute negation within himself."[8] Here Nishida begins his moral or valuational turn, for he allows a "better" and a "worse," a "higher" and a "lower" within the account of God thus far given: "The *highest* form must be one that *transforms* the *lowest* matter into itself."[9] Not that the lowest is to be overcome or destroyed, but that it will be raised up so as to include within one's conception of it the recognition of its higher dimensions.

Reflecting back to the theory of universals, it is not that objects are not objects, but that the very recognition of objects as objects requires that they also be objects for subjects, that subjects be teleologically oriented, and that the theologically intelligible world be lined with absolute nothingness. To utter the word "object" is implicitly to utter the word "divine," or "godly," or "nothingness." The double aperture keeps both senses alive in a vital contradictoriness. An object is the absolute, and the absolute is objects; samsara is nirvana, and nirvana is samsara. It is this that the term "transformation," in Nishida's "higher" transforming the "lower," refers to. Thus it is that "Absolute agape must reach even to the absolutely evil man."[10] It does so because the evil man is already good. He is already at his bottomlessness a determination of the absolute. Dōgen's description of the "unborn" stresses this fact, for the unborn as the absolute is also all that *is* born. "That which is born is, in some sense, the self-expression of that which is not."[11] The unborn is, contradictorily, the born, and the born is the unborn. That one does not know this is an original and sustaining sin. One is estranged by one's ignorance. Evil is the deprivation of good, the separation of the many from the absolute unity out of selfish arrogance and/or ignorance. To realize one's self-contradictory nature is, however, the religious turn whereby one comes to see that one's estrangement already assumes God (i.e., one's separation implies one's Godliness), and thus that one is intrinsically "divine." So it is that the human self, as the place/ *basho* of all realization, of the sinful and the godly, is the "battlefield" where the struggle between God and Satan takes place.[12] If God and Satan are contradictory, it also follows that absolute nothingness is the *basho*/field which underlies such conceptual contradiction. Beyond God and beyond Satan there is the nothingness out of which both arise. This is their *identity:* the identity behind the paradox. Fox, in describing Dōgen's perspective on the ultimate ground, writes that "the Ultimate Truth, the ground of our being, is that Reality or Absolute which we may call by many names, but which Dōgen often likes to call simply the Unborn."[13]

As the mirror image of God, the human self contains, in microcosm, the same contradictoriness of good and evil that God and Satan represent on the macrocosmic level. Yet agape enriches the evil by providing the realization that the evil is enveloped by the good, for the good is determined at its extreme of self-negation, i.e., estrangement from the source, as evil. Good and evil both exist as co-ingredients in the identity of contradiction in the absolute. One might well ask whether evil can also envelop the good. It seems that it cannot precisely because, for Nishida, evil is an act or perspective of separation, and not an embracive one. It is true, however, that evil can color one's perspective such that one might ignore, destroy or otherwise affect a circle of influence with which one is associated. But insofar as evil is the result of separation (estrangement) from the totality, it cannot envelop the whole. It could, however, infect the whole world. Evil is unaware or deluded particularization, and is present in any of the degrees of incomplete apprehension of the oneness of all things. Nishida warns that "this does not mean that God looks indifferently at good and evil."[14] This is the moral key! It is not that individuality, the many, or the objective should disappear, but that all particularity, selfhood, or objecthood should be seen for what it really is at its bottomless depths, *viz.* contradictory. A thing is an object because it isn't *just* an object; it is God-infused, or lined with the spiritual thrust-to-creation of absolute nothingness. A self is a self precisely because it is not a self at its bottomless depths. It is, rather, an image of and an expression of God, and so mirrors the whole universe in itself. Evil, as separation, is really not separation (or at least not *just* separation), but unification or identity as well. It is both separate and, at a deeper level, unity.

Still, it is only one approach to evil to conceive of it, negatively, as estrangement from the whole. Positive evil, i.e., the willful torture of human beings, the suffering in the Nazi camps of death, and the like, is not so easily dealt with. It is little comfort to a "moral" being to learn that Hitler, too, was an expression of the divine. Nishida has indicated that God, and by mirror extension we human beings, do not look *indifferently* at good and evil, at Hitler and Martin Luther King, at the extremes. The ground of this value preference is that the very act of religious realization is to throw out, or abandon altogether, the *self* itself.[15] Religiosity is utterly transformative in that it must be an abandoning of the self in its existential depths—a feeling of shame concerning the very existence of the self.[16]

This is exactly what one might expect from a thinker immersed in a cultural tradition, or a confluence of cultural traditions (Taoism and Buddhism, including Zen Buddhism), which promotes the abandoning of the self. Nishida quotes Dōgen on several occasions during this exposition of his position, and Dōgen's expression of the necessity of selflessness is perhaps the crispest in the literature. It is also formulated in the logical form of paradox—the identity of contradiction:

> Studying the Buddha Way is studying oneself. Studying oneself is *forgetting oneself.* Forgetting oneself is being enlightened by all things. Being enlightened by all things is causing the body-mind of oneself and the body-mind of others to be shed.[17]

AN ANALOGY

Borrowing an analogy from Nicholas of Cusa, Nishida writes of the world of the absolute present as "a bottomlessly self-contradictory sphere that reflects itself in itself," rather than just as "an infinite sphere of which, because there is no circumference, every point is the center," as Cusanus described it.[18] In Nishida's self-contradictory sphere, there *are* points of reference, and hence at least two directional indications. First, the centrifugal direction is a movement away from God, who represents the center of the sphere. This direction is evil, for it is the movement of separation from God, of individuality as *independent* objective existence, of estrangement from the center or souce of all things, including estrangement from one's own self-contradictory self. For to make one's self an object is to render it single-mindedly consistent, rather than self-contradictory. Second, the centripetal direction is the direction of goodness and is towards God. By drawing towards the center of the sphere, we discover the absolute subjectivity of the creative historical world, in contrast with the objectivity of the physical world. Recall, however, that the absolute is itself self-contradictory, and so both evil and good. God and Satan are but moments of, or directions in, the whole sphere, which itself is neither God nor Satan, and therefore both. The sphere is, ultimately, absolute nothingness, and therefore it is, immanently, exactly what it is: Godly and Satanic. And as mirrors of God, we, the places/ *bashos* where nothingness expresses itself through conscious acts, must also be mirrors of God and Satan:

> We, the centers of this bottomlessly contradictory world, are both satanic and divine. Hence my theology of the absolute present is neither theistic nor deistic—a theology neither of mere spirit nor of mere nature. It is the theology of the dynamic matrix of history itself.[19]

The direction of religiosity is centripetal, or spiritual, however. And while it is easy to see why God, as the pole of goodness, is not indifferent valuationally and morally, it is less obvious whether absolute nothingness can be said to prefer at all, but instead simply serves as the final enveloping reality of the good and the evil together.

Part of the confusion surrounding Nishida's analysis of the nature of God seems to have been brought on by Nishida himself. He appears to use the term "God" equivocally, sometimes referring to the centripetal determination of the indeterminate, and at other times using "God" as a synonym for the indeterminate final absolute, nothingness. It does seem at times that he intends to keep the term as the *penultimate* designation, but the problem arises precisely because "God" is the ultimate term in Western religious understanding, as St. Anselm's "that than which no greater can be conceived" makes amply evident. In much Eastern thought, "God" is not the ultimate notion, unless it is used as a synonym for absolute nothingness. But then its meaning or referent would be drastically different, even though Anselm's "God" and Nishida's "absolute nothingness" are both the *ultimate* notions of each cultural mainstream. In any case, "God" seems to carry the weight both of the ultimate-determinate-being and the ultimate-as-utterly-indeterminate.

The centripetal direction is the direction of *goodness,* and it is characterized by the abandoning of self. Nishida declares which direction is the better by stressing that the spiritual movement "means to see our essential nature, to see the true self."[20] Thus estrangement is somehow less true, or accidental, and a less deep or penetrating direction of understanding our nature. It is but the outer, or surface, layer of reality. It is partial, superficial, cut off from its deeper core. The inner layers and the core itself, however, presuppose, embrace, or carry along with them this outer layer. Two images are at work here, of course, for the core is also the most embracive, and therefore must be drawn both as the center of ontological priority and ontic "radiation," and as the outer ring in terms of its epistemic embrasiveness of each of the less deep and more superficial rings. These two attributes of the most real, the "true self" as the mirror of God, and God as the deeper dimension of spirit, require two different—indeed contradic-tory—depictions. By now, however, such paradox is old hat. In any case, Nishida is perhaps clearest when he explicates the Buddhist tradition to make clear his own position. For to "see" our essential nature or true self means within Buddhism "not to see Buddha objectively outside, but to see into the bottomless depths of one's own self."[21] Buddha, as the centripetal direction, is not external to us, but is an event in our own soul, the re-discovery of one's own Buddha-nature. Yet, while the direction is centripetal, even Buddha, or God, is a penultimate determination of the ultimate, which is experienced in the places of consciousness, as a "welling up from the bottomless depths of the soul."[22] And, as we have seen, the truth about the self is that it is not a self, but the ultimate... and *yet*, therefore, it is a self. This transform-ative realization, which moves us towards our true nature, is also an "absolute overturning of values.... For the proud moralist to gain religious faith may be said to be more difficult than for a camel to pass through the eye of a needle."[23]

MORALITY

Movement towards the deeper layers of self, which culminates in the realization of bottomless self-contradictory identity as the place where absolute nothingness arises and becomes uniquely conscious of itself, is contrasted with movement away from our essential nature, which is increasingly evil (estranged) as it covers over its deeper nature. Delusion, the traditional cause of evil in Buddhist thought, occurs when we mistake the objective self for the real or deeper self.[24] The logic of objects moves us in the wrong direction, whereas the logic of the identity of self-contradiction (paradox) is to move centripetally towards the absolute. The deep self and the absolute, "are always related in the paradoxical form of simultaneous presence and absence."[25] The religious awareness consists precisely in the realization of this contradictory identity of the true self and absolute nothingness. To "see" this is to have one's own experience of one's bottomlessness. Such an experience *is* a religious conversion. To transcend one's ordinary, empirical, or shallow self is to realize one's true or deep self, which is to lose one's self by recognizing one's essential identity with the absolute. The unexpected prize that is given at this point is one's individuality as ordinary and everyday selfhood. Each self is a center of the universe, for Buddha and one's self are not two. Indeed, the self, Buddha, and absolute nothingness are not three, but ultimately one and the same. Samsara is nirvana because nirvana manifests itself as samsara. The absolute embraces us because it has already given expression to us.

In personalistic terms, the spiritual emotion of embrace is agape. The self encounters the absolute by transcending the ordinary self, and the direction is inward. Love between persons "is the paradoxical identity of persons who face each other as individual selves."[26] Perfect, unconditional love—agape—is the love of the good and the bad. It is the embracing of all that exists.

NISHIDA'S ATTEMPTED SOLUTION

Agape is unconditional, but as Nishida cautions, "this does not mean that God looks indifferently at good and evil," but only that even evil is a part of the absolute. What is morally significant about this fact of the absolute's unconditional love as embrace, or envelopment-as-identity is that this unconditional envelopment of each being is exactly what infuses our moral life with the kind of spiritual feeling that makes it genuine, rather than being necessitated, or grudgingly performed. In Nishida's words:

> From this fact that we are embraced by God's absolute love… our moral life wells forth from the depths of our own minds. People do not seem truly to understand love. It is nothing instinctive. Instinct is not love; it is selfish desire. True love must be an interexpressive relation between persons between I and Thou. I say, therefore, that there must be God's absolute love in the depths of the absolute moral ought. If not, the moral ought degenerates into something merely legalistic.[27]

To use the analogy of the kimono again, what Nishida terms "God's love," (where "God" means absolute nothingness) is the lining which gives proper shape and form to a moral act and to a moral code. An understanding of this point of view is more easily achieved against the background of notions such as *kokoro* in the Japanese context. The thrust is towards a natural, spontaneous, genuine, intrinsic (rather than reward oriented) expression of fellow-feeling from the heart. *Kokoro*, a term which can refer to both mind and heart, is a term of praise of character. One has *kokoro* if one interacts with another lovingly, or in a thoroughly friendly way, for *no* ulterior or extrinsic reasons. One just spontaneously, and from one's depths expresses such warmth, caring, and concern. As stated in *A Study of Good*, "Our loving a thing means our casting aside the self and merging with the other."[28] This is not all, however, for the quality of spontaneity is also central:

> For example, when we are absorbed in that which the self likes, we are almost unconscious.… when with regard to the joys and sorrows of another person, there is absolutely no distinction between the self and the other and we feel in the self directly what the other person feels, laughing together and weeping together, at this time we are loving the other person and we also are knowing him. Love is to intuit the emotions of the other person.[29]

One envelops the other in good will. *Kokoro* is the natural and spontaneous springing up from the depths of feeling of a human being, from his or her "true heart" an aspiration to be friendly, and to live happily with everyone.[30] Nishida writes that "there must be pure love at the ground of Kant's kingdom of ends. The moral person is established only on that ground."[31] Such grounding projects mutual love and respect, through the I and Thou becoming one. When one expresses *kokoro,* one is other-regarding, that is, one reaches out to the other, and for a moment, one is selfless, or filled with the other person. To speak of "selflessness" is but to adapt Dōgen's adage that one must forget the self to be open to all things. Indeed, the complex East Asian Buddhist notion of dependent—or better, interdependent—origination may be taken to refer to the inextricable links, at the deep level of the "lining" between what is taken as oneself, and all other things. It is separation, destruction, uniqueness, individuality, and *selfishness* which are delusory. They are delusory in that they represent the most shallow account of who we are, and how we are related to others, to the historical world, and to the cosmos. Individuality is not illusory in the sense that it does not actually "happen"—it happens overwhelmingly—but it is unreal or delusory in a sense similar to the taking of the cover of a book as a complete account of the content of its pages. The cover is the first and most superficial exposure we have of the book. The book's deeper nature is the real substance of its inner pages. We must come to see the interconnection of each and every page, sentence, word, letter, and blank space of existence. Iino Norimoto interprets Dōgen as stating exactly this view of interdependence as the route to the selflessness of compassion, whereby all valuation is

> ...rooted in the one "Crimson Heart of Cosmic Compassion," which is one ethereal ship aboard which all mankind will be delivered to the Blessed Land of Enlightenment sooner or later. In fact, the whole cosmos is radiant with infinite compassion when we have our inner spiritual eyes opened through the practice of Zen. Zen is concentration on the truth of universal interdependence, which reveals the folly of the narrowness of self-centeredness.[32]

More strongly still, "If there is any remainder of selfishness in a man, he is not able to see the pervading presence of the cosmic compassion."[33] One remains an individual self, but not as interconnected at one's depths. As Nakamura Hajime puts it, "If we allow the virtue of compassion to grow in us, it will not occur to us to harm anyone else, any more than we would willingly harm ourselves."[34] Thomas Kasulis illustrates Dōgen's position as a variant interpretation of the biblical "Thou shalt not kill":

> Dōgen might argue that one first takes this to be a divine imperative, "*Do not kill,*" and thus one undertakes a religiously moral life. After some time, however, the efficacy of one's spiritual cultivation is such that one is no longer capable of murder. At that point, one suddenly sees the phrase as a description: "[You are such a person that] you will not kill."[35]

When Dōgen tells us to drop off both body and mind, he means the dropping off of our superficial and separate selfhood, in order to give full expression to our deep self, as interconnected. One's entire personality must undergo an about-face, a transformation "into pure compassion itself."[36] As a selfless or other-directed deep self, one finds joy in the joy of others, sorrow in the suffering of others. In another essay, Nishida quotes Dōgen, agreeing that the body and mind must drop off, and adds, "Dōgen tells us that it is not by the self subjectively going out to all things, but rather 'by all things advancing' that the self is enlightened."[37] Enlightenment or "intuitive wisdom in Buddhism" is more than intellectual; it is a lived awareness of "the working of God within us."[38] God and man are one, and as such they together are apprehended "in the form of a contradictory identity."[39]

Still, the scandal of Zen is said to rest on the intrinsic relativeness, or non-absoluteness, of the moral dualism of good and bad. All dualisms are mental constructs, and hence at least once removed from spontaneity. Conceptualizations, laws, prohibitions, even the noble truths and the eightfold way, like the Ten Commandments of Christianity, are but hundred-foot-poles, useful only in scaling the heights of a cliff, but not necessary once one has arrived at one's destination. To have arrived is not to reject the pole, but to have moved beyond it by means of its help and functionality. Life is now lived spontaneously, and the true foundation of all morality, spirituality as compassion, permeates all of one's actions, even those of eating, and the functions of the body.[40] So it is that "once the *buddha*hood of a man is revealed through Zen, all his activity is as full of compassion as the act of Zen itself."[41] The secular has been sacralized, and samsara is nirvana, because nirvana has self-negated and become samsara. Altruistic behavior is now a "spontaneous outburst."[42] Brear argues this thesis and writes that

> the real aim and result of the Zen life is precisely to be in a position to use morality as an instrument of free and creative living, and hence Zen masters continue to act in a way which is, relatively, moral, although without motivation or constraint by relative issues.[43]

D.T. Suzuki advises that

> …morality is always conscious of itself; it speaks of decisions and individual responsibilities…. Morality can never be innocent, spontaneous, self-forgetful and divinely or devilishly above all worldly concerns.
>
> The saintly man is, therefore, to be distinguished from the moral man. The saintly man may not be strictly all-moral or scrupulously correct. But the moral man can never be saintly as long as he remains on the plane of morality which is the plane of relativity.[44]

From the relative standpoint, actions are either good or bad, but because now one's "human nature is beastly,"[45] it is necessary to "forget" this objective and superficial self, and transform one's self by losing this shallowest self. En route to one's bottomless depths, one passes through *morality*, and when one reaches the deepest or religious "place," one continues to perform right actions, and to avoid evil ones, by simply and spontaneously acting, without attaching the qualities "goodness" or "badness" to one's actions. A Buddhist acts now from his own deep nature, and not out of duty, fear, or a desire to abide by the law. He acts, rather, from the deepest motivations. Even so, he performs generally what relative morality would dictate. As Dōgen affirmed, "Benevolence is the universal law."[46] Dōgen is further interpreted by Fox to be making the saying of the Buddha, "Do not commit evil," carry precisely this distinction between internalized vs. externally imposed morality:

> "Do not commit evil" must become my subjectivity; it must not remain an externally imposed rule. When it *is* truly my subjectivity and my true self,

then my self is no longer that separate, finite ego of which I once boasted, but is none other then the unborn, the Absolute, the Eternal Truth.[47]

The "fundamental principle of Buddhist ethics is that all men should develop an attitude of compassion.... By dissolving our human existence into component parts, we can get rid of the notion of ego, and through that meditation we are led to a limitless expansion of the self in a practical sense, because one identifies oneself with more and more living beings. The whole world and the individual are intimately and indissolubly linked.[48]

Compassion is the natural way of being. The "forms" of compassion are relatively determined by the structures, laws, rules, and codes of goodness. But to cling to the dualistic way of distinguishing the good from the bad will not lead one to enlightenment, to one's religious depths. If we are not yet enlightened, then, of course, we must discriminate, and learn to follow an ethical path. But if we have discovered that our self is the absolute, then we act in the only way that we can, compassionately, without calculation, for no personal gain or reward, but as expressions of the suchness of self and absolute.[49]

To characterize the transformation in chart form, one begins in ignorance, and ends in enlightenment:

Stage one selfish/evil/unconcerned about the well-being of the larger context	a state of **ignorance**
Stage two compassionate (but not yet selfless for one still thinks dualistically—self/other, good/bad, mine/yours) but *morally* oriented towards the "good"	a state of **ignorance**
Stage three selflessly compassionate, spontaneously expressing acts of other-directed, whole-oriented compassion.	a state of **enlightenment**

Dōgen reminds us that every Buddha-figure has admonished us not to commit evil. Not to commit evil is not a ritual, or a form of self-control, but "the very speaking of Enlightenment itself."[50] Not doing evil is but the spontaneous self-determination of the absolute itself:

> Being moved by the Supreme Enlightenment one learns to aspire to commit no evil, to put this injunction into practice, and as one does so the practice-power emerges which covers all the earth, all worlds, all time, and all existences without remainder.[51]

One is now freed from evil, and the absolute now simply expresses itself freely through these, spontaneously, and not because of a rule.

No doubt the root of this non-mental-construct viewpoint, which is not linguistically or rationally accessible, is *meditation* as a mode of awareness and a source of insight. Nakamura makes this link adeptly in his depiction of the meditative experience:

> Meditating...seeks to abolish our deep-rooted egoism in our own existence: it aims at cherishing compassion and love towards others. By dissolving our human existence into component parts, we can get rid of the notion of ego, and through that meditation we are led to a limitless expansion of the self in a practical sense, because one identifies oneself with more and more living beings.[52]

Compassion, equanimity, selflessness, nonattachment, joy in the joys of another, and sorrow at another's sorrow are traits that "should be deliberately practiced, beginning with a single object and gradually increasing until the whole world is suffused with them."[53]

Neither Buddhism in general, nor Nishida in particular, is uncommitted to goodness as such, but rather seeks to push the search towards the source or ground of goodness, i.e., for the spontaneity behind goodness. The goodness/badness dichotomy simply does not reach far enough. In addition, "Thinking not only fails to grasp the true nature of prereflective compassion; it often *obstructs* the expression of compassion.[54] Only without the ego can there be compassion without distinctions. It is in Dōgen's "unborn," and Nishida's bottomlessly self-contradictory identity where, in the depths of the self, is found that which transcends the self. The self, as deep self, is *also* not the self at all, it will be remembered, but absolute nothingness. It is both self and not-self, and neither.

Yet to argue that pureheartedness lies at the ground of Kant's ethical system that culminates in the "kingdom of ends," or to extend the thesis by observing that all conceivable ethical systems must rest ultimately on pureheartedness, love, or fellow-feeling, is not to show that *social* ethics is unimportant or bypassable. Rather, what it seemingly *ought* to imply is that ethical systems are never to be separated from that basic and fundamental feeling component without which all acts are but habit, cultivated reflex, or purely mechanical responses for selfish and/or instrumental reasons. It is important to observe that Nishida does not provide a social ethic in his voluminous writings, and that this omission is typical of most Mahāyāna Buddhist thinkers. That it is an omission is a regrettable fact, but it is not lamentable. To focus on ethics as not fundamental, or as a penultimate stage through which one may (must?) pass on one's way towards spirituality, seems both laudable and worthy of investigation. There would be reason for lament only if social ethics were rejected and abhorred in principle. Nishida, at least, does not take such a position, but instead attempts to infuse ethics with its originating impulse (fellow-feeling or love), and then pushes beyond ethical structures to religiosity itself. That ethics does not receive sufficient attention along the way is a matter for regret. It does not distort Nishida's vision to pause and implant ethical theory into his perspective. Natural and spontaneous feeling *(kokoro)* must, after all, take on form, and while all form is partial, less rich, and to some extent distortive of the whole (nothingness) of which it is an expression, it is imperative that the form expressed be the highest and most spiritually grounded of which we are capable. And each succeeding generation has precisely the same responsibility anew. It is when the task is not shouldered anew, or when the old form is out of accord with the feelings and cultural embodiments of a new age, that the system handed on loses its grounding of vitality, and becomes an empty shell, a form without life or passion. It is then that a conscious reexamination of one's reflex actions, one's cultural habits, must be undertaken anew. To do so is to be engaged in the development of a new social-ethical dimension. I will raise this issue again at the end of this book.

THE GROUND OF MORALITY

Moral norms are, in Buddhism as in most religions, leader-inspired. Buddhism codifies its ethical teachings in its eightfold path, its scriptures, its traditions, and its practices. But each of us is also Buddha, and we discover how to express this moral awareness spontaneously, through the revelation of this compassionate nature in meditation, and no doubt in numerous other religious practices. Nishida speaks of a "non-discriminating wisdom in the sense of a dimension of knowing that transcends and yet incorporates the judgments of abstract consciousness and determines their validity."[55] Such activity is "truly selfless" and "actively intuitive."[56] Indeed, "moral behavior is grounded in it, and that is why moral behavior is religious in its ground."[57] This confirms directly that Nishida does not seek to leave morality behind, and to wallow in a sea of valuational indifference. The superiority of the religious is a matter of envelopment of the less basic by the more basic. It is not that one ceases to be moral, but that one is now moral *and* religious. But the very recognition of the superiority of the religious is founded on the self-transformation that it necessarily entails, as an event in one's soul. This transformation makes it impossible for one to be moral in the same way that one understood the moral life before enlightenment. Morality is now the spontaneous expression of who one really is and, therefore, the self-determination of absolute nothingness itself. It is as though the specific meaning of Christ's insistence that insofar as you show generosity of spirit to another, you do it unto him, is given a Buddhist flavor. The expression of love is the expression not only of one's own divinity, but of nothingness itself. No wonder Nishida can assert so straightforwardly that "religious experience signifies that we are always embraced by the vow of absolute compassion."[58] The religiously transformed person is, *ipso facto*, a spontaneous vehicle of compassion, and thus of morality which is a revealment not only of itself, but also of its ground. Religious awareness does for morality what a virtuoso spontaneously accomplishes as a result of the exhausting years of routine and rigid rule-following leading to creative performance. Spontaneity comes only at the end of practice, discipline, memorization, obedience, and diligence. It could not occur without them. Yet virtuosity conceals them all, for it is something else altogether. It is spontaneous; interpretive rather than slavish with respect to the practice and the rules; an expression of freedom and originality from within, rather than a mimicking of external norms. It is akin to *kokoro*, the non-calculating welling up of spontaneous artistic feeling and enactment, expressed and given for no other reason than that, at least for this moment, it is one's nature, one's interpretive gestalt. In Nishida's words, "any true communication with another person takes place in this dimension of 'no thought and no conception'."[59] The spontaneity of ethical expression has no thought and no conception as its ground. The ground itself is the event of religious transformation in one's soul such that one now realizes one's endlessly contradictory self-identity. As a self, one must forget the self; as selfless, one can interact with others as a self, as though for the first time, and for the first time recognize others as selves of worth—because they are not just selves, but are joined with us in the interdependence that manifests itself, generally *and* in us, as compassion. Thus it is that "compassion always signifies that opposites are one in the dynamic reciprocity of their own contradictory identity."[60]

THE MORALITY OF CONTRADICTORY IDENTITY

That "oneself and Buddha are not two" is the teaching of the *Prajñāpāramitā Sūtra*.[61] Nishida takes this to say that "the whole mind is Buddha and the whole Buddha is oneself, in the form of the contradictory identity of the consciously active self and world, of the volitional individual and the absolute."[62] He then warns that this is not pantheism, where all things are God (i.e., taken together, the whole world of beings is God). Pantheism is a conception of object logic, and all object logic is thoroughly *dualistic* as its roots. X is a part of Y, because Y is simply all X's taken together. X and Y are thoroughly distinguished from each other, and this is what makes it possible to affirm that all X's are parts of Y. Yet how are we to make a sharp distinction between the pantheism of object logic and the paradoxicality of Nishida's concrete logic of contradictory identity? The reader may recall W. T. Stace's analysis of the "pantheistic paradox" discussed earlier.[63] Stace argued that pantheism asserted *both* that the world is identical with God, *and yet* that it is distinct from, or not identical with, God.[64] This is a real step taken in the understanding of the nature of religious experience, for it brings us to the point of recognizing the shortcomings of ordinary (object) logic. The law of non-contradiction has to be violated in order to say all that must be said about the experiential richness in hand. Nishida drives beyond this recognition of logical inadequacy, to a new logic, and to the metaphysical analysis of which even the new logic is but a schematic outline. The individual (any X) is not a *dualistic* part of the absolute, but an integral self-determination of it. This is not pantheism restated, *if* one is no longer operating from a dualistic logical base. Ken Wilber articulates this insight well when he writes:

> Thus the Absolute, the Buddha-Mind, the real Self cannot be attained. For to attain union with the Absolute implies bringing together two things, and yet in all reality there is only One without a second. The attempt to bring the soul and God together perpetuates the illusion that the two are separate . . . the Self is already present, and we're already It.[65]

The absolute "has no opposite,"[66] writes Wilber, and for Nishida this becomes the recognition that all seeming opposites are self-contradictorily *identical.* The "identical" is equivalent to Wilber's having no opposites, except that Nishida is at pains to also say that that which has no opposites, has, for that very reason, opposites as self-contradictory expressions of its own nature. *One must affirm both propositions.* Nishida has pinpointed the logical realization that what is non-dual cannot be said to be one, for to say "one," is to think dualistically by implying that which is not one, or a multiplicity which is somehow contrasted with the one. In a series of lectures delivered at Kyoto University in 1938, Nishida said that "manyness as ultimately the manyness-of-oneness [and thus as self-negating] is Nothingness, oneness as ultimately the oneness-of-manyness must also be Nothingness."[67] He sums this up with the words, "being is at the same time nothingness, nothingness is at the same time being."[68] The absolute embraces both unity and multiplicity, rather than simply being contrasted with, or opposed to the many. Similarly, the identity of absolute nothingness must embrace *both* God and Satan, good and evil, rather than simply being *opposed* to evil. *Kenshō,* which means to see into one's own nature, is "to penetrate to the roots of one's self."[69] To so penetrate to one's own bottomless yet ultimately real self is to discover that one's "self exists as the absolute's own self-negation."[70] At our depths we are self-contradictory (yet identically so), and since we are the absolute's own self-negation, the absolute is also, therefore, intrinsically self-contradictory (but no less an identity of such self-contradiction).

Nishida's distinction between the "transcendent transcendent," and the "immanently transcendent" helps to further explicate the precise relationship between self and absolute. These are two very different stances, or directions, with respect to "the self's existential condition of facing the absolute."[71] The Judeo-Christian (and typically Western) account of the man/God relationship is that of transcendent transcendence. That is, one takes God to be "out there" somehow, as a transcendent objective absolute, who is distinctly separate from us, even spatially. One is expected to obey the wishes and commands of such a God, who is represented as wholly other, or at least as other. By contrast, Nishida is closer to his account of the Mahāyāna Buddhist position (which, in its immanent transcendence, is typically Eastern he claims). In this stance, the individual encounters the absolute by transcending the self in an *inward* direction. In other words, the realization of transcendence can only occur within the immanent self. One's own subjectivity is the *place* where the absolute arises—it is a transcendence within the immanent, or an immanent transcendence. In a very complex passage, Nishida writes:

> As its own uniquely individual and volitional self, in this paradoxical structure of inverse polarity and biconditionality, the self faces the absolute by transcending itself outwardly, and, simultaneously, faces with the absolute by transcending itself inwardly.[72]

Rather than having to obey an external absolute, in the immanent transcendent form, the absolute *embraces* us! "It pursues and embraces us even though we are disobedient and try to flee. It is infinite compassion."[73] While compassion or love requires that there be two, the self and the other, it is also, paradoxically, an engulfing of that other. In divine love, "we experience an absolute love embracing us,"[74] and thus there is not the dualistic opposition of self and absolute other in embrace, but an embracing of self by virtue of the self actually being the absolute other; and, of course, the absolute other is, in reality, every self. The identity of contradiction embraces the relative, rather than being contrasted with it. Transcendent transcendence is a movement in one direction only, whereas immanent transcendence affirms (embraces) both the otherness and the sameness of the religious relationship.[75] Indeed, for one to truly love, one negates oneself in embracing and identifying with the other. Thus, "Christianity . . . teaches that God has created the world out of love. And this entails the self-negation of the absolute—that *God is love*."[76] God becomes what he loves, and thereby is immanent and incarnate. Love necessitates that we lose our own self-awareness in our awareness of the beloved. Love is self-negation, but its route is inwards, or immanent, for we must express in our loving the reality of the depths of feeling and volition within ourselves. It is not enough to love a corpse, nor is love the satisfaction of self-directed desire. Love is the totality of the expression of a self, who has lost him/herself in the other. God, too, as the absolute of contradictory identity, creates by negating himself/herself/ itself, and yet embraces fully and "selflessly" that which he/she/it has created, unconditionally. It is this unconditional *love-as-embrace* that forever bubbles up from the depths of existence, that is the spring-like source and true color of all *morality:*

> From this fact that we are embraced by God's absolute love, conversely, our moral life wells forth from the depths of our own souls.[77]

Otherwise, as has already been discussed, morality is separated from its source, and without its deep spring of feeling (or love), it dries up, and becomes lifeless and brittle legalism. Worse, it loses all contact with individuality, with distinct persons, and retains only the pallid complexion of the universal, the "to be obeyed," the commanded. In slightly different words, morality has regularly cut itself off from its source, and has become transcendently transcendent, and is to be obeyed as one obeys an external command, for fear of punishment. An immanently transcendent morality is an *internalized* morality, which bubbles forth from within, and infused with feeling as love, embraces its object.

Much Eastern morality is rigid and ritualistic in form. Most Western ethical theory, particularly at the present time, is justice oriented, and/or tested by means of its universalizability in the form of laws and principles. Either way, the standards are external ones in that they are to be obeyed, however one feels about them, as normative, impersonal (justice is impartial and universalization is the "everyman," the "archangelic," or "ideal observer"), and rationally binding. Yet reason's advantage is also its greatest flaw; it is impersonal. The ethics of agape, however, *does* preserve the distinctiveness of the individual. It is not enough to treat someone fairly from the agapistic perspective (and, therefore, impartially, if not impersonally). One must also treat the other humanely as an individual source and expression of worth.

If one looks at the perennial life raft and desert island examples in recent Anglo-American ethical theory (and in moral and values education in the schools), one quickly sees the need to pretend to be sure about all of the "relevant" factors involved in a moral decision-making situation. In real life, of course, one is never completely certain, even though one must nevertheless decide. We encapsulate or caricature complex personalities as types, thus making "relevant" only a handful of circumstantial likenesses. Rather than imposing conceptual grids *alone* on persons and situations, however, the agapist attempts to make goodness happen in a less than good world. This is acted out by being transparently personal, i.e., selfless, conceptless, and other-directed in an empathetic mode. To be morally loving as an agapist is to be relentlessly observant or aware of factors and nuances as they arise. Real, concrete life is forever unfolding, and so are revised rules, principles, universalized formulas, and mechanisms of fairness, as understanding and circumstances change.

And yet, as in ballet, one's originality, one's deepening of the tradition through *creative* expression and transformation, is based squarely on the shoulders of the history of the art and its practice. The agapist of dance is the virtuoso who maintains rigorously the spirit of the law, while altering from time to time the letter of the law. An agapist would know what to do only one moment at a time. If that creative breakthrough in one moment were to be repeated, it would regularly apply and work. But it would not be taken as a certain and sure ritual, but as a point of advance, to be used only so long as, and wherever, it fits, and until it is in turn overcome by a yet higher insight. The agapist would sometimes appear to be immoral or "radical." He/she would be a candidate for censure, or for a goblet of hemlock. Was it "just" for the prodigal son to receive so much more praise than the son who stayed at home? Should the latecomer to the vineyard have received as much pay as the individual who worked all day? Love is personal, however, not general. It arises out of and searches for uniqueness and specific appropriateness, and cannot assume some arbitrary equality. It transcends justice, impersonality, and universalization, as the ground out of which they arise, and of which they are determinations. One should not, however, mistake the specific determinations for the moral moon. The "moral life of the self" is "grounded in the world of the Buddha's compassionate vow."[78]

What kind of world is this that Nishida values, and identifies as the goal? "It is a creative world through mutual love and respect, through the I and the Thou becoming one."[79] We thus act out of the grace of

God, or of *Amida*, or of our human-heartedness, and not out of the rational selection of rules of universality. We are, at our depths, *Amida*, God, absolute nothingness. Thus, to act and live in grace is to act in accordance with our own bottomless depths. It is to act immanently. Yet that immanence is not just self-determination, it is also transcendent. To be who we are is to negate ourselves, and to see our divinity. And yet, to recognize our divinity is to see ourselves as the self-negation of the absolute, and hence to be who we are *as* individuals. The immanence is a transcendent one, i.e., an identity of opposites. This is how we transcend and yet incorporate the judgments and requirements of abstract consciousness, *viz.* by active intuition, a "non-discriminating wisdom" which is wholly lodged in the absolute present. It is the *allowing* of the whole drift, the direction of the entire universe, and of the absolute nothingness to flow through us and to determine us as us. For we are it, and it we. Non-discriminating wisdom is a truly selfless activity, and "moral behavior is grounded in it," and hence all moral behavior is ultimately religious behavior.[80] To know this, to feel this, and to act in this way is to understand what the "other-power" or grace of religiosity is. It is self-expression through self-negation.[81] The I and Thou are both preserved, and yet both self-negated. The absolute negates itself and creates the world, yet the world is a necessary part of the absolute's self-realization, or self-knowledge. By negating itself (creating the world out of love as spontaneous expression) the absolute sees itself, just as we find our self by losing it.

The non-dualistic realization that I am God, and God is me, is the basis of morality. Its form is that of contradictory identity. Its formlessness is not directly visible, except as the non-visible lining, and the effect it exerts on the hang of the directly visible garment. There is only the oneness without a second entity, as formless, and it is not separate from me, for there is no me, neither any longer is there God.[82] There is only my bottomlessness which, as formed, is an identity of self-contradiction. As formless, it is but bottomlessness, the void, the ineffable, or absolute nothingness. As religious consciousness, of its content "nothing can be said, except that it is 'experience'."[83] As absolute nothingness, "it is a determination without mediation by concept."[84] It is the ground of the so-called "irrational" [non-rational?] and "free."[85] The formless is never seeable as the formless, but is ever expressing itself as the formed. As the formed it is seen and yet not seen. As the formless it is unseeable, and yet is seen as the formed. This absolutely contradictory identity of the formed and the formless is, in part, manifested as the absolutely contradictory identity of God and man, as moments of self-determination (forms) of the absolute (God as the absolute, as the Western equivalent of absolute nothingness).

The God we can see is not the God-beyond-God of Tillich, but only the tentative God of conception, creed, doctrine, and ritual. The formless God, the Nishidan absolute, is always and necessarily formless.

COSMIC COMPASSION

The absolute as formless arises as creative expression through the formed. Each individual is such a place of arising. My bottomless depth is a place of "no thought and no conception" where the compassion of the absolute arises—as formed.[86] I, because I am not-I, open myself to another in empathetic identification, and it is then that compassion arises. "The religious will arises as the self-determination of this dimension of sympathetic coalescence."[87] This is sincerity, which Nishida defines as a "form of selflessness, a pure response to the other."[88] By becoming a no-self, i.e., by losing oneself, one can express one's bottomless compassion which can't be one's own alone, because it is also the absolute's, but since one is the absolute it therefore is one's own.

> Perfect sincerity is grounded in infinite compassion. It is this kind of perfect sincerity that I would place at the foundation of "practical reason" as well. Kant's ethics of practical reason was only a bourgeois ethics. A historically transformative ethics, I say, is one that is based on the vow of compassion.[89]

Religion envelops the moral; it does not abandon it.

THE TRANSFORMATION OF THE EVERYDAY

Nishida moves from the created to the creating in his account of the world as historical: "And it is the extremely 'ordinary and everyday' standpoint" through which he, and Zen, celebrate "the self-determination of the absolute present."[90] It includes eating rice, wearing clothes, taking rest, and attending to the bodily functions of elimination. All of these are "eschatological" because they are signs, or expressions, of the absolute. The secular has become sacred, but only because the sacred is the secular. The absolute, as absolute nothingness, *is* all of the things, events, life forms, and people of the world, for they are its creating, forming, expressive self-determination. Human consciousness is a spectrum which extends from the unaware and beastly natural, to the enlightened awareness of *kenshō* as the bottomless identity of contradictories of self as absolute, of absolute as self. The enlightened is *preferable,* but all are equally moments in the divine creation. The fact of minimal awareness is not the *télos* of the absolute, but one of its expressions. At the same time, at its bottomlessness, the minimally aware is the deep *télos* of the absolute. Thus, evil is no less a part of the absolute because of its evil, but its present *télos is* centrifugal, or movement away from the absolute (and its own *deep* nature), rather than centripetal. The *télos* of the centripetal is "God-like," or God-imitative. It is compassion oriented, and therefore preserving of the uniqueness of the person.

Nishida remains a personalist throughout. His recognition of the uniqueness of the person is the ground of pure freedom as well, for under such conditions one can express oneself spontaneously from one's bottomless depths, and feel that one is in harmony with the flow of the absolute, or with the whole of things. To be a "servant of God" is to flow spontaneously (freely) with the flow of the whole of the cosmos—indeed with the direction of the creating, which itself arises out of the absolutely formless. By losing the self, paradoxically again, "the self becomes truly individual, a real self,"[91] and as though for the first time expresses itself as it really is ... effortlessly. Significantly, in this discussion of authentic freedom, Nishida reaffirms that "true knowing and true moral practice arise in this horizon of true individuality."[92]

True morality is a free and spontaneous expression of the heart. It arises from one's deepest nature, and is compassionate. One's selfhood, now radically individual, stands out in sharp contrast against the absolute nothingness of which it is a unique expression. Of course, and at the same time, the focus shifts, bringing the background of nothingness to the foreground, which now stands out in bold contrast to the many unique individuals that form *its* background. The double aperture is but a dualistic way of depicting the paradoxicality of the self-contradictory as an identity. Now one sees that "each and every point is an Archimedean point."[93] Because a point is just the uniquely located point that it is, therefore it is a valuable opening onto the absolute. Of course, the opening is wider, more revealing, more transparent if it is more than simply a quest for the objective, or a mere expression of biological instinct, but is also religiously aware of the actual identity that diversity expresses. Only then is "the religious character of ordinary human experience"[94] apparent. It is only then that one is aware of the eschatological character of the everyday, in each and every moment of the absolute present. Everything already is the absolute, but only when our consciousness reaches its own bottomless depths, and mirrors "the absolute's own self-negation,"[95] do we actually realize this. To rid ourselves of the limits (ignorance) of the more superficial perspective, and hence to drop off body and mind, is to be transformed such that one is now able to see things as they really are. Or, if this is too uncritically boastful, it is at least to see things religiously, as a Zen Buddhist or a mystic might.

Ordinary experience has become thoroughly—indeed utterly—religious in character. In this sense, Nishida has come full circle, having re-affirmed the starting point of his first book, but now making clear that it is also the end point of achievable enlightenment: "Truth always returns to its point of departure in the immediately given."[96] Pure experience is the route of realization in one's movement towards spiritual awareness. It is also, in the final analysis, what one is ultimately aware of. Pure experience is revelatory of the absolute, and human consciousnesses are the places where this comes to be known. Hence, "the goal of true religion would lie in grasping eternal life in its own immediacy in our lives."[97] Samsara is now fully nirvana, and the ordinary mind is now without a doubt "the way."

ON HOW TO BECOME ENLIGHTENED

Spiritual awareness, or religiosity, is not a special kind of consciousness, nor the consciousness of special people.[98] Nishida struggles, perhaps too hard at times, to contrast his own position with the traditional mystical esotericisms. Indeed, the Zen figure who most forthrightly held such a non-elitist position was Dōgen. Dōgen made a point of stressing that to seek a special, paradigmatic *satori* experience was to miss the whole point of Zen. To be sure, the Sōtō and Rinzai schools do not see exactly eye to eye on this point, and there are grounds for maintaining that Rinzai Zen, which Nishida practiced, is more elitist because it stresses the enlightenment experience as a distinct break m ordinary consciousness. Dōgen and Sōtō Zen emphasize that only a few enlightenment experiences are so sudden and radically transformative. For most, it is more accurate to state that one is enlightened when one begins to take one's enlightenment seriously. To sit in *zazen* is to be enlightened. For to take one's own enlightenment seriously enough to question one's present state, and to *act* in search of a greater realization is already to have taken the religious turn. If one's sense of existential reality is that which is "nearest and most evident to us,"[99] then the very act of questing, or questioning of self, is to have *abandoned* the complacent, uncritical, and conventional standpoint that simply assumes that we are who we appear to be, and this even to the point of not even raising the issue or being reflective enough about those assumptions to begin questioning them. On the other hand, to put these assumptions in genuine doubt and to undertake the search for a deeper understanding of one's own complex nature *is the religious act itself.* Nothing else need be done except to let it happen, and to continue to walk in this turned direction. One is now facing in the right direction, and the religious act of placing oneself in profound doubt represents the quantum leap of spirituality. All else is growth, development, refinement, advancement, but none of these is different in kind from the initial religious or existential doubt that placed one on the path, or on one's *zazen* cushion *(zafu)*. In this spirit, then, all experience is now enlightened. Nothing is taken in its heretofore unquestioned "objective" sense. All is in flux and yet not in flux, and one is now able (however infinitesimally at first) to look at and then through all objects and events of consciousness towards their "lining." The very self-contradictoriness of experience causes us to see that the Buddha-nature is impermanence, as Dōgen says. Nishida states this as the identity of self-contradiction, thereby providing a much richer analysis of Dōgen's insight.

Religiosity continues in one's life-stance, however, and one's initial doubting, and the vague sensing that one's initial and conventional assumptions about self and world are insufficient, gives way to ever increasing unravelings of the self, until we eventually penetrate to the very depths of that self. The ultimate self-revelation is, as we have seen, that we are absolutely nothing, and therefore, that the finding of our innermost or bottomless self is in fact an absolute self-negation. We are a self-determination of absolute nothingness. We are, in this and every awareness, a self-determination of the absolute present, which is the only temporal place for experience to occur. In the temporal horizon of the absolute present, we encounter the absolute as every aspect of common or everyday experience, including the experience of ourselves, as manifestations of the absolute. "Even to set upon the quest for awakening is to go astray,"[100] because it separates the quest and its final achievement from the everyday. The quest is to *seek nothing else*, but to look at the grass under one's feet, and at one's feet, as self-determinations of the absolute in the absolute's theater of activity—and, therefore, in our theater of everydayness—the absolute present, the right now of pure experience. Writing of the Japanese spirit generally, Nishida contends that "the characteristic feature of Japanese culture" is to "negate the self" in order to become the thing apprehended in experience.[101] "To empty the self and see things, for the self to be immersed in things, 'no-mindedness' [in Zen Buddhism] or effortless acceptance of the grace of *Amida (jinenhōni)* [in True Pure Land teaching]—these, I believe, are the states we Japanese strongly yearn for."[102] Indeed, "the essence of the Japanese spirit must be to become one in things and events. It is to become one at the primal point in which there is neither self nor others.[103]

No wonder it must be continuously emphasized that such a standpoint is not a standpoint.[104] It is not a creed, a set of practices, or even the practice of *zazen* as distinct from relieving oneself. "The Way does not pertain to finding or not-finding,"[105] but in seeing that what is, already is nirvana. The holy is brought to earth, to immanence from transcendence, and made un-holy, i.e., ordinary and everyday. At the same time, the making un-holy of the ordinary is the making holy of the ordinary. Religion is a non-stance because it doesn't hold out the hope of a special awareness as something separate from the ordinary, a special transcendent object of holiness separate from the everyday, or a special place or practice distinct from ordinary actions and places. For Dōgen, Zen religiosity is exemplified in the way one washes and hangs up one's clothes to dry, in the way one walks and sleeps, and in the way one shows compassion. The true absolute must self-negate, or *empty*. As the absolute empties itself it negates itself as absolute, to self-negate is to create (or express) what is distinct from itself. To create is to love what one creates by embracing it unconditionally as of oneself, for such it is.

This is the ultimate ground of ethics. To ask why one cares about oneself is a ridiculous question for all but the masochist or the depressed. We say of these that they are not themselves, that they are out of balance. The vast majority of creatures, human and non-human, prefer pleasure over pain, happiness over unhappiness, satisfaction over dissatisfaction, and health over illness. These are rock-bottom judgments of value, and as with all rock-bottom stands, one cannot say anything in defense of them directly, for they are *foundations* of defense. One wants to be happy because one then feels better, finds life richer, and is able to contribute to society in some way. All of these judgments rest, ultimately, on rock-bottom judgments of the sort indicated above.[106]

So far, of course, we have but a "refined" egoism, or egoistic hedonism. The move beyond the self is, for Nishida, now almost effortless. If I am my neighbor, and he/she is me at my depths, then I have no more reason to do harm to him/her than to myself. If I am, at my bottomlessness, the whole cosmos, and all forms are forms of the absolute, then I would not wish to do harm to any part of the whole, any more than to the small part of it temporarily known as myself. Like the creator, our attitude must be that of compassion, for compassion is grounded in the capacity to leave behind the narrow limits of the empirical self-as-separate, and to compenetrate or empathetically identify with the other as a Thou. As "no-mind" one is able to become the other. Recall, "sincerity is a form of selflessness, a pure response to the other," and "perfect sincerity is grounded in infinite compassion."[107] By abandoning self-focus, one finds compassion. In compassion one can grasp the other as though for the first time, by "becoming that person." Then, and only then, is one truly lovable in return. One is now transparently who one is. One has made oneself available (disponibilité), in Marcel's terms. The result is that because one is now able to open to the other, the other can now open to you without terror, or with no need to break through the masks of individuality as ego. In the embracive relationship that follows, the two truly become one, and yet, as one, they are of necessity two-as-one. In the very act of giving up their masks of individuality, they find together their own truer, freer, and necessarily bottomless selves. They can now express individuality as it is and as it arises, in the spontaneity of the absolute present. There is no substantial and fixed self-identity to clog the way to full experience of the other, or to enclose the relationship of love. There is only the momentary-self-and-other-in-embrace, or in proximity, or at distance and yet fully in awareness. One's self is what it is fully, and in the moment of the moment of the absolute present. In order to be fully "there," the self must be a no-self, and the time must be a no-time as the eternity of the absolute present. One has become an aperture—a distinctive, unique, and penetratingly aware aperture—of the absolute as manifested in the absolute present. One has become who one is, or divine (and yet...), or freely compassionate out of one's own depth-nature. *All of one's actions are self-determinations of one's own true nature, just as one's nature is a self-determination of the absolute.* They now effortlessly well up from within, rather than being imposed from without. One doesn't obey, one spontaneously expresses compassion. One does not memorize the rules and moral laws, but acts from the depths of heart and mind *(kokoro),* manifesting fellow-feeling or human-heartedness out of one's own depths—which depths are, of course, transcendent of ordinary self: "In the depths of the self there is that which transcends the self,"[108] *viz.* the absolute which is absolutely bottomless (or absolutely nothing). Just as this absolute "empties" (self-negates) itself by creating the many, so we, as empty, express ourselves as compassionately concerned for, and identified with, the other.

The opposite of such God infusedness is a secular world that denies or forgets the religious dimension: "When the world loses itself and human beings come to forget God, mankind becomes boundlessly individual and selfish."[109] It is selfishness that constitutes real "sin" for Nishida. Only a tradition that understands the relation between selflessness and love, agape and compassion, would arrive at such a view of the ultimate sinfulness of rampant individuality or selfishness. It requires a sensitivity to the paradoxical strategy by means of which one finds the Self by losing the self.

CONCLUSION OF NISHIDA'S FINAL ESSAY

Nishida's final thoughts on religion in his final essay attempt to grapple with the Christ-figure in Dostoevsky's *The Brothers Karamazov.* The *silent* Christ, who listens to and then kisses the Grand Inquisitor who knows who he is and yet who will order him killed is, for Nishida, a symbol of the immanent-transcendent. The sacred is underfoot, even though it is either unrecognized or, much worse, rejected in favor of individualized human power and glory. Nishida's prescription for the future is that we "find the true God in the Place where there is no God,"[110] which surely refers to the formlessness of absolute nothingness, *and yet* to the emptying of absolute nothingness that is the absolutely divine immanence of the everyday, including the centrifugal Grand Inquisitor, who denies the sacred in the name of the sacred. Having lost the sense of true religion, he protects its semblance, its mask, its outer husk, at all costs. He has forgotten to kill his Buddha, in order to rest in the place where there is no God, which is, paradoxically, the only place where God arises. His orthodoxy will allow him to kill any true religiosity as and whenever it appears. The greatest killer of religiosity is religion. We must, therefore, probe beneath the masks of power and convention, to the bottomless place where there is no God. There, and only there, will we find what Nishida considers to be true spirituality. To discover the self one must forget the self, and to discover God, one must leave all gods behind. This is the move towards the un-holy which is the only route to the holy. If "this corrupt world reflects the Pure Land (Heaven), and the Pure Land reflects this corrupt world,"[111] then we must come to be able to discern the holy everywhere. To do so, however, will in no way deny the factuality of the centrifugal directional path called evil, symbolized by the Grand Inquisitor. Rather, it will but afford a perspective whereby the holiness even of the Grand Inquisitor may be understood, for he, too is on the path and has made the religious turn without understanding that he has done so. It may be that the kiss (by Christ, on the cheek of his persecutor), as a selfless act of sincere compassion, will cause just a flicker of existential doubt; will bring even the Grand Inquisitor to some understanding of his evil. Then, the Grand Inquisitor, too, will be on the path, consciously. That, and only that, is required; to sincerely doubt one's way heretofore is to move *centripetally*. This is the only genuine enactment of the truly religious, and the truly moral.

SEVEN

Values, Ethics and Feeling

The Japanese do not often concern themselves with the systematization of values and the types of valuation, but are more or less spontaneous valuationally. Of course, the same might be said about the man or woman on the street in Chicago or Toronto, but the difference is that the West has a lengthy and involved tradition of systematic and analytical philosophizing. Prior to Japanese utilization of Western techniques of logic and Western philosophical traditions (Hegel and Kant being in the forefront), philosophical ideas emerged from the Shintō, Buddhist, Confucian, Zen Buddhist, and Taoist traditions. They arose from the *"paideia"* of Japanese civilization transmitted to the lowest and highest ranking citizen in at least some measure, through art, ritual, etiquette, language, and so forth.[1] Nakamura Hajime emphasizes the non-rationalistic tendencies in the culture and its language.[2] The Japanese tend to emphasize the emotive rather than the cognitive factors in their use of their own language.[3] In describing the Japanese culture, Nishida contended that the distinctive characteristic of Japan lies in its being an emotional culture."[4] As such, it does not look to the transcendent beyond, to the future, or to eternity, but "moves immanently from thing to thing, without transcending time."[5] The Japanese language includes a rich vocabulary of words denoting aesthetic or emotional states of mind.[6]

VALUES AS IMMEDIATE

The Japanese find value *imbedded in this-worldly activity.* The acceptance of the phenomenal *now* is absolute, both in language and cultural attitude, and connects man most strongly with his immediate experience. Kishimoto Hideo observes that the central and common concern of all Japanese religions is the internal state of well-being, tranquility, harmony, happiness, and joy of the *individual*.[7] In other words, the prime focus is on the *quality of an individual's immediate positive value experience*. The abiding and profound love of nature among the Japanese serves to further heighten the enjoyment of the phenomenal present. To savor the majestic roar of a waterfall, the subtle sounds of pebbles washing over pebbles in a man-made pot-hole next to a Japanese inn, the irregularity of a garden rock, the perfect symmetry of a single flower (or its equally exquisite asymmetry), or the color, texture and smell of tree bark in Spring is to gain immediate positive value experiences that are never repeated. Yet such experiences are generally predictable as sources of profound value.

We can say, then, that the Japanese emphasize intrinsic values (i.e., value immediately found, and found satisfactory in the direct experience of it) which are states of human awareness both immediate and momentary, running the gamut from the slightly pleasant to the ecstatic and joyful (with their converse ranging from the slightly negative or unpleasant to the horrendous or traumatic). Intrinsic values, then, are all relational or involve a subject, and emphasize the subjective state of consciousness in terms of its pleasurable content, its state of satisfaction (to eliminate desires is to be not unsatisfied), its tranquility, harmony, and its gusto or life-affirmation. In this connection, I think Archie Bahm is correct in his statement that "...there are at least four distinguishable kinds of intrinsic value, namely, feelings of pleasure, enthusiasm, satisfaction, and contentment."[8]

There are countless examples of the Japanese encouraging individuals to learn to concentrate through mental and emotional discipline of one kind or another—to meditate, for example, while deaf to a bass drum a few feet away. The tea room requires that you leave all cares and class distinctions behind you for you must crouch through a tiny doorway in order to enter this new world. Yet the significance of such concentration derives not only from concentration on the phenomenal present as though it were one's entire world, but also from actually seeing the entire universe in any concentrated experience. "The philosophy of the infinite," Suzuki writes, "enters into every corner of finite realities. One is not just one, it comes out of the infinite so that we can say that the latter is in every finite number."[9]

Shintōism may be more of a direct influence on this way of seeing than Zen. Quoting from a Nō song entitled "The Great Shrine," by Yokyoku Taisha, Nakamura writes, "Nowhere is there a shadow in which a god does not reside: in peaks, ridges, pines, cryptomerias, mountains, rivers, seas, villages, plains, and fields, everywhere there is a god."[10] Such "nature mysticism," as it has often been called, does not use rational argument to justify such "god talk," nor does the notion of God in our monotheistic sense apply, for the key to divinity is feeling the divinity directly in one's heart.[11] In fact, the worshipper may not know the deity's name, or care to know. Emphasis is solely on the immediate experience of religious joy or value. On this point I am struck by the parallels between the emphasis on the quality of immediacy in experience, and Ernst Cassirer's account of mythical as opposed to scientific or discursive conceptualizing. He writes,

> The aim of theoretical thinking ... is primarily to deliver the contents of sensory or intuitive experience from the isolation in which they originally occur.... It proceeds "discursively," in that it treats the immediate content only as a point of departure, from which it can run the whole gamut of impressions in various directions, until these impressions are fitted together into one unified conception, one closed system.
>
> Mythical thinking...bears no such stamp; in fact, the character of intellectual unity is directly hostile to its spirit. For in this mode, thought does not dispose freely over the data of intuition, in order to relate and compare them to each other, but is captivated and enthralled by the intuition which suddenly confronts it. It comes to rest in the immediate experience; the sensible present is so great that everything else dwindles before it. For a person whose apprehension is under the spell of this mythico-religious attitude, it is as though the whole world were simply annihilated; the immediate content, whatever it be, that commands his religious interest so completely fills his consciousness that nothing else can exist beside and apart from it. The ego is spending all its energy on this single object, lives in it, loses itself in it.[12]

Surely such recognition of the richness of immediate experience is reminiscent of James's and Nishida's pure experience. In Japan, there is an inseparable relation between religious and aesthetic value, and the power of concentration and "seeing" must yield experiences of positive and immediate value to be perfected and worthy.[13] To be religious, to be an artist, to be a samurai, is to be open to such experiences in ever-increasing and profound intensity. When one comes back from the death of such ecstasy, concentration, involvement, the world is transformed because one is uplifted, transformed, cleansed, or enlightened.[14] In R. S. Hartman's words, such valuation "is the capacity of complete concentration on a thing or person, the personal involvement of the artist, the inventor, the teacher.... It is possible only in a person who is himself integrated and has all his powers available for reaching out to and actually meeting persons or things."[15] Certainly the ideal of integration of personality is a central aspect of mental and emotional training in Japan:

> Conflicting desires are the cause of worries and anxieties. Desires as such are not only the cause of worries and anxieties, but are also the cause for all life-activities.... But desires should be given a right structure.[16]

Central to Hartman's analysis is the notion of interpenetration, compenetration, or fusion of the valuer and the valued. Intrinsic valuation "joins the concrete richness of the valued, in an infinity of meanings." As expressed by Nishitani Keiji, "just in our being really in contact with things within the things themselves, is our being really in contact with ourselves."[17]

It is in precisely this sense that the distinction between subject and object breaks down and is purposefully eliminated by the Buddhists and Zen Buddhists. "As long as the field of separation between 'internal' and 'external' is not broken through, . . . contradictions will always prevail."[18] Thus, Nishitani writes of a *psychic sympathy*[19] or empathy which allows a direct contact with whatever is being apprehended, for all things are psychically akin and emerge from the same nothingness. Now the metaphysics of the foregoing is more than controversial, but the image or content of experience being the interfusion or co-penetration of beholder and beheld such that the very distinctions seem unimportant and inappropriate is a key notion in the higher continuum range of intrinsic valuation—that approaching joy or ecstasy. In Hartman's words "Thing and observer are one continuous entity. At its maximum, intrinsic value means the interpenetration of the valuer and the valued, as in love, in artistic creation and appreciation, in mystic rapture, in the satori experiences of Zen, and others."[20]

Hartman's emphasis on the singularity and uniqueness of intrinsic valuation also serves to emphasize the concrete and particular. One simply attends to and intuits *in toto* that which is before one. Intrinsic value derives from or attaches to such intense, concentrated, singular, and all-consuming experiential awareness. Such experiences are directly known as such to be of fundamental worth. Their worth is worth-in-itself and for-its-own-sake—both formulations of the intrinsically valuable.

JOY

Experiences of intrinsic value, at their highest or purest, are characterized not merely as pleasant or yielding satisfaction, but as joyful. The greatest creative achievements in art and science, Ohe Seizo argues, "are usually accompanied with a great joy of unique purity, a joy of being entirely absorbed in creative work."[21] Joy may result from social mindedness, for example "in witnessing a devoted act of brotherly love,"[22] or from the exuberance of health. Thus, genuinely creative activity may predictably yield that intense immediate value experience termed joy.[23] Joy is positive value experience that transforms, allows one to see a thing as though for the first time, completely absorbs one (becomes one's whole world), and takes one beyond subject/object distinctions to the intuition of oneness wherein we can see the ultimate in a blade of grass, or God, or nothingness in any heretofore trivial thing. In Hartman's sense, all things are uniquely what they are—the whole world, which is a continuum of what used to be me and it. Now we are a new totality—suchness.

FEELINGS AS MORAL CRITERIA

Emphasis in ethics on spontaneity, a pure heart, and the desire to help another for little or no extrinsic reason of reward, or with little or no premeditated calculation for self gain, is typically Buddhist, at least in the ideal of theory. It is, however, also typically Christian in theory. Agape is selfless love, to be distinguished from a love based on desire *(érōs)*. Desire is, on most accounts, self-directed, and has a *télos* of self-satisfaction of some sort. Selfless love is simply and freely given, without expectation—even without the possibility—of satisfaction or reward. Jesus, as God incarnate, serves as the Christian paradigm of agapistic action. Jesus, as God become man, gave his life "selflessly," literally with no hope of gainful return. It was a self-sacrifice and, being a sacrifice of self, the goal was not to achieve something for oneself, but to selflessly do the *necessary because it is one's nature, and, therefore, one's deepest inclination, to do so,* as well as being God's law. Thus, Christian theologians such as the Swedish theologian, Anders Nygren, maintain that agape is a central, if not the essential, characteristic of Christianity, and its distinguishing mark.[24] Yet surely it is as much a mistake to give the franchise on the agapistic paradigm to Christendom, as it would be to view the religion of nothingness, and Nishida's Kyoto school as having made Christianity obsolete by going "beyond" it. In fact, one has to grant high marks generally to the major world religions for presenting consistent, and profoundly humane, self-legislating systems of thought and action. Each standpoint pays a price, nevertheleess, for whatever emphasis it encourages. Kant's stress on doing one's duty as the only proper moral motivation appears to all but Kantians as a depreciation of the wider range of feelings and desires. Similarly, the Christian or Buddhist emphasis on love and compassion seems to underplay systematic thinking and regulation in moral decision making. Evelyn Shirk urges just this point in her discussion of character and the role of feeling:

> But to rely on the mere fact of desire alone to create the good is folly. In the first place, man can want and yearn for evil as well as for good. The mere presence of desire gives no assurance regarding how that desire is to be

expressed. It can deceive us. We can feel like saints while acting like vipers; we can feel holy while committing crimes. We can be delighted with that which ultimately has disastrous consequences. Feelings give notoriously unreliable testimony regarding themselves.[25]

Old feeling habits or inclinations can also block change for the better, in an environment of altered circumstances. One may not "catch" the feeling of a "liberation movement," and thereby respond in a reactionary way. As well, one may not feel at all as one is supposed to. Surely then one *ought* to follow the moral rules of action which otherwise might have arisen spontaneously. Feelings are also notoriously difficult to "teach," and no doubt this, in part, accounts for the gulf between one generation and another, as the feelings of the one lose force for the other, and vice versa.

Shirk's critique of feeling alone as a sufficient guide for ethics includes the suggestion that we can yearn for evil as well as for good. The Zen Buddhist, Buddhist, Christian, etc., could well argue that to be tuned into the other in love means that the desire to do evil cannot arise because one is now transparently, or selflessly, identified with the well-being of the other. Yet Shirk's point remains, that it is not always easy to know what is in the interest of the other, nor what to do if the interests of several others conflict. Social ethics is the dimension that seems most lacking in Buddhism generally, and in Nishida's thought as well.

The ground of most ethical theory, as well as the strategy of most social ethics in the West, is the intellect. In contrast with the Eastern emphasis on feelings, which "magnifies one aspect of the ethical situation," *viz.* "the person who chooses rather than on what he chooses,"[26] both deontological and teleological ethics in the West concentrate on *what is chosen*. Deontologists like Kant, Prichard, and Ross stress the dutiful, or intuitively *prima facie*, rightness or obligatoriness of the act chosen. Utilitarians and other teleologists emphasize not the nature of the act, but the goodness of the consequences of the act. Rule-utilitarianism and act-deontology are hybrid positions, in which aspects of the best of the deonotological and teleological perspectives are woven together in the hope of describing a theory that can be sensitive both to the nature of an act (e.g., keeping one's promise), and to its consequences. Either way, stress is still on the act, not on the agent. It should be pointed out that there are major exceptions in the West, and it may even be that they have become the new vitality in ethical theory and moral education. Books such as *On Caring*, by Milton Mayeroff, *Caring: A Feminine Approach to Ethics and Moral Education*, by Nell Noddings, *The Role of Feeling in Morals*, by William Neblett, Carol Gilligan's *In a Different Voice*, and R. S. Peters's *Reason and Compassion*, all emphasize the place of caring and empathy in ethics,[27] and Alasdair MacIntyre (in *After Virtue*) is exemplary in having breathed new life into the Aristotelian emphasis on the virtue of the agent.[28] Noddings distinguishes an ethic of caring from a moral reasoning approach by its "locating morality primarily in the pre-act consciousness of the one-caring."[29] To care is to be receptive to the other, the capacity to "feel with" the other person.[30] Similar ideas have been expressed in Western philosophical and religious circles throughout time. One beautifully phrased example is by W. T. Stace, whose work we have already encountered in the context of mysticism:

> What, then, are the special parts of human nature which give birth to morality? They are, in my opinion, two.... The first is *the social nature of man*. The second—which is closely connected with the first, but not identical with it—is the *capacity for being made happy in some degree by the bare fact of the happiness of other persons*....
>
> This social nature of man . . . is the most primitive source and perhaps the most important. It is this which in the first instance forced morality upon us....
>
> The other reason is now before us. That I am, willy nilly, made directly happy by the happiness of others, and unhappy by their unhappiness, means that I can only attain complete happiness for myself through unselfishness, through seeing others happy and making them happy.[31]

It is evident that one must not claim that altruistic sentiment is an Eastern trait, nor that many of the details of Nishida's approach are not elsewhere echoed. Neblett's thesis, for instance, seems to be remarkably in line with Nishida's insistence that morality must be from the heart:

> An ideally good person feels all of the morally good feelings with such intensity and passion that he always succeeds in doing what is right and avoiding what is wrong. His feelings always find appropriate expression in moral action. The possibility of human morality, therefore, resides in the doubly-faceted human capacity, "to feel morally good feelings that issue into morally right actions," or to phrase this alternatively, in the twin human capacities of (i) feeling morally good feelings and (ii) performing morally right actions. These two capacities are both judged to be fundamental to moral goodness...[32]

Neblett incorporates his thesis in his "Moral Maxim of Feeling: We Ought to Care About, and We Ought to Act Considerately in Regard To, the Feelings of Others."[33] He concludes that to be morally good

> ...is first and foremost to be good in one's heart, even if circumstances, or deficiency of talent or intelligence or bodily mobility severely limit one's capacity to do good, just as to be bad is first and foremost to be bad in one's heart, even if circumstances or personal deficiencies severely limit one's capacity to do bad.[34]

Neblett, like Nishida, calls for a passionate inferiority in ethical theory, and reacts against an ethics of external form. Yet form is inescapable, and so Neblett does concern himself with the "utility" of actions, while emphasizing that consequences must not be severed from the possession, expression, and affecting of feelings in oneself and others.[35] It would not stretch things very far to recast Neblett's thesis in the language of *kokoro*. The form always arises out of the formless (or less formed) ground, in this case of feeling. One feels empathy with another, and one wishes to express one's fellow-feeling or love so as to help, or simply to positively affect, another. One gives form to one's feelings as action. Laws, rules, principles, commandments, and etiquette are only less than complete and non-particular general guidelines. Their validity for this specific situation arises out of generalization, cultural history, and context, *plus* the nature of the feelings of the caring one and the one cared for. It seems that it is in feelings that the particular is to be found, and it is here that the uniqueness of the individual-in-this-situation-here-now is attended to. It is here that change is accounted for, both in terms of the individuals involved as changing flesh and blood people, and as people in inevitably changing circumstances. The immediacy of pure experience catches us and the world in process, whereas our conceptual analysis of it into parts, concepts, judgments, yields only static ingredients.

Moral life, too, is characterized by change, yet the change is always contrasted with the more fixed and historical continuities of humankind. Here again we encounter paradox, and the reality of our existence is more adequately accounted for only when the opposing facts and tensions are taken together. It is the moral agent who is the place, as identity of self-contradiction, where morality arises and the ethical life persists in everchanging yet continually recognizable form. Nishida's uniqueness is to be found in the way he builds his theory on both Buddhist and Western philosophical underpinnings. If he did not work out a satisfactory and detailed social ethic, he may well have laid a better groundwork for it in his careful analysis of the role of spontaneous love in ethics, and of the relation between morality and religion.

Nishida and East Asian Buddhism generally focus on the feelings or the psychological state of the agent *(kokoro)*, rather than on the act itself or its consequences. One must perform a kind act because one wants to, i.e., as an outward manifestation of an inward welling up of spontaneous fellow-feeling, and not as a result of any sort of calculation by the intellect. One is not to act because it is one's duty, or because it is a right action, or because it would bring about more good. The assumption is that to act from the right motivation is, automatically, to do what really is one's duty, and that the best results will follow in its wake. Character and good intentions are not always guarantees of right action. Part of the reason why this is so is that moral action is less fixed in nature than we often suppose. To do the right thing, in the right manner, at the right time, for the right reasons, and to the right person (to paraphrase Aristotle) is not reducible to a simple formula.

Particularly as the context changes due to societal flux, social improvement, and the general alteration of the circumstances of existence, what is now the right thing to do may be quite different from what was thought to be the morally correct or valuationally preferable just a few years earlier. To keep up with the inevitably changing times, one must not only "feel" one's way into the other's needs and expectations, but must actually examine one's own social context in a critical manner. The tension between the past values and the present values of a culture is philosophically complicated by the recognition that neither what is old nor what is new is, on that account alone, good.

The moral or valuational practitioner must critically reflect upon what it is that people think good for themselves and good for others, in an attempt to ascertain whether what is held as a social good is in fact as good as is thought, or perhaps even evil. This deliberative scrutiny is an intellectual and calculative act, and not just an act of feeling. It is social criticism, and not just personal moralizing, as it requires judgments about what is "better" for most citizens of a culture. Social ethics is the systematic inquiry into correct behavior in a given culture and, at the same time, is a forum for criticism of that culture in an attempt to improve on past regulations, and to cull out bad, ineffective, or no longer prudent social requirements. Rational calculation, at its best, attends to the present context of moral requirements; at its worst, it rigidifies such requirements, and loses touch with the contextual. Feeling, too, can become habituated, and so lose touch with contextual needs and change. Critical rational scrutiny is likely the surest way of keeping alert to the changing needs and circumstances of one's moral decision-making. Social ethics, as the continuing self-critical scrutiny of one's culture's rules, regulations, and value preferences seems essential to social justice, social improvement (however specific and limited), and social happiness. At the same time, any and all critical activity can become antithetical to genuine human feeling, as can rational calculation and the reliance on laws, rules, and moral formulae. Such "outer" trappings of moral sentiment can cause sentiment itself to wear thin and to become but a threadbare unlined garment.

Nishida's emphasis on nothingness serves as a continual reminder that all forms are expressions of an inner force which is both intellectual and emotional. Not only is the kimono lined with deep feeling, but it is also stitched with the activity of critical re-appraisal. His philosophic analysis seeks to ground the belief that we must discover our deep consciousness in order to align ourselves with our cosmic source. In doing so he adopts both rationally calculative and affective means to achieve a volitional harmony with the whole of things. Nishida is a bridge between East and West precisely because he identifies himself with neither alleged perspective and sees more often than most that the work of philosophy is neither Eastern nor Western, but takes as its material the overlapping insights of people anywhere in the world, and produces from that material totality of thought transcending any particular cultural perspective. Each of us, if we are good at building our own philosophical world view, must glean insights from many cultural directions. To be "postmodern" means to have moved from the orthodoxy of any single cultural perspective to the liberation—and sometimes the confusion—of a multicultural and ongoing (open-ended) creation of a perspective that is truly one's own. Quality philosophizing is world philosophy by nature, and Nishida serves as one of the better examples of this in the twentieth century. He has painstakingly analyzed the empirical outer form, without becoming blinded and thereby desensitized to the various linings of the inner or deeper significance lying beneath. In any case, "It is obvious that whether the emphasis is on feeling or on calculation neither can avoid the insistent presence of the other."[36] It is in the sense that Nishida's meticulous analysis of the role of feeling in ethics contributes to our understanding of the fuller role of the moral agent, and of the religious agent in ethical activity. The result may be a more adequate vantage point from which to decide what it means to be a human being, for oneself and for others.

CONCLUSION

Zen Buddhism is not itself an intellectual or strictly philosophical school of thought. Indeed, Zen koans, *zazen* meditation, and the ordinary life of practice of the Zen Buddhist strive to break the iron grip of thinking, conceptualizing, abstracting, and intellectualizing. The first crisis of self for the Zen novice is the letting go of his/her dependence on thinking, or trying to reason things out. Zen is not thinking, whatever else it may be. How can Nishida have hoped to succeed in his philosophical attempt to understand Zen experience? How could not-thinking be grasped by means of thinking? Will not any thought-analysis distort not-thought?

That the answer is both "yes" and "no" will not come as a surprise. Zen is not thinking, and so to think about Zen is not to do Zen. Similarly, to think about loving someone is not to love. A biologist studying frogs need not hop. Systematic thinking may be applied to anything at all, and it is problematic only if the thinking is taken as the subject matter itself, rather than as the method by means of which understanding of that subject matter is (partially) achieved. Zen and thinking stand in opposition only if the one is confused with the other. Nishida's study of Zen is not a study of Zen thinking and Zen logic, as though thinking and logic were the primary training and practice of the Zen monk. Rather, Nishida began his lifework by becoming clear about the fact that the primary ground of Zen is experience itself; not just ordinary mediated-by-thinking-and-concepts experience, but non-mediated, pure and immediate experience. In his foreword to *A Study of Good* he wrote that he "would like to clarify everything in the light of the claim that pure experience is the only real reality."[37] It was William James who helped him see this clearly in philosophical terms, and while he only adopted as much of James as he could adapt to his own project of understanding, it was James's "pure experience" that provided the insight Nishida needed to begin the process of unraveling the philosophical topography of the Zen landscape.

Pure experience is the beginning of Zen. It is awareness stripped of all thought, all conceptualization, all categorization, and all distinctions between subject-as-having-an-experience, and an experience-as-having-been-had-by-a-subject. It is *prior* to all judgment. Pure experience is without all distinction; it is pure no-thingness, pure no-this-or-that. It is *empty* of any and all distinctions. It is absolutely nothing at all. Yet its emptiness and nothingness is a chock-a-block fullness, for it is all-experience-to-come. It is rose, child, river, anger, death, pain, rocks, and cicada sounds. We carve these discrete events and entities out of a richer-yet-non-distinct manifold of pure experience.

A successor to Nishida's chair at Kyoto University, Ueda Shizuteru, accurately interprets Nishida to be embodying the Buddhist methodology for inhibiting substantializing thought-activity. Thus, "absolute nothingness, the nothingness that dissolves substance-thinking, must not be clung to as nothingness. It must not be taken as a kind of substance...."[38] As I have contended throughout this study, it is in the self that nothingness arises, and it is the self which is the *basho,* the field, the place where all experience arises, including pure experience. Even this is not quite right, however, for the self is itself nothing. Empty the self itself, lose the ego, and there is but pure experience. But how do we convey this point philosophically? The self is empty, or simply the self is the emptying insofar as it is the place where pure experience arises, and yet, to recognize it as pure experience is already to be separate from it, to be a subject aware of it as an object of consciousness, and to contrast it with something else, and hence to classify it in thought. Empty "pure experience" once more, and empty the "self" as well. Empty emptiness itself, and keep everything non-substantial and in the flow of movement in being-time. Empty being-time, too, so that it points to the going on of events, and then empty the event of any fixity or substance. Nothingness is the empty, or the emptying, or the filling and emptying, or the empty as full, or the emptied as filling, and the filled as emptying—for it is the *process* that one is to focus on and come to grasp.

How else can any of this be said, except paradoxically? Not to speak paradoxically is to fix the focus, to stop the flow, to carve out a discrete time and event, and to privilege oneself or some-thing as the center from which all else is distinguished and located. One is, of course, privileged in being the place where all arises, but now one must empty even this self-place-substance. The true Zen "man is able to say of himself, 'I am I *and likewise* I am not I'."[39] Yet this *not I* is not the point, or the resting place, for if the I is not an I, then it is for that very reason an I…and the process of emptying continues. To grasp absolute nothingness is to comprehend the "coincidence of ceaseless negation and straightforward affirmation."[40] The self, the I, is never "there," but is at each moment in the process of transformation, now losing every trace of itself in nothingness, now blooming selflessly with the flowers and like one of them, now meeting another and making the encounter into its own self.[41]

Herein arises the ethical dimension in Zen and Nishida. As I am not I, I am whatever I purely experience. I am the gamut of pure experiences as experienced by me: flowers, trees, and another human being. "For the self in its selflessness, whatever happens to the other happens to itself."[42]

As Ueda depicts this, the space of the hyphen between Martin Buber's I-Thou is the place-as-nothingness where the two meet and become one.[43] Yet in order to be one, the one had to be two. Hence, neither the one nor the two is the point, but rather the one-as-two and the two-as-one as a continuous flow back and forth. Thus we have the "nothingness of nothingness," as the process of desubstantializing all permanence, all fixity, all boundaries, all egos, all concepts, and all distinctions altogether. Then, as though to fill the nothingness of nothingness, each thing is now just-as-it-is, *thus (Tathāta)!* The mountains are mountains again, and I am I. As a reflex, each of us now qualifies the above, and instantly we add, "and so the mountains are not mountains, and I am not I, and yet I am I and not-I, and the mountains are mountains and not-mountains." Paradoxicality is the form of expression that most nearly captures the process and, when unpacked, forces us to deny, affirm, deny, affirm, without ceasing. Nishida's identity of self-contradictories depicts a process that is precisely what it is, at the same time that it is never ending. The self, too, is discrete and therefore is everything else in its awareness, and is both of these, yet not as substance, but as place-as-identity of the arising of both the affirmation and the denial. Because I am I, I am not my brother and my sister, and yet I am not-I and so I am my brother and my sister, and what makes me fully human is the identity of both facts existing together in contradictory tension. In losing my ego, I not only find the other *not* as myself but myself as the other. To put oneself in another's shoes; that is, to truly implement the logical requirement of ethical universalization, one must become transparent. One becomes as transparent as one can by forgetting oneself, and mirroring or reflecting the other. In the very act of recognizing the other in his/her otherness, one discovers who one truly is. One is constituted as a self precisely because one can become the other, whether a lover or an ant. Empathetic identification depends on this capacity to see the other just-as-he/she/it-is-from-out-of-him/her/itself.[44] It is a cosmic consciousness, an experiential sense of the ecological whole of things. It is in me as not-me, and in the me as me, that the entire consciousness arises in experience. The universe of experience is the experience of one as not two. Yet neither are experiences simply one. They are both one and two, yet only when taken *dynamically,* as a process whereby to be distinct is to be identical, since to be identical is to be distinct as well. All that is, is in constant transformation, and it is only in the instant, in the moment, in the *now* that this transformation-as-reality can be met. The eternal and everpresent now of Zen is the place where reality manifests itself, and it does so as pure experience. Not only does Nishida clarify everything in the light of pure experience, everything clarifies itself to itself through pure experience, and it does so within the nothingness wherein pure experience itself arises. It does so within us.

NOTES

INTRODUCTION

1. Walter Watson, *The Architectonics of Meaning: Foundations of the New Pluralism* (Albany: State University of New York Press, 1985), p. 13.
2. It is my hope that readers who are not already open to calling theoretical undertakings from other cultures "philosophy" will come to do so after discovering that Nishida is a kindred spirit with philosophers everywhere in reaching for conceptual foundations (starting points) and in raising the age-old philosophical questions of epistemology, logic, ethics, ontology, valuation, etc. The flavor of Nishida's work is often Japanese and/or Buddhist, but its substance and method are clearly epistemological and probingly philosophical in the broadest sense.
3. Martin Heidegger, *On the Way to Language*, Peter D. Hertz, tr. (San Francisco: Harper & Row, 1959), p. 5.
4. *Ibid.*
5. Robert E. Carter, *Dimensions of Moral Education* (Toronto: University of Toronto Press, 1984), pp. 24-30.
6. Gilles Deleuze and Félix Guattari, *Capitalisme et Schizophrenie: Milles Plateaux* (Paris: les éditions de Minuit, 1980), pp.238, 272, *passim.* An English translation is forthcoming from the University of Minnesota Press, entitled *A Thousand Plateaus*, Brian Mussumi, tr.

CHAPTER 1. PURE EXPERIENCE

1. Nishida Kitarō, *A Study of Good*, V. H. Viglielmo, tr. (Tokyo: Printing Bureau, Japanese Government, 1960), p. 1.
2. *Ibid.*, pp. 1-2.
3. *Ibid*, p. 3. On pp. 2-3, Nishida comments, "Now let us consider for a moment the characteristics of this pure experience which is thus directly related to us and which is the cause of all psychical phenomena. First of all, the problem arises of whether pure experience is simple or complex. When we look at it from the standpoint that, even though it be immediate, direct experience, it is a thing which is composed of past experience, or that it can be broken down into its individual elements, it may be correct to say it is complex. No matter how complex pure

experience is, however, at the moment of its happening it is always one simple event. Even if it is reconstruction of past experience, at the time when it is unified within present consciousness and becomes one element, acquiring a new meaning, we can no longer say that it is the same as past consciousness."

4. *Ibid.*, p. 3.
5. Joseph C. Flay, "Experience, Nature, and Place," *The Monist,* Vol. 68, no. 4 (Oct. 1985), p. 472.
6. *Ibid.*, p. 473.
7. *Ibid.*, p. 476.
8. Joseph C. Flay, "Pure Experience Revisited," unpublished manuscript, pp. 8-9. This paper was read before the Society for the Advancement of American Philosophy.
9. William James, *Pragmatism, and Four Essays from the Meaning of Truth*, R. B. Perry, ed. (New York: A Meridian Book, New American Library, 1955 [first published in 1909]), p. 199.
10. Flay, "Experience, Nature and Place," p. 477.
11. *Ibid.*
12. Nishida, *Study of Good*, p. 175.
13. *Ibid.*, p. 33.
14. *Ibid.*, p. 36.
15. William James, *The Principles of Psychology* (New York: Dover Publications, Inc., 1950 [first published in 1890]), Vol. 1, p. 139.
16. Nishida, *Study of Good*, p. 36.
17. *Ibid.*
18. David Dilworth, "The Initial Formations of 'Pure Experience,' in Nishida Kitarō and William James," *Monumenta Nipponica*, Vol. XXIV, nos. 1-2, p. 109.
19. William James, *Essays in Radical Empiricism* (Cambridge, Mass.: Harvard University Press, 1976), p. 4.
20. *Ibid.*, p. 14.
21. Charlene H. Seigfried, *Chaos and Context: A Study in William James* (Athens, Ohio: Ohio University Press, 1978), p. 40.
22. James, *Essays*, p. 66.
23. *Ibid.*, p. 13.
24. Thomas R. Maitland, Jr., *The Metaphysics of William James and John Dewey* (New York: Philosophical Library, 1963), p. 85.
25. Nishida, *Study of Good*, p. 8.
26. *Ibid.*, p. 28.
27. James, *Essays*, p. 7.
28. Edward C. Moore, *William James* (New York: Washington Square Press, 1966), pp. 164-165.

29. William James, *Some Problems of Philosophy* (London: Longmans, Green & Co., 1948), p. 50.
30. James, *Essays*, p. 13.
31. *Ibid.*, p. 263.
32. James, *Problems*, p. 65.
33. Maitland, *The Metaphysics*, p. 92.
34. James, *Psychology*, (I), p. 467.
35. James, *Problems*, p. 73.
36. *Ibid.*, p. 78.
37. *Ibid.*, p. 79.
38. *Ibid.*, p. 101.
39. *Ibid.*, p. 97.
40. *Ibid.*
41. *Ibid.*
42. *Ibid.*, p. 86.
43. William James, Letter to Arthur O. Lovejoy, 1909, in Ralph Barton Perry, *The Thought and Character of William James*, Vol. II (Philosophy and Psychology) (Boston: Little, Brown & Co., 1935), p. 596.
44. James, *Psychology*, I, p. 482.
4S. Seigfried, *Chaos and Context*, p. 49.
46. *Ibid*
47. *Ibid.*
48. *Ibid.*, p. 51.
49. Nishida, *Study of Good*, p. 7.
50. Seigfried, *Chaos and Context*, p. 49.
51. James, *Essays*, p. 46.
52. James, *Psychology*, I, p. 251.
53. William James, *The Varieties of Religious Experience* (New York: Modern Library, 1902), p. 378.
54. *Ibid.*, p. 379.
55. Dilworth, "The Initial Formations," p. 110. Italics added.
56. Nishida, *Study of Good*, p. 1.
57. James, *Essays*, p. 22. In a footnote on p. 33, James comments on the quasi-chaotic nature of experience, on the continuity of the person as body, and on the discontinuity of inter-subjective experiences, concluding that, "Round their several objective nuclei, partly common and partly discrete, of the real physical world, innumerable thinkers, pursuing their several lines of physically true cogitation, trace paths that intersect one another only at discontinuous perceptual points, and the rest of the time are quite incongruent; and around all the nuclei of shared 'reality' floats the vast cloud of experiences that are wholly

subjective, that are non-substitutional, that find not even an eventual ending for themselves in the perceptual world—the mere day-dreams and joys and sufferings and wishes of the individual minds. These exist *with* one another, indeed, and with the objective nuclei, but out of them it is probable that to all eternity no inter-related system of any kind will ever be made."

58. James, *Pragmatism...Truth*, p. 199.
59. James, *Essays*, p. 22.
60. James, *Psychology*, I, p. 243.
61. *Ibid.*, pp. 245-246.
62. Seigfried, *Chaos and Context*, p. 13.
63. James, *Psychology*, I, p. 284.
64. Ames, *Pragmatism ... Truth*, pp. 246-247.
65. Nishida, *Study of Good*, p. 10. On p. 11 Nishida quotes from James's "The World of Pure Experience," and adds, "Formerly it was traditionally felt that thought and pure experience were wholly differing kinds of physical activity.... thought activity also is a kind of pure experience."
66. *Ibid.*, p. 17.
67. *Ibid.*, p. 27.
68. *Ibid.*, p. 31.
69. *Ibid.*, pp. 33-34.
70. *Ibid.*, p. 34.
71. *Ibid.*
72. *Ibid.*
73. *Ibid.*, p. 35.
74. *Ibid.*, p. 36.
75. *Ibid.*
76. *Ibid.*
77. *Ibid.*
78. James, *Problems*, p. 51.

CHAPTER 2. THE LOGIC OF BASHO

1. Nishida Kitarō, "The Logic of the Place of Nothingness and The Religious Worldview" (NKZ, ["Collected Works"] vol. XI, pp. 371-464, written in 1945), in *Last Writings: Nothingness and the Religious Worldview*, with intro. by David A. Dilworth, tr. (Honolulu: University of Hawaii Press, 1987).
2. Lao Tzu, *Tao Te Ching*. This particular translation is by D. C. Lau (New York: Penguin Books, 1963), p.57, but another, which focuses on the linguistic issues, is by Witter Bynner (New York: Capricorn Books, 1962), p. 25:

Existence is beyond the power of words
To define:
Terms may be used
But are more than absolute.
In the beginning of heaven and earth them were no words,
Words came out of the womb of matter;
And whether a man dispassionately
Sees to the core of life
Or passionately
Sees the surface,
The core and the surface
Are essentially the same,
Words making them seem different
Only to express appearance,
If name be needed, wonder names them both:
From wonder into wonder
Existence opens.

3. Lao Tzu, *Tao Te Ching*, Lin Yutang, tr. (New York: Modern Library, 1948), p. 41: "The Nameless is the origin of Heaven and Earth; The Named is the Mother of All Things."

4. Charles A. Moore, "Editor's Supplement: The Enigmatic Japanese Mind," in Charles A. Moore, ed., *The Japanese Mind: Essentials of Japanese Philosophy and Culture* (Honolulu: The University Press of Hawaii, 1967), p. 289.

5. Toshihiko Izutsu, *Toward a Philosophy of Zen Buddhism* (Tehran: Imperial Iranian Academy of Philosophy, 1977), p. 131.

6. Fung Yu-lan (in A Short History of Chinese Philosophy [New York: The Free Press, 1966], pp. 80-92) writes that "the term *Ming chia* has sometimes been translated as 'sophists,' and sometimes as 'logicians' or 'dialecticians.' It is true that there is some similarity between the *Ming chia* and the sophists, logicians, and dialecticians, but it is also true that they are not quite the same. To avoid confusion, it is better to translate *Ming chia* literally as the *School of Names*. This translation also helps to bring to the attention of Westerners one of the important problems discussed by Chinese philosophy, namely that of the relation between *ming* (the name) and *shih* (the actuality)" (p. 80).

7. Plato, *Seventh Letter*, L.A. Post, tr., in *Plato: Collected Dialogues*, Edith Hamilton and Huntington Cairns, eds. (New York: Bollingen Foundation, 1963), p. 1590 (342e-343a).

8. Werner Jaeger, *Aristotle: Fundamentals of the History of His Development*, Richard Robinson, tr. (Oxford: Oxford University Press, 1962), p. 82.

9. Joseph Owens, C.Ss.R., "Aristotle's Notion of Wisdom," *Apeiron* (vol. 3, 1987), pp. 1-16; see especially p. 9.

10. John Herman Randall, Jr., *Artistotle* (New York: Columbia University Press, 1960), p. 7.

11. Marjorie Grene, *A Portrait of Aristotle*, (London: Faber & Faber, Ltd., 1963), p. 73.

12. Aristotle, *Posterior Analytics*, Bk. II, ch. 19, 100b, 15-18, in *The Basic Works of Aristotle*, Richard McKeon, ed. (New York: Random House, 1941), p. 185.

13. Jaakko Hintikka, "The Varieties of Being in Aristotle," in Simo Knuuttila and Jaakko Hintikka, *The Logic of Being* (Dordrecht, Holland: D. Reidel Publishing Co., 1986), p. 95.

14. Charles H. Kahn, "Retrospect on the Verb 'To Be' and the Concept of Being," in Knuuttila and Hintikka, eds., *Logic of Being*, pp. 21-22.

15. *Ibid.*, p. 22.

16. Hintikka, "Varieties," p. 95.

17. Nishida Kitarō, *Fundamental Problems of Philosophy*, David A. Dilworth, tr. (Tokyo: Sophia Universiq, 1970), p. 4.

18. *Ibid.*

19. *Ibid.*

20. *Ibid.*,p.39.

21. *Ibid.*,p.4.

22. *Ibid.*, p. 5.

23. See chapter one above.

24. Nishida, *Fundamental Problems*, p. 7.

25. *Ibid.*, pp. 6-7.

26. Philip Wheelwright, *Heraclitus* (New York: Atheneum, 1964), pp. 91-92.

27. *Ibid.*,p.92.

28. *Ibid.*,p.90.

29. *Ibid.*, p. 89.

30. Aristotle, *Posterior Analytics*, Bk. II, ch. 19, 100a, 13.

31. Aristotle, *Metaphysics*, Bk. XII, ch. 7, 1073a, 3-4 (McKeon, tr., *supra*), p. 881.

32. Aristotle, *Nicomachean Ethics*, in J. A. K. Thomson, tr., *The Ethics of Aristotle* (Baltimore: Penguin Books, 1953), p. 307.

33. John Herman Randall, Jr., *Aristotle* (New York: Columbia University Press, 1960), p. 142.

34. Aristotle, *Metaphysics*, Bk. XII, chs. 8 and 9, especially p. 1074b.

35. *Ibid.* The central passage from Aristotle is the second chapter of his *Categories*.

36. Robert Joseph Wargo, *The Logic of Basho and the Concept of Nothingness in the Philosophy of Nishida Kitarō*, Ph.D. Dissertation, University of Michigan, 1972 (Ann Arbor: Universiq Microfilms International), p. 247.

37. Grene, *A Portrait*, pp. 78-85: "That things do sort themselves out in some way may seem on the face of it obvious.... Things as he saw them sorted themselves

out in defiance of the philosophers.... Surely it was the arperience of the practicing biologist, who can tell a placental from an ordinary dogfish, or the catfish now known as Parasilurus Aristotelis from other species, and specify the reason for his distinctions. He can tell, too, that a chicken will hatch out of a hen's egg, not only after the obvious twenty-one days, but after just these precise stages of development" (pp. 78-79).

38. Wargo, *The Logic*, p. 193.
39. Aristotle, *Posterior Analytics*, Bk. ll, ch. 19.
40. Wargo, *The Logic*, p. 250.
41. *Ibid.*, p. 251.
42. *Ibid.*, p. 253.
43. Randall, *Aristotle*, p. 7.
44. Wargo, *The Logic*, p. 264.
45. Masao Abe, "Nishida's Philosophy of 'Place'," unpublished manuscript, p. 10.
46. Wargo, *The Logic*, p. 288.
47. Wargo translates the salient passage from Vol. V of Nishida's *Collected Works* as follows: "The sum of Descartes's *'cogito ergo sum'* does not mean subject (g[rammatical]) existence, but must have predicative existence. That 'I' is a thinking 'I' and not a thought 'I'; it can never be found in the direction of the subject (g) of judgment and, further, all subjective (g) things must be located in it" (p. 18).
48. Nishida Kitarō, "Affective Feeling," *Analecta Husserliana*, Vol. VII, Nitta and Tatematou, eds. (Dordrecht, Holland: D. Reidel Publishing Co., 1978), p. 225.
49. *Ibid.*, p. 226.
50. *Ibid.*, p. 228.
51. Translation by Robert J. Wargo, *The Logic*, pp. 314-315, and taken from Vol. V of Nishida's Collected Works, p. 161.
52. *Ibid.*, p. 312.
53. *Ibid.*, p. 313.
54. Nishida, "Affective Feeling," p. 223.
55. *Ibid.*
56. *Ibid.*, p. 227.
57. *Ibid.*, p. 228.
58. *Ibid.*, p. 332.
59. Nishida Kitarō, *Intelligibility and the Philosophy of Nothingness: Three Philosophical Essays* (reprint), Robert Schinzinger, tr. (Westport, Conn.: Greenwood Press, 1973, originally published in 1958 by Maruzen Co., Ltd., Tokyo), p. 134.
60. *Ibid.*, pp. 134-135.
61. *Ibid.*, p. 136.
62. *Ibid.*

63. *Ibid.*, p. 133.
64. *Ibid.*
65. *Ibid.*, p. 135.
66. *Ibid.* p. 137.
67. Nishida Kitarō, *Last Writings: Nothingness and the Religious Worldview*, with intro. by David A. Dilworth, tr. (Honolulu: University of Hawaii Press, 1987), pp. 108-109.
68. W. T. Stace, *Mysticism and Philosophy*, (London: MacMillan 8' Co., Ltd., 1961), p. 297.
69. *Ibid.*
70. *Ibid.*
71. Steven T. Katz, "Language, Epistemology, and Mysticism," in Steven T. Katz, ea., *Mysticism and Philosophical Analysis* (London: Sheldon Press, 1978), p. 54.
72. *Ibid.*, p. 70.
73. Nishida, *Intelligibility*, p. 137. The poem's author is the Japanese Zen Buddhist Kanemitsu Kogun.
74. *Ibid.*, p. 138.
75. Miura Isshū, *The Zen Koan: Its History and Use in Rinzai Zen*, Ruth Fuller Sasaki, tr. (New York: A Helen and Kurt Wolff Book, Harcourt, Brace & World, Inc., 1965), p. x.
76. Chung-Ying Cheng, "On Zen (Ch'an) Language and Zen Paradoxes," *Journal of Chinese Philosophy*, Vol. I, no. 1 (December 1973), p. 85.
77. *Ibid.*, p. 90.
78. *Ibid.*, p. 92.
79. *Ibid.*
80. *Ibid.*
81. *Ibid.*, p. 95.
82. Stace, *Mysticism and Philosophy*, p. 305.
83. Cheng, "On Zen (Ch'an) Language," p. 93.
84. Miura, *The Zen Koan*, p. 44.
85. *Ibid.*, p. xi.
86. *Ibid.*, p. 37.
87. Ha Tai Kim, "The Logic of the Illogical: Zen and Hegel," *Philosophy East and West*, Vol. V (1955-56), p. 21.
88. *Ibid.*, p. 29.
89. *Ibid.*, p. 23.
90. *Ibid.*, pp. 23-24.
91. Nishida Kitarō, *Intuition and Reflection in Self-Consciousness*, Valdo H. Viglielmo, with Takeuchi Yoshinori and Joseph S. O'Leary, tr. (Albany: State University of New York Press, 1987), p. viii.

CHAPTER 3. SELF-CONTRADICTORY IDENTITY

1. Michiko Yusa, *'Persona' Originalis': 'Jinkaku' and 'Personne,'* According to the *Philosophies of Nishida Kitaro and Jacques Maritain,* Ph.D. Dissertation (University of California at Santa Barbara, 1983), p. 223. The quoted passage is Michiko Yusa's translation from *Nishida's Collected Works,* Vol. Xll, p. 290 (1938).

2. *Ibid.,* p. 230. Yusa's translation of Nishida, *Collected Works,* Vol. IX, p. 73.

3. From a letter written by Nishida to a "colleague" and member of Nishida's "inner circle," Mutai Risaku, on Dec. 21, 1944, and translated under my direction by Tom Hino (from *Collected Works,* Vol. 19, [2nd ed.], pp. 367-368).

4. Nishida Kitarō, *Intelligibility and the Philosophy of Nothingness* (reprint), Robert Schinzinger, tr. (Westport, Conn.: Greenwood Press, Publishers, 1973), p. 163 ff.

5. Yusa, *'Persona Originalis,'* p. 202.

6. From a letter written by Nishida to a "colleague," Matsutsuna Doi, on Sept. 6, 1943, and translated under my direction by Tom Hino (from *Collected Works,* Vol. 19 [2nd ed.], p. 258).

7. Nishida Kitarō, "The World as Identity of Absolute Contradiction" (1939), draft manuscript translation by David A. Dilworth.

8. David A. Dilworth, "Introduction" to Nishida's *Last Writings: Nothingness and the Religious Worldview* (Honolulu: University of Hawaii Press, 1987), p. 3.

9. Yusa, *'Persona Originalis,'* p. 281.

10. David A. Dilworth, "Introduction" to *Last Writings,* p. 29.

11. Nakamura Hajime, *Ways of Thinking of Eastern Peoples: India-China Tibet-Japan* (Honolulu: East-West Center Press, 1964), pp. 350ff.

12. Robert Schinzinger, "Introduction to 'The Unity of Opposites,'" in Nishida Kitarō, *Intelligibility,* p. 55.

13. Nishida Kitarō, "Active Intuition" (from *Collected Works,* Vol. VIII [1937], pp. 541-75), David A. Dilworth, tr., draft manuscript, 1983, p. 9.

14. David J. Kalupahana, *Nāgārjuna: The Philosophy of the Middle Way* (Albany: State University of New York Press, 1986), p. 86.

15. *Ibid.,* p. 92.

16. *Ibid.,* p. 84.

17. *Ibid.,* pl. 80.

18. T. P. Kasulis, *Zen Action/Zen Purpose* (Honolulu: The University Press of Hawaii, 1981), p. 17. Italics added.

19. *Ibid.,* p. 27

20. *Ibid.,* p. 28.

21. *Ibid.,* p. 21.

22. *Ibid.*, pp. 21-22.
23. *Ibid.*, p. 28.
24. Nishida, "The World as Identity of Absolute Contradiction" (1939), p. 13.
25. Nishida Kitarō, *Fundamental Problems of Philosophy* (Tokyo: Sophia University, 1970), p. 2.
26. Nishida, "Active Intuition," p. 14.
27. *Ibid.*, p. 8.
28. Schinzinger, *Intelligibility*, p. 165.
29. *Ibid.*, p. 168.
30. Nishida, "Active Intuition," p. 11.
31. Yusa, *Persona Originalis*, p. 229.
32. From a letter written by Nishida to a "colleague," Matsutsuna Doi, on Sept. 6, 1943, and translated under my direction by Tom Hino (from *Collected Works*, Vol. 19 [2nd ed.], p. 258).
33. Schinzinger, in *Intelligibility*, p. 37.
34. Nishida Kitarō (NKZ XI, 451), tr. by and quoted in Yusa, *Persona Originalis*, p. 229.
35. Schinzinger, *Intelligibility*, p. 11.
36. Ueda Shizuteru, "Emptiness and Fullness: Śūnyatā in Mahāyāna Buddhism," *The Eastern Buddhist*, Vol. XV, no.1 (Spring 1982), pp. 9-37. The text dates from the twelfth century, and an early translation was done by M. H. Trevor (*The Ox and His Herdsman* [Tokyo: The Hokuseidō Press, 1969]). The ten classic drawings are by Kuo-an.
37. *Ibid.*, p. 15.
38. Daisetz Teitaro Suzuki, *Essays in Zen Buddhism*, First Series (London: Rider & Co., 1949), p. 369.
39. *Ibid.*, p. 371.
40. *Ibid.*, p. 372.
41. *Ibid.*
42. *Ibid.*, p. 373.
43. *Ibid.*
44. *Ibid.*, p. 374.
45. *Ibid.*, p. 19.
46. *Ibid.*
47. *Ibid.* The Zen notion of "no-mind" is based on the Mahāyāna Buddhist insight that all reality is empty, and intuitive knowledge (prajñā) reveals that the mind, too, is empty. Our real state is prior to mind-form; it is mind-form-less, or no-minded.
48. *Ibid.*, p. 19.
49. *Ibid.*

50. *Ibid.*, p. 21.
51. *Ibid.*
52. *Ibid.*
53. Yusa, *Persona Originalis*, p. 221.
54. Nishida Kitarō, *A Study of Good*, V. H. Viglielmo, tr. (Tokyo: Printing Bureau, Japanese Government, 1960), p. 167.
55. *Ibid.*, p. 182.
56. *Ibid.*, p. 183.
57. *Ibid.*, p. 186.
58. *Ibid.*
59. *Ibid.*, p. 188.
60. Yusa, *Persona Originalis*, p. 227. The words are Nishida's [NKZ, Vol. X], Michiko Yusa, tr., p. 470.
61. *Ibid.*
62. *Ibid.*, [NKZ, Vol. IX], Michiko Yusa, tr., p. 75-76.
63. *Ibid.*, [NKZ, Vol. VI], Michiko Yusa, tr., p. 6.
64. *Ibid.*, [NKZ, Vol. XI], Michiko Yusa, tr., pp. 397-398.
65. Schinzinger, *Intelligibility*, pp. 15-16.

CHAPTER 4.. GOD AND NOTHINGNESS

1. Paul Tillich, *Systematic Theology*, Vol. II, Existence and the Christ (Chicago: University of Chicago Press, 1957), p. 9.
2. Tillich, *Systematic Theology*, Vol. II, p. 9.
3. *Ibid.*
4. Paul Tillich, *The Courage to Be* (New Haven: Yale University Press, 1952), p. 187.
5. Tillich, *Systematic Theology*, Vol. II, pp. 7-10.
6. Abe Masao, "Non-being and *Mu*: The Metaphysical Nature of Negativity in the East and the West," *Religious Studies* II (Tune 1975), p.181.
7. Nishida Kitarō, "Affective Feeling," *Analecta Husserliana*, Vol. VII, Nitta and Tatematsu, eds. (Dordrecht, Holland: D. Reidel Publishing Co., 1978), p. 223.
8. Nishida, "Affective Feeling," p. 225.
9. *Ibid.*, p. 227.
10. Nishida Kitaro, *A Study of Good*, V. H. Viglielmo, tr. (Tokyo: Printing Bureau, Japanese Government, 1960) p. 175.
11. Abe Masao, "God, Emptiness and the True Self," *The Eastern Buddhist*, Vol. II, no. 2 (Oct. 1969), p. 23.
12. *Ibid.*

13. D. T. Suzuki and Ueda Shizuteru, "The Sayings of Rinzai," *The Eastern Buddhist,* Vol. VI, no. 1 (May 1973), p. 93.

14. *The Encyclopedia of Philosophy,* Paul Edwards, ed. (New York: Macmillan and The Free Press, 1967), Vol. 3, p. 344.

15. Nishida, "Affective Feeling," p. 225: "Now, I have argued above that feeling remains after all content of consciousness has been intellectually objectified. From the intellectual standpoint, it might be considered to be without content and indeterminate."

16. Nishitani, "The Standpoint of Śūnyatā," p. 78; quoted in Hans Waldenfels, *Absolute Nothingness* (New York: Paulist Press, 1980), p. 111. Nishitiani, *Religion and Nothingness,* Jan Van Bragt, tr. (Berkeley and Los Angeles: University of California Press, 1982), p. 159: "The self is, at every moment of time, ecstatically outside of time. It was in this sense that we spoke above of the self of each man as a bottom preceding world and things."

17. Dependent origination has several meanings within the various Buddhist traditions, including (1) the interconnection of the karmic forces according to causal laws giving formation to a life, (2) the manifestation of all phenomena out of a fundamental consciousness, and (3) the interpenetration of all things in the universe throughout the past, present, and future, in that nothing can exist separately from other things.

18. Nishitani, "The Standpoint of Śūnyatā," as quoted in Waldenfels, *Absolute Nothingness,* p. 14; see Nishitani, *Religion and Nothingness,* p. 272.

19. Nishida Kitarō, *Intelligibility and the Philosophy of Nothingness.* Three Philosophical essays, Robert Schinzinger, tr. (Westport, Conn.: Greenwood Press Publishers, 1958), p.130. The *kimono* image is amplified by Schinzinger on p. 32.

20. Abe, "God, Emptiness and the True Self." p. 24.

21. Nishitani, *Religion and Nothingness,* pp. 279-280.

22. *Ibid.,* p. 279.

23. Robert S. Hartman, "The Logic of Value," *Review of Metaphysics* XIV (Mar. 1961), p. 408, and "The Logic of Value," unpublished manuscript, p. 32.

24. Nishida, *Fundamental Problems of Philosophy,* p. 246.

25. *Ibid.,* p. 247.

26. Wargo, *The Logic of Basho and the Concept of Nothingness in the Philosophy of Nishida Kitarō,* Ph.D. Dissertation, University of Michigan, 1972 (Ann Arbor: University Microfilms International), p. 332.

27. Nishida Kitarō, "The Logic of the Place of Nothingness and the Religious Worldview" (NKZ ["Collected Works"], Vol. XI), pp. 371-464, in *Last Writings: Nothingness and the Religious Worldview,* written in 1945, with intro. by David Dilworth, tr. (Honolulu: University of Hawaii Press, 1987), p. 47.

28. *Ibid.,* p. 2.

29. *Ibid.*

30. *Ibid.*, p. 4.

31. *Ibid.*

32. *Ibid.*, p. 7.

33. *Ibid.*, p. 9.

34. *Ibid.*, p. 10.

35. *Ibid.*, p. 12.

36. *Ibid.*, p. 23.

37. *Ibid.*, p. 32.

38. *Ibid.*, p. 34.

39. *Ibid.*

40. *Ibid.*

41. *Ibid.*, p. 38.

42. *Ibid.*, p. 39. The quoted passage is from the *Diamond Sutra,* and Nishida's gloss is that "God must always, in St. Paul's words, empty himself. That God is transcendent and at the same time immanent is the paradox of God. This is the true absolute."

43. *Ibid.*, p. 38.

44. *Ibid.*, p. 39.

45. *Ibid.*

46. Plato, *Symposium,* 210-212d.

47. Nishida, *Study of Good,* p. 186.

48. *Ibid.*

49. Nishida, *Intelligibility,* p. 133.

50. *Ibid.*

51. *Ibid.*, p. 138.

52. *Ibid.*

53. *Ibid.*, p. 140.

54. *Ibid.*

55. Nishida Kitarō, "Towards a Philosophy of Religion with the Concept of Pre-established Harmony as Guide," David A. Dilworth, tr., in *The Eastern Buddhist,* New Series 3, 1 (1970), p. 35.

CHAPTER 5. THE DIALECTICAL WORLD OF "ACTION INTUITION"

1. Noda Matao, "East-West Synthesis in Kitarō Nishida," *Philosophy East and West,* Vol. 4, no. 4 (Apr. 1954-Jan. 1955), pp. 349-50.

2. G.S. Axtell, "Comparative Dialectics: Nishida Kitarō's Logic of Place and Western Dialectical Thought," *Philosophy East and West*, vol. 41, no. 2 (April 1991), p. 169.

3. *Ibid.*, p. 171. Axtell writes that "the 'form' and the 'formless' characterizations of reality have an intriguing degree of parity. Each mode of conceptualization seeks transcendence of the historical life-world, but achieves it only through a kind of reduction, carried through on the shoulders of contrasting metaphors of the spatial and the temporal."

4. *Ibid.*, p. 350.

5. *Ibid.*

6. David A.Dilworth, "The Concrete World of Action in Nishida's Later Thought," *Analecta Husserliana*, Nitta Yoshihiro and Tatematsu Hirotaka, eds., vol. VIII (Dordrecht: D. Reidel Publishing Company, 1978), pp. 260-61.

7. *Ibid.*, p. 352.

8. Woo-Sung Huh, "The Philosophy of History in the 'Later' Nishida: A Philosophical Turn," *Philosophy East and West*, Vol. 40, no. 3 (July 1990), pp. 343-374.

9. Dilworth, David. "The Concrete World of Action in Nishida's Later Thought," in Yoshihiro and Hirotaka, eds., p. 252.

10. Discussed in many places, especially in *Fundamental Problems of Philosophy* (Tokyo: Sophia University, 1970): "The fact that the world is changing means that the 'that in which' is changing, and vice versa. To think of change in this way implies a structure which is a continuity of discontinuity. The world of change is the world of coming into being and passing away" (p. 6).

11. Yuasa Yasuo, *The Body: Toward an Eastern Mind-Body Theory*, Thomas P. Kasulis, ed., Nagatomo Shigenori & Thomas P. Kasulis, trs. (Albany: State University of New York Press, 1987), p. 199.

12. *Ibid.*

13. *Ibid.*

14. *Ibid.*, p. 200.

15. *Ibid.*

16. Eugen Herrigel, *Zen in the Art of Archery* (New York: Pantheon Books Inc., 1953). In the Introduction by D.T. Suzuki, a crisp summary is provided of what I take to be the oneness of action and intuition: "If one really wishes to be master of an art, technical knowledge of it is not enough. One has to transcend technique so that the art becomes an 'artless art' growing out of the Unconscious. ... Man is a thinking reed but his great works are done when he is not calculating and thinking. 'Childlikeness' has to be restored with long years of training in the art of self-forgetfulness. When this is attained, man thinks yet he does not think. He thinks like the showers coming down from the sky; he thinks like the waves rolling on the ocean; he thinks like the start illuminating the nightly heavens; he

thinks like the green foliage shooting forth in the relaxing spring breeze. Indeed, he is the showers, the ocean, the stars, the foliage" (pp. 10-11).

In Herrigel's words, "Bow, arrow, goal and ego, all melt into one another, so that I can no longer separate them. And even the need to separate has gone. For as soon as I take the bow and shoot, everything becomes so clear and straightforward and so ridiculously simple" (p. 88). And again, "What is true of archery and swordsmanship also applies to all the other arts. Thus, mastery in ink-painting is only attained when the hand, exercising perfect control over technique, executes what hovers before the mind's eye at the same moment when the mind begins to form it, without there being a hair's breadth between" (pp. 104-05.

17. Yuasa, *The Body*, p. 200.

18. Deshimaru, Jean Taisen, *The Zen Way to the Martial Arts*, Nancy Amphoux, tr. (New York: Arkana, Published by the Penguin Group, 1991), p. 17.

19. *Ibid.*, p. 55.

20. *Ibid.*

21. This is hinted at in Geoffrey Payzant's *Glenn Gould: Music & Mind* (Toronto: Van Nostrand Reinhold Ltd., 1978), p. 1. The event referred to was described in a CBC radio broadcast, at a time now forgotten by me: "When Gould was three years old it became evident that he possessed exceptional musical abilities, including absolute pitch and some ability to read staff notation."

22. Yuasa, *The Body*, p. 200.

23. Nishida Kitarō, *Intelligibility and the Philosophy of Nothingness: Three Philosophical Essays*, tr. with Intro. by Robert Schinzinger (Honolulu: East-West Center Press, 1958), P. 198.

24. Yusa Michiko, *"Persona Oricrinalis": "Jinkaku" and "Personne," According to the Philosophies of Nishida Kitarō and Jacaues Maritain*. Ph.D. Dissertation, University of California at Santa Barbara, 1983 (Ann Arbor: University Microfilms International), p. 231. Yusa refers to Nishida's *Collected Works* (NKZ VIII, 138-9), adding an additional quotation from that source: "The self without the body would be just a ghost": She refers as well to the same volume, pp. 428 *et passim.*

25. Nishida, *Intelligibility*, p. 50. From the Introduction by Robert Schinzinger.

26. *Ibid.*, pp. 54-5. From the Introduction by Robert Schinzinger.

27. *Ibid.*, p. 184.

28. *Ibid.*, p. 168.

29. R.P. Peerenboom, "The Religious Foundations of Nishida's Philosophy," *Asian Philosophy*, Vol. 1, no. 2 (1991), p. 169.

30. *Ibid.*

31. Nishida, *Intelligibility*, p. 187.

32. Nishida, *Fundamental Problems*, p. 134.

33. *Ibid.*, p. 246.

34. G.S. Axtell, "Comparative Dialectics," p. 164.

35. *Ibid.*

36. *Ibid.*, p. 170

37. *Ibid.*, p. 171

38. Nishida, *Fundamental Problems*, p. 2.

39. Wing-Tsit Chan (*A Source Book in Chinese Philosophy* [Princeton: Princeton University Press, 1963]), in commenting on ch. 2 of the *Chuang Tzu*, writes that "things are not only relative, they are identical, for opposites produce each other, imply each other, are identical with each other, and are both finite series. In some respects Chuang Tzu is surprisingly similar to Hegel and Nagarjuna ... It must be quickly added, however, that both the dialectic of Hegel and the relativity of Nagarjuna are much more conceptual than Chuang Tzu's synthesis of opposites" (p. 183). Gia-Fu Feng and Jane English (*Chuang Tsu: Inner Chapters* [New York: Vintage Books, 1974]) translate the passage from the *Chuang Tzu* as follows: "Every thing can be a 'that'; every thing can be a 'this.' ... Therefore it is said, '"that" comes from "this," and "this" comes from "that"'—which means 'that' and 'this' give birth to one another. Life arises from death and death from life. ... So he sees 'this,' but this' is also 'that,' and 'that' is also 'this.' ... When there is no more separation between 'this' and 'that,' it is called the still-point of Tao. At the still-point one can see the infinite in all things. ... All things may become one, whatever their state of being. Only he who has transcended sees this oneness" (pp. 29-30).

40. Nishida, *Intelligibility*, p. 177.

41. *Ibid.*

42. Axtell, "Comparative Dialectics," p. 174.

43. *Ibid.*

44. Woo-Sung Huh, "The Philosophy of History in the 'Later' Nishida: A Philosophical Turn," *Philosophy East and West*, Vol. 40, no. 3 (July 1990), p. 343. See also Woo-Sung Huh, *A Critical Exposition of Nishida's Philosophy*. Ph.D. Dissertation, University of Hawaii, August 1988 (Ann Arbor: University Microfilms International).

45. Hans Waldenfels, *Monumenta Nipponica*, Vol. 21 (1966), p. 363, n. 38.

46. Thomas P. Kasulis, in correspondence with me, August 19, 1996.

47. Ueda Shizuteru, "Pure Experience, Self-awareness, 'Basho'," *Etudes Phenomenologiques*, no. 18 (1993), p. 75.

48. *Ibid.*, pp. 69-70.

49. *Ibid.*, p. 70.

50. *Ibid.*

51. *Ibid.*

52. *Ibid.*, p. 75.

53. *Ibid.*

54. *Ibid.*
55. *Ibid.*, pp. 76-7.
56. *Ibid.*, p. 65.
57. Huh, "The Philosophy of History," p. 343.
58. Ibid., p. 368.
59. Noda, "East-West Synthesis," p. 354, n. 23. Noda's translation of a passage from Nishida's "Philosophical Essays," Vol. III (1939), from the *Works of Nishida Kitarō* (NKZ), pp. 94-95: "The historical world is the only real world. From this world are derived various other worlds. Hitherto one has been apt to fall into the error of conceiving the historical world from outside of it."
60. Nakamura Hajime, *Ways of Thinking of Eastern Peoples: India-China-Tibet-Japan* (Honolulu: East-West Center Press, 1964), pp. 350-361: "In the first place, we should notice that the Japanese are willing to accept the phenomenal world as Absolute because of their disposition to lay a greater emphasis upon intuitive sensible concrete events, rather than upon universals. ... What is widely known among post-Meiji philosophers in the last century as the 'theory that the phenomenal is actually the real' has a deep root in Japanese tradition" (p. 350).
61. Nishida, *Intelligibility*, p. 168.
62. *Ibid.*, p. 173: "Only when it comes to man, where the Self, as monad, is mirroring the world, and is, at the same time, itself a (viewpoint of) perspective of the world, there is activity through action-intuition [originating] from seeing things in a world of objects."
63. *Ibid.*, pp. 184-85.
64. Nishida, *Fundamental Problems*, p. 124.
65. *Ibid.*, p. 123.
66. Nishida, *Intelligibility*, p. 196.
67. *Ibid.*, p. 208.
68. *Ibid.*
69. *Ibid.*, p. 237.
70. Nishida Kitarō, *Last Writings: Nothingness and the Religious Worldview*, tr. with intro. by D.A. Dilworth (Honolulu: University of Hawaii Press), p. 97.
71. *Ibid.*, p. 98.
72. Nishida, *Intelligibility*, p. 209.
73. *Ibid.*, p. 133.
74. Nishida, *Fundamental Problems*, p, 29.
75. *Ibid.*, p. 29.
76. Nishida, *Last Writings*, p. 111.
77. Ueda, "Pure Experience, Self-awareness, '*Basho*," p. 67.
78. Ueda, p. 83.
79. *Ibid.*, p. 84.
80. *Ibid.*, p. 85.

81. Nishitani Keiji, *Nishida Kitarō*, Yamamoto Seisaku and James W. Heisig, trs. (Berkeley: University of California Press, 1991), p. 181.
82. *Ibid.*

CHAPTER 6. RELIGION AND MORALITY

1. Nishida Kitarō, *Last Writings: Nothingness and the Religious Worldview* (NKZ, Vol. XI, pp. 371-464, written in 1945), with intro. by David A. Dilworth, tr. (Honolulu: University of Hawaii Press, 1987), p. 74.
2. The moral psychologist Lawrence Kohlberg provides a stage-theory of development which may serve to sharpen the point I am trying to make. Kohlberg argues that the process of moral development, like the process of intellectual or cognitive development, can be described as the movement through distinct stages of awareness, with the later stage being more "adequate" or better than the earlier. They are not mere theory, but are argued to be empirical abstractions. They are inductive generalizations.
3. Nishida, *Last Writings*, p. 74.
4. *Ibid.*
5. *Ibid.*
6. *Ibid.*
7. *Ibid.*
8. *Ibid.*, p. 75.
9. *Ibid.* Italics added.
10. *Ibid.*
11. Douglas A. Fox, "Zen and Ethics, Dōgen's Synthesis," *Philosophy East and West*, Vol. 21, no. 1 Jan. 1971), p. 35.
12. Nishida, *Last Writings*, p. 75.
13. Fox, "Zen and Ethics," p. 35.
14. Nishida, *Last Writings*, p. 75.
15. *Ibid.*, pp. 76-77.
16. *Ibid.*, p. 77.
17. Thomas E Cleary, *Shōbōgenzō: Zen Essays by Dōgen*, Thomas E Cleary, tr. (Honolulu: University of Hawaii Press, 1986), p. 32. Italics added. Another recent translation is *Moon in a Dewdrop: Writings of Zen Master Dōgen*, Tanahashi Kazuaki, ed. (San Franciso: North Point Press, 1985), p. 70: "To study the Buddha-way is to study the self. To study the self is to forget the self. To forget the self is to be actualized by myriad things. When actualized by myriad things, your body and mind as well as the bodies and minds of others

drop away. No trace of realization remains, and this no-trace continues endlessly."

18. Nishida, *Last Writings*, p. 76.

19. *Ibid.*

20. *Ibid.*, p. 77.

21. *Ibid.*

22. *Ibid.*, p. 78.

23. *Ibid.*, p. 79.

24. *Ibid.*

25. *Ibid.*, p. 83.

26. *Ibid.*, pp. 99-100.

27. *Ibid.*, p. 101.

28. Nishida Kitarō, *Study of Good*, V. H. Viglielmo, tr. (Tokyo: Printing Bureau,, Japanese Government, 1960), p. 186.

29. *Ibid.*, p. 187.

30. A glimpse of *kokoro*, too, in transition from its meaning as "the heart of things" (e.g., Lafcadio Hearn, *Kokoro: Hints and Echoes of Japanese Inner Life* [Rutland, Vermont: Charles E. Tuttle Co., 1972], first published in 1896), to *kokoro* as a constraining, lonely, and confining quality of the heart, may be found in Soseki Natsume's *Kokoro* (Tokyo: Charles E. Tuttle Co., 1957), which charts and laments the major changes in Japanese thought, character, and culture, from the Meiji Restoration in 1868 to the modern era.

31. Nishida, *Last Writings*, p. 101.

32. Iino Norimoto, "Dōgen's Zen View of Interdependence," *Philosophy East and West*, Vol. 12 (Apr. 1962), p. 52.

33. *Ibid.*

34. Nakamura Hajime, "Interrelational Existence," *Philosophy East and West*, 17, nos. 1-4 (1967), p. 109: "Ryonin (1072-1132), the founder of the Yūzū Nembutsu sect of Japan, is said to have seen Amida Buddha appear and to have presented a poem to him, saying, 'One person is all persons; all persons are one person; one meritorious deed is all meritorious deeds; all meritorious deeds are one meritorious deed. This is called deliverance to the Pure Land by the grace of Amida.' Dōgen (1200-1253) also advocated unification of the self with other selves, saying, 'Oneself and others should be benefitted at the same time.'" Nakamura traces this notion to the Chinese Hua-Yen school, where "the idea of interrelational existence thus became the principle of altruistic deeds," for the entire universe is "motivated by the 'Great Compassionate Heart'" (p. 109).

35. T. P. Kasulis, *Zen Action/Zen Person* (Honolulu: The University Press of Hawaii, 1981), p. 96.

36. Iino, "Dōgen's Zen View of Interdependence," p. 52.

37. Nishida Kitarō, "Towards a Philosophy of Religion By Way of Leibniz's Concept of Pre-established Harmony (1944)," a draft translation by David A. Dilworth, unpublished manuscript, p. 36.

38. *Ibid.*

39. *Ibid.*, p. 34.

40. Nishida, *Last Writings*, p. 90.

41. A. D. Brear, "The Nature and Status of Moral Behavior in Zen Buddhist Tradition," *Philosophy East and West*, Vol. XXIV, no. 4 (Oct. 1974), p. 54.

42. *Ibid.*, p. 57.

43. *Ibid.*, p. 434.

44. D. T. Suzuki, "Ethics and Zen Buddhism," in Ruth Nanda Anshen, ed., *Moral Principles of Action; Man's Ethical Imperative* (New York: Harper & Brothers, Publishers, 1952), pp. 606-607.

45. Brear, "The Nature and Status," p. 51.

46. Dōgen Kigen, *Shōbōgenzō, Bodaisatta shishōhō* fascicle ("The Four Integrative Methods of Bodhisattvas").

47. Fox, "Zen and Ethics," p. 37.

48. Nakamura Hajime, "The Basic Teachings of Buddhism," in *The Cultural, Political, and Religious Significance of Buddhism in the Modern World*, Heinrich Dumoulin and John C. Maraldo, eds. (New York: Collier Books, 1976), pp. 28-29.

49. Brear, "The Nature and Status," p. 432: "The activity of the Zen master, then, is as that of the *bodhisattva*—it involves the same apprehension of the nonduality of samsara and nirvana (hence its highly practical nature), the apprehension of which is *prajñā*. Any statements made by such a one about behavior are uttered, therefore, from the other side, with the benefit of the eye of wisdom. Statements, for instance, on the relativity of moral canons are true from the absolute plane but may not be interpreted as guides to behavior on the relative plane. Before enlightenment, behavior is seen to be neither good nor bad absolutely, but still so relatively. 'Good' actions, rather than 'bad' continue to be performed, but their nature is truly seen—they are merely 'actions,' without qualities of goodness or badness."

50. Fox, "Zen and Ethics," p. 36: "The ... Enlightenment spoken of here cannot be separated from Ultimate Reality itself." Quoting Dōgen, Fox adds, "'Commit no evil' is the self-expression of the Unborn, and the *practice* of it is the Unborn itself in action. He [Dōgen] says, 'Do not commit evil' is not something contrived by any mere man. It is the *Bodhi* (the Supreme Enlightenment) turned into words.... It is the (very) speaking of Enlightenment."

51. *Ibid.*

52. Nakamura, *Buddhism in the Modern World*, p. 29.

53. Ibid. See also Fox, "Zen and Ethics," p. 39: ". . . that the Unborn fragments itself and that you and I are respectively pieces of it; in its essence it remains undivided, and it 'expresses itself' as you and as me. Consequently, to be enlightened is to know yourself as the Absolute; but it is also to know, quite paradoxically, that I, too, am the Absolute and that the story of our relationship at this relative level is, as D. T. Suzuki puts it, a story about the interpenetration of Absolutes. This means that the evil we do to each other is what the strange blindness and ignorance of one manifestation of the Absolute does to another, yet at the supraempirical level the Absolute is not damaged."

54. T. P. Kasulis, *Zen Action/Zen Person*, p. 98.

55. Nishida, *Final Writings*, p. 102.

56. *Ibid.*

57. *Ibid.*

58. *Ibid.*, p. 107.

59. *Ibid.*

60. *Ibid.*

61. *Ibid.*, p. 95.

62. *Ibid.*, p. 96.

63. See above ch. 2.

64. W. T. Stace, *Mysticism and Philosophy* (London: Macmillan, 1961), p. 212.

65. Ken Wilber, *Eye to Eye: The Quest for the New Paradigm* (New York: Doubleday, 1983), p. 299.

66. *Ibid.*, p. 297.

67. Nishida Kitarō,, "The Problem of Japanese Culture," in *Sources of Japanese Tradition*, Vol. II, Wm. Theodore de Bary, ed. (New York: Columbia University Press, 1964), p. 359.

68. *Ibid.*

69. Nishida Kitarō, *Final Writings*, p. 108.

70. *Ibid.*

71. *Ibid.*, p. 98.

72. *Ibid.*, p. 99.

73. *Ibid.*

74. *Ibid.*, p. 100.

75. Takeuchi Yoshinori, in coining the term "transcending-transcending," offers a reinterpretation of one strand of Christianity, by warning that Tillich's position is not one of human passivity in the face of God's active grace. "The grace of God alone is active insofar as the believer has arrived ex-statically transcending-transcending on the way of encounter, but not like a car bumping into a careless pedestrian on the street. Even reason can become ex-static of itself if it reaches its own ground through the contradiction of itself and, resuming its activity from there, allows itself to enter into communication with the

transcendent—in a word, insofar as it is authentically dialectical" (from *The Heart of Buddhism: In Search of the Timeless Spirit of Primitive Buddhism* [New York: Crossroad Publishing, 1983], p. 58). But Nishida, in line with much Eastern Buddhism, is emphatically dialectical in urging that the *mutuality* of the immanent as already transcendent, and the transcendent as already immanent, yields a thoroughgoing interpenetration (or copenetration) of the spiritual and the earthly, nirvana and samsara.

76. *Ibid.*, p. 100.

77. *Ibid.*, pp. 100-101.

78. *Ibid.*, p. 101.

79. *Ibid.*

80. *Ibid.*, p. 102.

81. *Ibid.*, p. 103.

82. Nishida Kitarō, *Intelligibility and the Philosophy of Nothingness: Three Philosophical Essays* (reprint), Robert Schinzinger, tr. (Westport, Conn.: Greenwood Press, 1973), pp. 137-138.

83. *Ibid.*, p. 136.

84. *Ibid.*, p. 135.

85. *Ibid.*, pp. 135-136.

86. Nishida Kitarō, *Last Writings*, pp. 101-102.

87. *Ibid.*

88. *Ibid.*

89. *Ibid.*

90. *Ibid.*, p. 108.

91. *Ibid.*, p. 111.

92. *Ibid.*

93. *Ibid.*

94. *Ibid.*, p. 112.

95. *Ibid.*, p. 113.

96. *Ibid.*, p. 114.

97. *Ibid.*, p. 115.

98. *Ibid.*

99. Walter Watson, *The Architectonics of Meaning: Foundations of the New Pluralism* (Albany: State University of New York Press, 1985), p. 42.

100. Nishida, *Last Writings*, p. 115.

101. Nishida Kitarō, "The Problem of Japanese Culture," (see footnote no. 67), p. 362.

102. *Ibid.*

103. *Ibid.*

104. *Ibid.*, p. 115.

105. *Ibid.*
106. See my *Dimensions of Moral Education* (Toronto: University of Toronto Press, 1984), pp. 153-155: What I call "basic values" are "self-justifying in the sense of being rock-bottom, given as evident, the primitive ground, beginning, or starting point of all valuation" (p. 154). See also my "Contemporary Value Theory: An inquiry into the notion of 'intrinsic value' in contemporary Western and Japanese philosophy," *Journal of Value Inquiry*, Vol. XIII, no. 1 (Spring 1979), pp. 33-56.
107. Nishida, *Last Writings*, p. 107.
108. *Ibid.*, p. 88.
109. *Ibid.*, p. 119.
110. *Ibid.*, p. 121.
111. *Ibid.*, p. 123.

CHAPTER 7. VALUES, ETHICS, AND FEELING

1. Cf. Muraoka Tsunetsugu, *Studies in Shintō Thought*, D. M. Brown and J. T. Araki, trs. (Tokyo: Japanese National Commission for UNESCO, Ministry of Education, Japan, 1964), p. 50: "If what we call 'Japanese philosophy'—in contradistinction, of course, to Western philosophy, but especially to Oriental philosophy—is to be established, it probably will result from digging deeply into that which is Japanese, or that which is Shinto; and also it will take form by giving these a theoretical base. Actually, it is inconceivable that a Japanese philosophy will be established without considering, in some sense, that which is Japanese or Shintō."
2. Nakamura Hajime, *Ways of Thinking of Eastern Peoples: India-China Tibet-Japan*, Phillip P. Wiener, ed. (Honolulu: East-West Center Press, University of Hawaii, 1964). See in particular ch. 36, pp. 531-576.
3. *Ibid.*, p. 531.
4. Nishida Kitarō, *Fundamental Problems of Philosophy*, David A. Dilworth, tr. (Tokyo: Sophia University, 1970), p. 247.
5. *Ibid.*
6. Nakamura, *Ways of Thinking*, p. 532.
7. Ha Tai Kim, "The Logic of the Illogical: Zen and Hegel," *Philosophy East and West* (Vol. V, 1955-56), p. 112.
8. Archie J. Bahm, "Axiology as an Inductive Science," *Journal of Human Relations*, Vol. XXI, no. 1 (first quarter, 1973), pp. 82-83: ". . . four subjectivistic theories have been with us for a long time: (1) Hedonism, holding that intrinsic good consists in pleasant feeling and intrinsic evil in unpleasant feeling. (2) Volunta-

rism, for which intrinsic good consists in feeling of satisfaction and intrinsic evil in feelings of frustration. (3) Romanticism, for which intrinsic good consists in good feelings of desirousness such as enthusiasm, gusto, zest, and intrinsic evil in feelings of apathy. (4) Anandism, for which intrinsic value (*ananda*) consists in feelings of contentment, and intrinsic evil in feelings of disturbance or anxiety.... My prolonged study of value experiences under the influence of these theories has led me to formulate a fifth (5) 'Organicism,' for which intrinsic good consists in enjoyment of any one of the four, i.e., feelings of pleasantness, satisfaction, enthusiasm or contentment, alone or in combination, and either when focused upon as such or as aspects of any other experience. Intrinsic evil consists in suffering feelings of unpleasantness, frustration, apathy or disturbance, singly or intermingled with each other and either as pure suffering, if that is possible, or suffering experiences crowded with other contents." Bahm also correctly observes that "all of the intrinsic values mentioned above are intuited. They are known directly. They are not always distinguished clearly" (p. 83). Professor Bahm offers supplementary explication of his thesis in "The Aesthetics of Organicism," *Journal of Aesthetics and Art Criticism,* Vol. XXVI, no. 4 (Summer 1968), pp. 449-459, and in "Four Kinds of Intrinsic Value" *Darshana International,* Vol. V, (July 1965), pp. 22-31.

9. Daisetz T. Suzuki's introduction, "How to Read Nishida," in Nishida Kitarō, *A Study of Good* (Tokyo: Printing Bureau, Japanese Government, 1960), p. v. Suzuki explains that Kegon "is the climax of Chinese speculative thought as influenced by Indian metaphysics which developed within the system of Mahāyāna Buddhism," which entered "into the fabric of Zen thought," and in which Nishida was profoundly interested.

10. Nakamura, *Ways of Thinking,* p. 350.

11. Kishimoto Hideo, "Some Japanese Cultural Traits and Religions," in Charles A. Moore, ea., *The Japanese Mind: Essentials of Japanese Philosophy and Culture* (Honolulu: East-West Center Press, University of Hawaii, 1967), p. 110.

12. Ernst Cassirer, *Language and Myth,* Susanne K. Langer, tr. (New York: Dover Publications, 1946), pp. 32-33.

13. Kishimoto, "Some Japanese Cultural Traits ...," p. 115.

14. Clavell grasps this transforming power with clarity and accuracy in a moving passsage in his novel *Shogun: A Novel of Japan* (New York: Atheneum, 1975), p. 452. The English ship's pilot has just learned that an entire village will be put to death unless he learns to speak Japanese in six months. Existential encounters with death are often occurrences for renewed concentration on and enjoyment of everyday activities:

"Mariko leaned over and touched him compassionately. 'Anjin-san, forget the village. A thousand million things can happen before those six months occur. A tidal wave or earthquake, or you get your ship and sail away, or Yabu dies, or we all die, or who knows? Leave the problems of God to God and *karma* to *karma*. Today you're here and nothing you can do will change that. Today you're alive and here and honored, and blessed with good fortune. Look at this sunset, it's beautiful, *neh?* This sunset exists. Tomorrow does not exist. There is only *now*. Please look. It is so beautiful and it will never happen ever again, never, not this sunset, never in all infinity. Lose yourself in it, make yourself one with nature and do not worry about *karma*, yours, mine, or that of the village.'

"He found himself beguiled by her serenity, and by her words. He looked westward. Great splashes of purple-red and black were spreading across the sky.

"He watched the sun until it vanished."

Such transformation of an individual's power of seeing, appreciation, and enjoyment may be discerned in the Zen account of an ordinary person seeing mountains (and other ordinary things) and then, after beginning Zen training, not being able to see the mountains any longer.

After enlightenment, however, the Zen man is able to see the mountains once again. What is only hinted at is that the mountains now speak of the whole, and of the nothingness that underlies and unites all things.

15. Robert S. Hartman, "The Nature of Valuation," p. 20. Spanish version published in *Anuario Humanitas* (Centro de Estudios Humanisticos, Universidad de Nuevo Leon, Monterrq, Mexico), 1968.

16. Kishimoto, "Some Japanese Cultural Traits ...," p. 115.

17. Nishitani Keiji, "What is Religion?," *Philosophical Studies of Japan* (Vol. II, 1960), p. 29.

18. *Ibid.*, p. 30.

19. *Ibid.*, p. 31.

20. Hartman, "The Logic of Value," unpublished manuscript, p. 32. D. T. Suzuki, *Zen Buddhism* (New York: Doubleday, 1956), contains an essay on "The Role of Nature in Zen Buddhism," describing the annihilation of subjective/objective perspectives with considerable point and force: "In Zen there is no such separation between worker [in this case, Ungan who is sweeping the ground] and observer, movement and mover, seer and seen, subject and object. In the case of Ungan, the sweeping and the sweeper and the broom are all one, even including the ground which is being swept" (p. 243).

21. I am indebted to Professor Ohe Seizo, of Nihon University, Tokyo, who proposed the threefold list of basic requirements. In "Toward a More Concrete Ethics," *Personalist*, (Vol. 38, no. 2, Spring 1957), pp. 149-161, Professor Ohe recommended a thought experiment to determine fundamental requirements and necessities if human beings are to function fully as healthy and fulfilled beings.

22. Ohe Seizo, "Toward a More Concrete Ethics", p. 159.

23. *Ibid.*, pp. 158-160.

24. Swedish theologian Anders Nygren (1890-) distinguished *érōs* and *agape*, and saw the latter as the essential and identifying characteristic of Christianity. His principal writings include *Eros and Agape* (1930), *Commentary on Romans* (1944), and *Meaning and Method* (1971).

25. Evelyn Shirk, *The Ethical Dimension: An Approach to the Philosophy of Values and Valuing* (New York: Appleton-Century-Crofts, 1965), p. 237.

26. *Ibid.*, p. 238.

27. Milton Mayeroff, *On Caring* (New York: Harper & Row [Perennial Library], 1971); Nell Noddings, *Caring: A Feminine Approach to Ethics and Moral Education* (Berkeley and Los Angeles: University of California Press, 1984); William Neblett, *The Role of Feelings in Morals* (Washington, D.C.: University Press of America, Inc., 1981); Carol Gilligan, *In a Different Voice* (Cambridge, Mass.: Harvard University Press, 1982); Richard S. Peters, *Reason and Compassion* (London: Routledge and Kegan Paul, 1973).

28. Alasdair MacIntyre, *After Virtue* (Notre Dame, Ind.: University of Notre Dame Press, 1981).

29. Noddings, *Caring*, p. 28.

30. *Ibid.*, p. 30.

31. W. T. Stace, *The Concept of Morals* (New York: Macmillan, 1962), pp. 262-274. Emphasis in original.

32. Neblett, *Role of Feelings*, p. 102.

33. *Ibid.*, p. 9.

34. *Ibid.*, p. 102.

35. *Ibid.*, p. 2.

36. *Ibid.*, p. 239.

37. Ueda Shizuteru, "'Nothingness' in Meister Eckhart and Zen Buddhism," in Frederick Franck, ed., *The Buddha Eye: An Anthology of the Kyoto School* (New York: Crossroad Publishing, 1982), p. 164. Ueda's translation of this sentence is from the foreword to *A Study of Good*, which does not appear in the only English translation presently available. A new translation by Abe Masao and Thomas P. Kasulis will appear shortly.

38. *Ibid.*, p. 161.

39. *Ibid.*

40. *Ibid.*, p. 160.

41. *Ibid.*, p. 163.

42. *Ibid.*, p. 162.

43. *Ibid.*

44. *Ibid.*

BIBLIOGRAPHY

PRIMARY SOURCES IN ENGLISH TRANSLATION

A Study of Good. Tr. V. H. Viglielmo (Tokyo: Japanese Government Printing Bureau, 1960.

"Affective Feeling." Tr. D. A. Dilworth and V. H. Viglielmo, in Yoshihiro Nitta and Tatematsu Hirotaka, eds., *Japanese Phenomenology* (Dordrecht, Holland: D. Reidel Publishing Co., 1978), pp. 223-247.

An Inquiry into the Good , Masao Abe and Christopher Ives, trs.(New Haven: Yale University Press, 1990).

Art and Morality. Tr. D. A. Dilworth and V. H. Viglielmo (Honolulu: University Press of Hawaii [An East-West Center Book], 1973).

"The Forms of Culture of the Classical Periods of East and West as Seen from a Metaphysical Perspective." Tr. D. A. Dilworth, in *Japanese Religions*, Vol. 5, no. 4 (1969) pp. 26-50.

Fundamental Problems of Philosophy. Tr. with Intro. by D. A. Dilworth (Tokyo: Sophia University, 1970).

Intelligibility and the Philosophy of Nothingness. Tr. with Intro. by Robert Schinzinger. (Honolulu: East-West Center Press, 1958).

Intuition and Reflection in Self-Consciousness. Tr. Valdo H. Viglielmo, withTakeuchi Yoshinori and Joseph S. O'Leary (Albany: State University of New York Press, 1987.

Last Writings: Nothingness and the Religious Worldview. Tr. with Intro. by D. A. Dilworth (Honolulu: University of Hawaii Press, 19871

"The Logic of Topos and the Religious Worldview (I)." Tr. Yusa Michiko. *Eastern Buddhist*, Vol. 19, no. 2 (Autumn 1986), pp. 3-29.

"The Problems of Japanese Culture." Tr. Abe Masao in W. T. deBary, *et al.*, eds., *Sources of Japanese Tradition* (New York: Columbia University Press, 1958), pp. 858 - 872.

"Religious Consciousness and the Logic of the Prajñāpāramita Sutra." Tr. D. A. Dilworth, in *Monumenta Nipponica*, Vol. 25, nos.1-2 (1970), pp. 203-216.

"Towards a Philosophy of Religion with the Concept of Pre-Established Harmony as Guide." Tr. D. A. Dilworth, *Eastern Buddhist*, Vol. III, no.1 (1970), pp. 19-46.

I have also benefited greatly from a number of translations in manuscript form, either unpublished or in press, generously supplied by Prof. David A.Dilworth of S.U.N.Y. at Stony Brook, including the following Nishida Kitarō writings:

"Active Intuition," 1937 [Nishida Kitarō Zenshū, Vol. 8, pp. 541-571].

"The Self-Determining Historical World," 1937 (*Nishida Kitarō Zenshū*, Vol. 8, pp. 572 ff).

"The World as Dialectical Universal," 1935 (*Nishida Kitarō Zenshū,*, Vol. 8, pp. 2129-2168).

"The World as Identity of Absolute Contradiction," 1939 (*Nishida Kitarō Zenshū,*, Vol. 9, pp. 305-335.)

SECONDARY SOURCES

Abe, Masao. "God, Emptiness and the True Self," *Eastern Buddhist,* Vol. II, no. 2 (Oct. 1969), pp. 15 - 30.

_____. "'Inverse Correspondence' in the Philosophy of Nishida: The Emergence of the Notion." *International Philosophical Quarterly,* Vol. 32, no. 3 (September 1992), pp. 325-344.

_____. "The Logic of Absolute Nothingness, As Expounded by Nishida Kitarō." *Eastern Buddhist,* Vol. 28, no. 2 (Autumn 1995), pp. 167-74.

_____. "Nishida's Philosophy of 'Place,'" unpublished manuscript. This paper was originally published in a Japanese philosophical journal, *Riso,* No. 541, June 1978. The English manuscript edition is translated by Christopher A. Ives.

_____. "Non-being and *Mu*: The Metaphysical Nature of Negativity in the East and the West." *Religious Studies,* Vol. II (June 1975). Reprinted in Abe Masao, *Zen and Western Thought,* ed. William R. LaFleur (Honolulu: University of Hawaii Press, 1985), pp. 121-134.

_____. *Zen and Western Thought,* ed. William R. LaFleur (Honolulu: University of Hawaii Press, 1985).

Aiken, Robert. *A Zen Wave: Basho's Haiku and Zen* (New York: Weatherhill, 1978).

_____. *The Mind of Clover: Essays in Zen Buddhist Ethics* (San Francisco: North Point Press, 1984).

_____. *Taking the Path of Zen* (San Francisco: North Point Press, 1982).

Anshen, Ruth Nanda, ed. *Moral Principles of Action; Man's Ethical Imperative* (New York: Harper and Brothers, 1952).

Arima Tatsuo. "Nishida Kitarō: The Epistemological Character of Taisho Japan," in *The Failure of Freedom: A Portrait of Modern Japanese Intellectuals* (Cambridge, Mass.: Harvard University Press, 1969), pp. 7-14.

Aristotle. *The Basic Works of Aristotle,* ed. Richard McKeon (New York: Random House, 1941).

_____. *The Ethics of Aristotle,* tr. J. A. K. Thomson (Baltimore: Penguin Books, 1953).

Axtell, G.S. "Comparative Dialectics: Nishida Kitarō's Logic of Place and Western Dialectical Thought." *Philosophy East a West,* Vol. 41, no. 2 (1991), pp. 163-184.

Bahm, Archie, J. "The Aesthetics of Organicism." *Journal of Aesthetics and Art Criticism*, Vol. 26, no. 4 (Summer 1968), pp. 449-459.

_____. "Axiology as an Inductive Science." *Journal of Human Relations*, Vol. 21, no. 1 (first quarter, 1973), pp. 81-90.

_____. "Four Kinds of Intrinsic Value." *Darshana International*, Vol. 5 (July 1965), pp. 22-31.

Barthes, Roland. *Empire of Signs*, tr. Richard Howard (New York: Hill & Wang, 1982).

deBary, Wllliam Theodore, ed. *The Buddhist Tradition in India, China and Japan* (New York: Vintage Books, 1972).

Bellah, Robert N. *Beyond Belief* (New York: Harper & Row, 1970).

Benoit, H. *Let Go!: Theory and Practice of Detachment According to Zen*, tr. Albert W. Low (New York: Samuel Weiser, 1973).

_____. *The Supreme Doctrine: Psychological Studies in Zen Thought* (New York: Viking Press, 1979).

Brear, A. D. "The Nature and Status of Moral Behavior in Zen Buddhist Tradition." *Philosophy East and West*, Vol. 24, no. 4 (Oct. 1974), pp. 429-441.

Caputo, John D. *The Mystical Element in Heidegger's Thought* (New York: Fordham University Press, 1986).

_____. *Radical Hermeneutics: Repetition, Deconstruction, and the Hermeneutic Project* (Bloomington: Indiana Universiq Press, 1987).

Carter, Robert E. "Contemporary Value Theory: An Inquiry into the Notion of 'Intrinsic Value' in Contemporary Western and Japanese Philosophy." *Journal of Value Inquiry*, Vol. 13, no. 1 (Spring 1979), pp. 33-56.

_____. *Dimensions of Moral Education* (Toronto: University of Toronto Press, 1984).

_____. "The Nothingness Beyond God." *Eastern Buddhist*, Vol. 28, no. 1 (Spring 1985), pp. 120 - 130.

_____. "Toward a Philosophy of Zen Buddhism: Prolegomena to an Understanding of Zen Experience and Nishida's 'Logic of Place.'" *Eastern Buddhist*, Vol. 13, no. 2 (Autumn 1980), pp. 127-130.

Cassirer, Ernst. *Language and Myth*, tr. Susanne K. Langer (New York: Dover Publications, 1946).

Chang, Chung-yuan. *Original Teachings of Ch'an Buddhism* (New York: Pantheon Books, 1969).

_____. *Tao: A New Way of Thinking* (a translation of the Tao Te Ching with an Introduction and Commentaries) (New York: Harper & Row, [Perennial Library], 1977).

Chang, Garma C. *The Buddhist Teaching of Totality: The Philosophy of Hwa Yen Buddhism* (Harrisburg, Pa.: Pennsylvania State University Press, 1971).

Cheng, Chung-Ying. "On Zen (Ch'an) Language and Zen Paradoxes." *Journal of Chinese Philosophy*, Vol. 1, no. 1 (Dec. 1973), pp. 77-102.

Clavell, James. *Shogun: A Novel of Japan* (New York: Atheneum, 1985).

Cleary, Thomas F. Entry into the *Inconceivable: An Introduction to Hua-Yen Buddhism* (Honolulu: University of Hawaii Press, 1983).

_____ and J. C. Cleary, trs. *The Blue Cliff Record*, 3 vols. (Boulder: Shambhala Publications Inc., 1977).

_____, tr. *Shōbōgenzō: Zen Essays by Dōgen* (Honolulu: University of Hawaii Press, 1986).

Conze, Edward. *Buddhism: Its Essence and Development* (New York: Harper & Brothers, 1951).

Cook, Francis Dojun. *How to Raise an Ox: Zen Practice as Taught in Zen Master Dōgen's Shōbōgenzō* (Los Angeles: Center Publications, 1978).

Delenze, Gilles and Guattari, Felix. *Capitalisme et Schizophrenie: Milles Plateaux* (Paris: les éditions de Minuit, 1980). An English translation is forthcoming from the University of Minnesota Press, entitled *A Thousand Plateaus*, tr. Brian Massumi.

Deshimaru, Jean Taisen, *The Zen Way to the Martial Arts*, Nancy Amphoux, tr. (New York: Arkana, Published by the Penguin Group, 1991).

Dilworth, David A. "The Initial Formations of 'Pure Experience' in Nishida Kitarō and William James." *Monumenta Nipponica*, Vol. 24, nos. 1-2 (1969), pp. 93-111.

_____. "Nishida and Whitehead," unpublished manuscript.

_____. "Nishida's Early Pantheistic Voluntarism." *Philosophy East and West*, Vol. 20, no. 1 (1970), pp. 409-421.

_____. "Nishida's Final Essay: The Logic of Place and a Religious Worldview." *Philosophy East and West*, Vol. 20, no. 4 (1970), pp. 355-367.

_____. "Nishida Kitarō's "Philosophy of the Tópos of Nothingness as the Negative Space of Experiential Immediacy." *International Philosophical Quarterly* (1973), pp. 463-483.

_____. "The Phenomenology and Logic of Interpresence in Watsuji Tetsurō and Nishida Kitarō." *Studies on Japanese Culture*, Vol. 2 (1973), pp. 112-121.

_____. "Philosophical Texts as World Texts: A Comparative Hermeneutical Analysis," unpublished manuscript.

_____. "The Concrete World of Action in Nishida's Later Thought." In Nitta Yoshihiro and Tatematsu Hirotaka, eds., *Japanese Phenomenology* (Dordrecht, Holland: D. Reidel Publishing Co., 1978), pp. 249-270.

_____. "The Range of Nishida's Early Religious Thought." *Philosophy East and West*, Vol. 19, no. 4 (1969), pp. 409-421.

Dumoulin, Heinrich. *A History of Zen Buddhism* (Boston: Beacon Press, 1963).

_____. *Christianity Meets Buddhism*, tr. John C. Miraldo (LaSalle, IL: Open Court Publishing Co. 1974).

_____, and John C. Maraldo, eds. *The Cultural, Political, and Religious Significance of Buddhism in the Modern World* (New York: Collier Books, 1976).

_____. *Zen Buddhism in the 20th Century* (New York: Weatherhill, Inc., 1992).

_____. *Zen Enlightenment: Origins and Meaning*, tr. John C. Maraldo (New York: Weatherill, 1976).

von Durckheim, Karlfried Graf. *Hara: The Vital Centre of Man*, tr. Sylvia Monica von Kospoth (London: Mandala Books, Unwin Paperbacks, 1977).

Edwards, Paul, ed. *The Encyclopedia of Philosophy*. (New York: Macmillan, and the Free Press, 1967).

Feenberg, Andrew, and Arisaka, Yoko. "Experiential Ontology: The Origins of the Nishida Philosophy in the Doctrine of Pure Experience." *International Philosophical Quarterly*, Vol. 30, no. 2 (June 1990), pp. 173-205.

Flay, Joseph C. "Experience, Nature, and Place," *The Monist*, Vol. 68, no. 4 (Oct. 1985), pp. 467-80.

_____. "Pure Experience Revisited," unpublished manuscript. This paper was read before the Society for the Advancement of American Philosophy.

Fox, Douglas A. *The Vagrant Lotus: An Introduction to Buddhist Philosophy* (Philadelphia: The Westminster Press, 1973).

_____. "Zen and Ethics, Dōgen's Synthesis." *Philosophy East and West*, Vol. 21, no. 1 Jan. 1971), pp. 33-41.

Franck, Frederick. *The Buddha Eye: An Anthology of the Kyoto School* (New York: Crossroad Publishing, 1982).

Fromm, Erich, Daisetz Suzuki, and Richard de Martino. *Zen Buddhism and Psychoanalysis* (New York: Harper & Row, 1960).

Fung Yu-lan. *A Short History of Chinese Philosophy* (New York: The Free Press, 1966).

Gilligan, Carol. *In a Different Voice* (Cambridge, Mass.: Harvard University Press, 1982).

Gray, Wallace. "Mu and Pneuma: A Projective Comparison of Kitarō Nishida and Nels Ferre." *Asian Profile*, Vol. 1, no. 1 (1973), pp. 171-184.

_____. "The Shock of the Universal." *Asian Profile*, Vol. 2, no.2 (1974), pp. 219-255.

Grene, Marjorie. *A Portrait of Aristotle* (London: Faber & Faber, Ltd., 1963).

Hartman, Robert S. "The Logic of Value," *Review of Metaphysics*, Vol. XIV, no. 3 (Mar. 1961), pp. 389-432.

Haver, William. "Thinking the thought of that which is strictly speaking unthinkable: On the thematization of alterity in Nishida-philosophy." *Human Studies*, Vol. 16 (1993), pp. 177-192.

Hearn, Lafcadio. *Kokoro: Hints and Echoes of Japanese Inner Life* (Rutland, Vermont: Charles E. Tuttle Co., 1972).

Heidegger, Martin. *Discourse on Thinking*, tr. John M. Anderson and E. Hans Freund (New York: Harper & Row, 1959).

_____. *On the Way to Language*, tr. Peter d. Hertz (San Francisco: Harper & Row, 1971).

Heine, Steven. *Existential and Ontological Dimensions of Time in Heidegger and Dōgen* (Albany: State University Press of New York, 1985).

Heisig, James, & Maraldo, John C., eds. *Rude Awakenings: Zen. the Kyoto School. & the Question of Nationalism* (Honolulu: University of Hawaili Press, 1995).

Herrigel, Eugen. *The Method of Zen* (London: Routledge and Kegan Paul, 1960).

_____. *Zen in the Art of Archery* (New York: Vintage Books, 1971).

Hirai Tomio. *Zen and the Mind* (Tokyo: Japan Publications, Inc., 1978).

Hisamatsu Shin'ichi. *Zen and the Fine Arts* (Tokyo: Kodansha, 1971).

_____. "Characteristics of Oriental Nothingness." *Philosophical Studies of Japan*, Vol. 2 (Tokyo: Japan Society for Promotion of Science, 1960), pp. 65-97.

Hoover, Thomas. *Zen Culture* (New York: Vintage Books, 1978).

_____. *The Zen Experience* (New York: New American Library, 1980).

Huh, Woo-Sung. "A Critical Exposition of Nishida's Philosophy." Ph. D. Dissertation, University of Hawaii, 1988 (Ann Arbor: University Microfilms International).

_____. "The Philosophy of History in the 'Later' Nishida: A Philosophic Turn." *Philosophy East and West*, Vol. 40, no. 3 (July 1990), pp. 343-374.

Inada, Kenneth. *Nāgārjuna: A Translation of His Mulamadhyamakakarika with an Introductory Essay* (Tokyo: The Hokuseidō Press, 1970).

_____. "Some Basic Misconceptions of Buddhism." *International Philosophical Quarterly* (1969), pp. 101-119.

_____. "The Metaphysics of Buddhist Experience and Whiteheadian Encounter." *Philosophy East and West*, Vol. 25 (1975), pp. 465-488.

Ino, Norimoto. "Dōgen's Zen View of Interdependence." *Philosophy East and West*, Vol. 12 (Apr. 1962), pp. 51-57. Ives, Christopher. *Zen Awakening and Society* (Honolulu: University of Hawaii Press, 1992).

Izutsu Toshihiko. *The Structure of Selfhood in Zen Buddhism* (Zurich: Rhein Verlag, 1971).

_____. *Towards a Philosophy of Zen Buddhism* (Tehran: Imperial Iranian Academy of Philosophy, 1977).

Jacobson, Nolan Pliny. *Buddhism & the Contemporary World: Change and Self-Correction* (Carbondale: Southern Illinois University Press, 1983).

_____. *Buddhism: The Religion of Analysis* (Carbondale: Southern Illinois University Press, 1966).

_____. *Understanding Buddhism* (Carbondale: Southern Illinois University Press, 1986).

James, William. *Essays in Radical Empiricism* (Cambridge, Mass.: Harvard University Press, 1976).

_____. *Pragmatism, and Four Essays from The Meaning of Truth*, ed. R. B. Perry (New York: A Meridan Book, New American Library, 1955 [first published in 1909]).

_____. *The Principles of Psychology*, 2 vols. (New York: Dover Publications, Inc., 1950 [first published in 1890]).

_____. *Some Problems of Philosophy* (London: Longmans, Green and Co., 1948).

_____. *The Varieties of Religious Experience* (New York: Modern Library, 1902).

Kalupahana, David J. *Buddhist Philosophy: A Historical Analysis* (Honolulu: The University Press of Hawaii, 1976).

_____. *Nāgārjuna: The Philosophy of the Middle Way* (Albany: State University of New York Press, 1986).

Kapleau, Philip, ed. *The Three Pillars of Zen: Teaching, Practice and Enlightenment* (New York: Harper & Row, 1966).

_____, ed. *The Wheel of Death: A Collection of Writings from Zen Buddhist and Other Sources on Death—Rebirth—Dying* (New York: Harper & Row, 1971).

_____. *Zen: Dawn in the West* (Garden City: Anchor Books, 1979).

Kasulis, Thomas. "The Two Strands of Nothingness." *International Philosophical Quarterly*, Vol. 19, no. 1 (Mar. 1979), pp. 61-72.

_____. *Self as Body in Asian Theory and Practice* (Albany: State University of New York Press, 1993).

_____. "The Kyoto School and the West: Review and Evaluation." *Eastern Buddhist*, Vol. 15, no. 2 (1982), pp. 125-144.

_____. *Zen Action/Zen Person* (Honolulu: The University Press of Hawaii, 1981).

_____. "Zen Buddhism, Freud and Jung." *Eastern Buddhist*, Vol. 10, no. 1 (May 1977), pp. 68-91.

Katz, Steven T., ed. *Mysticism and Philosophical Analysis* (London: Sheldon Press, 1978).

Kim, Ha Tai. "The Logic of the Illogical: Zen and Hegel." *Philosophy East and West*, Vol. V (1955-56), pp. 19-29.

Kim, Hee-Jin. *Dōgen Kigen—Mystical Realist* (Tucson: University of Arizona Press, 1975).

_____, tr. *Flowers of Emptiness: Selections from Dōgen's Shōbōgenzō* (Lewiston, N.Y.: The Edwin Mellen Press, 1980).

Kishimoto Hideo. "Some Japanese Cultural Traits and Religions." In Charles A. Moore, ed. *The Japanese Mind: Essentials of Japanese Philosophy and Culture* (Honolulu: East-West Center Press, University of Hawaii, 1967), pp. 110-121.

_____. "The Immediacy of Zen Experience and Its Cultural Background," *Philosophical Studies of Japan*, Vol. III (1961), pp. 25-32.

Knauth, Lothar. "Life is Tragic: The Diary of Nishida Kitarō." *Monumenta Nipponica*, Vol. 20, nos. 3-4 (1965), pp. 335-358.

Knuuttila, Simo, and Jaakko Hintikka. *The Logic of Being* (Dordrecht, Holland: D. Reidel Publishing Co., 1986).

Kodera Takashi James. *Dōgen's Formative Years in China* (London: Routledge & Kegan Paul, 1980).

Kreeft, Peter. "Zen in Heidegger's *Gelassenheit.*" *International Philosophical Quarterly*, Vol. 11 (Dec. 1971), pp. 521-545.

LaFleur, William R., ed. *Dōgen Studies* (Honolulu: University of Hawaii Press, Studies in East Asian Buddhism, no. 2, 1985).

Lao Tzu, *Tao Te Ching*, tr. D.C. Lau (New York: Penguin Books, 1963). *Tao Te Ching*, tr. Lin Yutang (New York: Modern Library, 1948).

_____. *The Way of Life*, tr. Witter Bynner (New York: Capricorn Books, 1962).

Leggett, Trevor. *Zen and the Ways* (Boulder: Shambhala Publications, Inc., 1980).

Linssen, Robert. *Living Zen*, tr. Diana Abrahams-Curiel (New York: Grove Press, 1958).

MacIntyre, Alasdair. *After Virtue* (Notre Dame, Ind.: Notre Dame University Press, 1981).

Maezum Hakuyu Taizan, and Bernard Tetsugen Glassman. *The Hazy Moon of Enlightenment* (Los Angeles: Center Publications, 1978).

Magliola, Robert. *Derrida on the Mend* (West Lafayette, Indiana: Purdue University Press, 1984).

Maraldo, John C. "Translating Nishida." *Philosophy East and West*, Vol. 39 (October 1989), pp. 465-496.

_____. "The Problem of World Culture: Towards an Appropriation of Nishida's Philosophy of Nation and Culture." *Eastern Buddhist*, Vol. 28, no. 2 (Autumn 1995), pp. 183-97.

Maitland, Thomas H., Jr., *The Metaphysics of William James and John Dewey* (New York: Philosophical Library, 1963).

Mayeroff, Milton. *On Caring* (New York: Harper and Row [Perennial Library], 1971).

Merton, Thomas. *Mystics and Zen Masters* (New York: Delta, 1967).

_____. *Zen and the Birds of Appetite* (New York: New Directions, 1968).

Miura Isshū, and Ruth Fuller Sasaki. *Zen Dust* (New York: Harcourt, Brace & World, 1966).

_____. *The Zen Koan: Its History and Use in Rinzai Zen* (New York: Harcourt, Brace & World [A Helen and Kurt Wolf Book], 1965).

Moore, Charles A., ed. *The Japanese Mind* (Honolulu: An East-West Center Book, The University Press of Hawaii, 1967).

Moore, Edward C. *William James* (New York: Washington Square Press, 1966).

Muraoka Tsunetsugu. *Studies in Shintō Thought*, tr. D. M. Brown and J. T. Araki (Tokyo: Japanese National Commission for UNESCO, Ministry of Education, 1964).

Murti, T. R. V. *The Central Philosophy of Buddhism* (London: George Allen & Unwin, 1960).

Nakamura Hajime. "The Basic Teachings of Buddhism," in *The Cultural, Political, and Religious Significance of Buddhism in the Modern World*, Heinrich Dumoulin and John C. Maraldo, eds. (New York: Collier Books, 1976), pp. 3 - 31.

_____. *Buddhism in Comparative Light* (New Delhi: Islam and the Modern Age Society, 1975).

_____. "Interrelational Existence." *Philosophy East and West*, Vol. 17, nos. 1-4 (1967), pp. 107-112.

_____. *Parallel Developments. A Comparative History of Ideas* (Tokyo, New York: Kōdansha, 1975).

_____. *Ways of Thinking of Eastern Peoples: India-China-Tibet-Japan* (Honolulu: East-West Center, 1964).

Naranjo, Claudio and Robert E. Ornstein. *On the Psychology of Meditation* (New

Neblett, William. *The Role of Feelings in Morals* (Washington, D.C.: University Press of America, Inc., 1981).

Nishitani Keiji. "Nihilism and Śūnyatā," *Eastern Buddhist*, Vol. IV, no. 2 (1971), pp. 30-49.

_____. "The Personal and the Impersonal in Religion," *Eastern Buddhist*, Vol. III, no. 1 (1970), pp. 1 - 18; Vol. III, no. 2 (1970), pp. 71 - 88.

_____. *Religion and Nothingness*, tr. Jan Van Bragt (Berkeley and Los Angeles: University of California Press, 1982).

_____. "The Awakening of Self in Buddhism," *Eastern Buddhist*, Vol. I, no. 2 (1966), pp. 1-11.

_____. "Two Addresses by Martin Heidegger," *Eastern Buddhist*, Vol. I, no. 2 (Sept. 1968), pp. 48-77.

_____. "What is Religion?" *Philosophical Studies of Japan*, Vol.2 (1960), pp. 21-64.

Noda Matao. "East-West Synthesis in Kitarō Nishida." *Philosophy East and West*, Vol. 4, no. 4 (Apr. 1954-Jan. 1955), pp. 345-359.

Noddings, Nell. *Caring: A Feminine Approach to Ethics and Moral Education* (Berkeley and Los Angeles: University of California Press, 1984).

Odin, Steve. *Process Metaphysics and Hua-Yen Buddhism: A Critical Study of Cumulative Penetration vs. Interpenetration* (Albany: State University of New York Press, 1982).

Ohe, Seizo. "Toward a More Concrete Ethics." *Personalist*, Vol. 38, no. 2 (Spring 1957), pp. 149 - 161.

Otto, Rudolf. *Mysticism East and West* (London: Macmillan, 1932).

Owens, Joseph, C.Ss.R. "Aristotle's Notion of Wisdom." *Apeiron*, Vol. 3 (1987), pp. 1-16.

_____. *The Doctrine of Being in the Aristotelian Metaphysics* (Toronto: Pontifical Institute of Mediaeval Studies, 1951).

Panikkar, Raimundo. "Nirvana and the Awareness of the Absolute," in *The God Experience*, tr. T. Whelan (New York: Newman Press, 1971), pp. 82-99.

Peerenboom, R.P. "The Religious Foundations of Nishida's Philosophy." *Asian Philosophy*, Vol. 1, no. 2 (1991), pp. 161-173.

Perry, Ralph Barton. *The Thought and Character of William James*, 2 vols. (Boston: Little, Brown & Co., 1935).

Peters, Richard S. *Reason and Compassion* (London: Routledge & Kegan Paul, 1973).

Piovesana, Gino. "The Philosophy of Nishida Kitarō, 1870-1945." *Recent Japanese Philosophical Thought*, 1862-1962: A Survey (Tokyo: Sophia University Press, 1968).

Piper, R. F. "Nishida, Notable Japanese Personalist." *Personalist*, Vol. 17, no. 1 (1936), pp. 21-31.

Plato. *Collected Dialogues*, ed. Edith Hamilton and Huntington Cairns, (New York: Bollingen Foundation, 1963).

Randall, John Herman, Jr. *Aristotle* (New York: Columbia University Press, 1960).

Reps, Paul, comp. *Zen Flesh, Zen Bones: A Collection of Zen and Pre-Zen Writings* (New York: Doubleday [Anchor Books], 1961).

Reynolds, David K. *Morita Psychotherapy* (Berkeley: University of California Press, 1976).

_____. *Playing Ball on Running Water* (New York: Quill, 1984).

_____. *The Quiet Therapies* (Honolulu: University Press of Hawaii, 1980).

_____. *Water Bears No Scars: Japanese Lifeways for Personal Growth* (New York: William Morrow, 1987).

Rosemont, Henry, Jr. "The Meaning is the Use: *Koan* and *Mondo* as Linguistic Tools of Zen Masters." *Philosophy East and West*, Vol. 20 (Apr. 1970), pp. 109-119.

Ross, Nancy Wilson. *The World of Zen: An East-West Anthology* (New York: Vmtage Books, 1980).

Seigfried, Charlene H. *Chaos and Context: A Study in William James* (Athens, Ohio: Ohio University Press, 1978).

Shaner, David Edward. *The Bodymind Experience in Japanese Buddhism* (Albany: State University of New York Press, 1984).

Shaner, David Edward and Duval, R. Shannon. "Conservation Ethics and the Japanese Intellectual Tradition." *Environmental Ethics*, Vol. 11 (Fall, 1989), pp. 197-214.

Shibata, M. "The Diary of a Zen Layman: The Philosopher Nishida Kitarō." *Eastern Buddhist*, Vol. 14, no. 2 (19811 pp. 121-131.

Shibayama Zenkie, tr. and intro. *Zen Comments on the Mumonkan* (New York: New American Library [Mentor], 1974).

Shigematsu Soiku. *A Zen Forest: Sayings of the Masters* (New York: Weatherhill, 1981).

Shimomura Torataro. "Nishida Kitarō and Some Aspects of His Philosophy." In *A Study of Good* [by Nishida Kitarō], tr. V. H. Viglielmo (Tokyo: Japanese Government Printing Bureau, 1960), pp. 191-217.

Shirk, Evelyn. *The Ethical Dimension: An Approach to the Philosophy of Value and Valuing* (New York: Appleton-Century-Crofts, 1965).

Soseki, Natsume. *Kokoro* (Tokyo: Charles E. Tuttle Co., 1957).

Spae, Joseph J. *Buddhist-Christian Empathy* (Chicago: The Chicago Institute of Theology and Culture; Tokyo: Oriens Institute for Religious Research, 1980).

Sprung, Mervyn. *Lucid Exposition of the Middle Way* (London: Routledge & Kegan Paul, 1979).

Stace, W. T. *Mysticism and Philosophy* (London: Macmillan, 1961).

_____. *The Concept of Morals* (New York: Macmillan, 1962).

Stcherbatsky, Th. *Buddhist Logic* (Osnabruck, W. Germany: Bilio Verlag, 1970).

_____. *The Central Conception of Buddhism* (Calcutta: Sisil Gupta (India) Ltd., 1923).

Streng, Frederick J. *Emptiness—A Study in Religious Meaning* (Nashville: Abingdon Press, 1967).

Suzuki Daisetz Teitaro. *An Introduction to Zen Buddhism* (New York: Grove Press, 1964).

_____. *Essays in Zen Buddhism*, 3 vols. (London: Rider & Company, 1953).

_____. *The Field of Zen* (New York: Harper & Row [Perennial Library], 1969).

_____. *Japanese Spirituality*, tr. Norman Waddell (Tokyo: Japan Society for the Promotion of Science, 1969).

_____. *Manual of Zen Buddhism* (London: Rider & Co., 1950).

_____. *Mysticism: Christian and Buddhist* (New York: Harper & Brothers, 1947).

_____. *Outlines of Mahāyāna Buddhism* (New York: Shocken Books, 1963).

_____. *Shin Buddhism: Japan's Major Religious Contribution to the West* (London: George Allen & Unwin, 1970).

_____. *Studies in Zen*, ed. Christman Humphreys (London: The Buddhist Society, Rider Publishers, 1957).

_____. *The Awakening of Zen*, ed. Christman Humphreys (Boulder: Prajna Press, 1980).

_____, and Ueda Shizuteru. "The Sayings of Rinzai." *Eastern Buddhist*, Vol. VI, no. 1 (May 1973), pp. 92-110.

_____. *Sengai, The Zen Master* (Greenwich, Conn.: New York Graphic Society, 1971).

_____. *The Training of the Zen Buddhist Monk* (Berkeley: Wingbow Press, 1974).

_____. *The Zen Doctrine of No-Mind: The Significance of the Sutra of HuiNeng (Wei-Lang)* (London: Rider & Co., 1959).

_____. *Zen and Japanese Buddhism* (Tokyo: Japan Travel Bureau, Inc., 1973).

_____. *Zen and Japanese Culture* (Princeton: Princeton University Press [Bollingen Paperback], 1970).

_____. *Zen Buddhism: Selected Writings of D. T. Suzuki,* ed. William Barrett (Garden City: Doubleday [Anchor Books], 1957).

_____. *Zen Mind, Beginner's Mind,* ed. Trudy Dixon (New York: Weatherhill, 1970).

Tachibana, S. *The Ethics of Buddhism* (London: Curzon Press [Barnes & Noble Books], 1975).

Takeda Hiromichi. "Nishida's Doctrine of Universals," *Monumenta Nipponica,* Vol. 23, nos. 3 - 4 (1960), pp. 497 - 502.

Takeuchi Yoshinori. "Nishida's Philosophy as Representative of Japanese Philosophy." In *Encyclopaedia Britannica* (1966), Vol. 12, pp. 958-962.

_____. *The Heart of Buddhism: In Search of the Timeless Spirit of Primitive Buddhism* (New York: Crossroad Publishing, 1983).

_____. "The Philosophy of Nishida Kitarō." *Japanese Religions,* Vol. 3, no. 4 (1963), pp. 1-32.

Tanabe Hajime. *Philosophy as Metanoetics,* tr. Takeuchi Yoshinori (Berkeley: University of California Press, 1986).

Tanahashi Kazuaki. *Moon in a Dewdrop: Writings of Zen Master Dōgen* (San Francisco: North Point Press, 1985).

Tillich, Paul, and Shin'ichi Hisamatsu. "Dialogue, East & West. Paul Tillich and Hisamatsu Shin'ichi," *Eastern Buddhist* (1971), pp.89-107; (1972), pp. 107-128; (1973), pp. 87-114.

Tillich, Paul. *Systematic Theology.* 3 vols. (Chicago: University of Chicago Press, 1951-1963).

_____. *The Courage to Be* (New Haven: Yale University Press, 1952).

Tu Wei-Ming. *Confucian Thought: Selfhood as Creative Transformation* (Albany: State University of New York Press, 1985).

Ueda Shizuteru. "Des 'Nicht' bei Meister Eckhart und im Zen-Buddhismus unter besonderer Berucksichtigung des Granzbereiches von Theologie und Philosophie," in *Transzendenz und Immanenz, Philosophie und Theologie in der veranderten Welt,* D. Papenfuss, & J. Soring, eds. (Stuttgart: Kohlhammer, 1976), pp. 257-266.

_____. "Emptiness and Fullness: Śūnyatā in Mahāyāna Buddhism." *Eastern Buddhist,* Vol. XV, no. 1 (Spring 1982), pp. 9-37.

_____. "Pure Experience, Self-Awareness, 'Basho'." *Etudes Phenomenologicrues* (Editions Ousia: Bruxelles), no. 18 (1993), pp. 63-86.

_____. "The Difficulty of Understanding Nishida's Philosophy." Eastern Buddhist, Vol. 28, no. 2 (Autumn 1995), pp. 175-82.

Viglielmo, V. H. "Nishida Kitarō: The Early Years." In Donald Shively, ea., *Tradition and Modernism in Japanese Culture*. (Princeton: Princeton University Press, 1971), pp. 507-562.

Waldenfels, Hans. "Absolute Nothingness: Preliminary Considerations on a Central Notion in the Philosophy of Nishida Kitarō and the Kyoto School." *Monumenta Nipponica*, Vol. 21, nos. 3-4 (1966), pp. 354-391.

_____. *Absolute Nothingness*. (New York: Paulist Press, 1980).

Wargo, Robert Joseph. *The Logic of Basho and the Concept of Nothingness in the Philosophy of Nishida Kitarō*. Ph.D. Dissertation, University of Michigan, 1972 (Ann Arbor: University Microfilm International).

Watson, Walter. *The Architectonics of Meaning: Foundations of the New Pluralism* (Albany: State University of New York Press, 1985).

Watsuji Tetsurō. *Climate and Culture: A Philosophical Study*, tr. Geoffrey Bownas (Ministry of Education, Japan, The Hokuseidō Press, 1961).

_____. "The Significance of Ethics as the Study of Man," tr. D. A. Dilworth. *Monumenta Nipponica*, Vol. 26, nos. 3-4 (1971), pp. 395-413.

Wheelwright, Philip. *Heraclitus* (New York: Atheneum, 1964).

Wienpahl, Paul. *Zen Diary* (New York: Harper & Row, 1970).

Wilber, Ken. *Eye to Eye: The Quest for the New Paradigm* (New York: Doubleday, 1983).

_____. *No Boundary: Eastern and Western Approaches to Personal Growth* (Los Angeles: Center Publications, 1979).

_____. *The Spectrum of Consciousness* (Wheaton, IL.: Quest Books, 1977).

Woods, Richard, ed. *Understanding Mysticism* (New York: Image Books, 1980).

Yokoi Yūhō. *Zen Master Dōgen: An Introduction with Selected Writings* (New York: Weatherhill, 1976).

Yuasa Yasuo. *The Body: Toward an Eastern Mind-Body Theory*, ed. Thomas P. Kasulis, tr. Nagatomo Shigenori and Thomas P. Kasulis (Albany: State University of New York Press, 1987).

Yusa Michiko. *"Persona Originalis": "Jinkaku" and "Personne," According to the Philosophies of Nishida Kitaro and Jacques Maritain*. Ph.D. Dissertation, University of California at Santa Barbara, 1983 (Ann Arbor: University Microfilms International).

_____. "Nishida in Translation: Primary Sources in Western Languages." *Eastern Buddhist*, Vol. 28, no. 2 (Autumn 1995), pp. 297-302.

_____. "Reflections on Nishida Studies." *Eastern Buddhist*, Vol. 28, no. 2 (Autumn 1995), pp. 287-96.

INDEX

Abe Masao, 35; on distinguishing Nothingness from Christian God, 85; monistic principle of, 82-83; on ultimate reality, 88

aboriginal sensible muchness, 56

absolute: *télos* of, 154; things as, 54-55; and compassion, 153

absolute nothingness, *xvi*, 44-47, 60-61; and emptying, 98-99; and mirroring, 78-79. *See also* nothingness

abstract universals, 33

act-deontology, 168-169

acting intuition (*see kōiteki chokkan*), *xiv, xvi*

action intuition, 120-121, 125; Herrigal on, 191-192n16; introduced, 104; model of, 126; as ordinary, 107

action understanding, 123

aesthetic values, 41-42

affective feeling, 87

"Affective Feeling" (Nishida), 38-39

After Virtue (MacIntyre), 169

agape, 122; vs. desire, 167; ethics of, 150 as spiritual embrace, 137

agapist, behaviour of, 150-152

altruism, 141, 196-197n34

Amida, 151-152; in True Pure Land teaching, 157-158

anandism, 200n8

anātman, 95

Anaximander, 53

Anglo-American ethical theory, 150-151

Anselm, St., 135

antinomies, of Kant, 63, 93-94

ápeiron, 53

apperception, as reality, 6

arche, 115

archery, 106

archic elements, *xxii*

archic intuition, *125*

Archimedean point, 124

Aristotle, *xxii*, 17; approach to knowledge of, 21-24; and grammatical subject, 59; individual substance, 100-101; and language, 20; logic, 111-113; per Nishida, 20, 30-31; vs. Nishida, 54-57; on predication, 22-23

artistic intuition, 42

Augustine, St., 85-86

awareness, 84, 114

Bahm, Archie, 163

basho (place), *xiv*; as absolute, 126-127; of being, *xv*; as bright opening, 116; defined, 30-31, 32; final, 102-103, 115; of relative nothingness, *xv*

beauty, 39, 41-42

behavior, Brear on, 197-198n49

behaving self, 45

being, as understanding, 81; as starting point, 109

Blessed Land of Enlightenment, 139

Body: Toward and Eastern Mind Body Theory, The (Yuasa), *xiv*

body-mind: oneness of, 107

Brear, A.D., 112, 197-98*n*49

Brothers Karamazov, The (Dostoevsky), 160-161

Buber, Martin, 176

Buddhahood, 50-51, 53

Buddha-nature, impermanence of, 156-157

Buddhism: Eightfold path of, 129-130; "scandal" of, 129; ultimate goal of, 129

Buddhist tradition, 162; background, 102

Buddhist utterance, paradox of, *xxiii*

budō (martial arts), 106-107, 125-126

Candrakīti, 64

Caring, A Feminine Approach to Ethics and Moral Education (Noddings), 169

Cassirer, Ernst, 164

cause and effect, 43-44

change, 22-23, 58-59, 191fn10; and moral life, 171; and time, 35

Cheng, Chung-Ying, 50-51; an non-attachment, 52

China, Japan's defeat of, *xi*

Chinese, as pragmatists, 18-19

Christ-figure *(Brothers Karamazov)*, 160-161

Christian, 121

Chuang Tzu, 112; Wing-Tsit Chan on, 193n39

circumsessional interpenetration, 89

citizen(s), 101-02

Collingwood, R.G., *x*

compassion, 139-144, *passim*, 149, 158-159; in Buddhist ethics, 142; cosmic, 124

conception, and reality, 6-7

concrescere, 100

concrete individual, 34

concrete universal, 100, 102; how grasped, 103

concreteness, 29

Confucian tradition, 162

conscience, 43

consciousness, 2-3, 4; deep (dark), 107-108; in general, 39; kinds of, per James, 9; religious, 122; surface (bright), 106-108, 126

contemplation, and happiness, 25

content, as ideas, 40-44 *passim*

contradiction, 35-36; in knowledge, 33

contradictory identity, 2-3; morality of, 145-153

contradictory self identity, 32-33

creatus to *creans*, 118-119

"Crimson Heart of Cosmic Compassion," 139

deconstruction, *xxi, xxv*

delusion, 136-137, 139

deontologists, 168-169

dependent origination, 102, 189*n17*

Descartes, René, 36-37; concept of God, 104

Deshimaru Taisen, 107

desires, 165, 167

Dharma, 52, 96

dialectical universal, 110

dialectical world: of action, 103; as the historical world, 118; as individuals, 102

"Dialogue on Language between a Japanese and an Inquirer, A" (Heidegger), *xxiv*

die gottheit, 99

Dilworth, David A., *xxii, 102-103*; on Nishida's pure experience, 3-4

Ding-an-sich, 94

direct experience, 109

disponibilité, 159

dō ("way"), 107

Dōgen, *xxiii, 105, 114*; and evil, 143; on seeking religious experience, 156; on selfless love, 139; on selflessness, 134, 139-140

Dostoevsky, Fyodor, 160

double aperture, 32, 58-59

dualism, 8

dualistic consciousness, 13-14

dual structure: introduced, 105

dying, paradox of, 95-96

East vs. West, 90-91

Eckhart, Meister, *xxiii*, 86

eightfold path, 140

eisagōgē, *xxi*

emotive self, 37

empirical ego, 74

emptying, as absolute self-negating, 160-161; emptying the empty, 66-67, 97; the self, 157-58, 175; principle of (emptiness), 85; as recast, 74-75

enlightenment (*see jikaku, kaku*) 114; of Buddhism, 140; how to reach, 156-160; stages of, 142

environment, and the individual, 67-68

Ereignis, 114

eternal negation, 95

ethics, Western, 150-151

evil, 77-78; characteristics of, 132-133; defined, 132; as separation from God, 132-134

existential contradiction, 94

experience: relations among things in, 9-10; richest, 9-15

experience of immediacy, of Zen, *xxiii*

expression, 77, 119; of absolute nothingness, 78-79; consciousness as, 93-94

fact vs. value, xii-xiii, *xvi-xvii*

feeling, 39; in direct experience, 83

field/subject/predicate, 30

field theory, *xiv-xv*, 29, 32-33, 101

Final Writings (Nishida), 121

first universal, 33-37

Flay, Joseph, 1-3

flowing. *(See* change)

form of the formless, 81, 83, 84-85, 101; Axtell on, 191n3

formed and forming, 109

Fox, Douglas, A., 132, 141-142

Fragment 108 (Heraclitus), 24

France, expansion of, in 19th Century, *xi*

free will, 43-44

freedom, 43-44, 84-85; Kantian, 87

Frege, 28

Fundamental Problems of Philosophy, The (Nishida), 105, 112

fusion of horizons, 126

Gilligan, Carol, 169

God, 44; absolute contradictory identity of, 152-153; as being, 81-82; Christian conception of, 85; as creator, 88; and evil, 128-134; grace of, 199n75; Judeo-Christian, 85-86; Kantian, 87; as manifested by universe, 77; of Nishida, 131-133; and nothingness, 81-99, 110; paradox of, 190n42; as pure experience, 88, 92; as pure *nous*, 25; and religion, 92-96; and Satan, 134-

135; and self-negation, 79; tran-
scendence and immanence of, 96-
97; as transcendent subject, 46-47
Golden Rule, 89-90
good (value), 40, 42-44
good/bad, and Zen, 140
goodness/badness dichotomy, 143
Gould, Glenn, 107
Grand Inquisitor (*Brothers Karamazov*),
160-161
Great Britain, expansion of, in 19th
Century, *xi*
Great Compassion, 75, 89
"Great Shrine, The", (*Taisha*), 164
Great Understanding, 75
Grene, Marjorie, 26-27

happiness, 25, 159-159
Hartman, Robert S., 89, 165-166
Ha Tai Kim, 53
hedonism, 159, 201*n*8
Hegel, Georg, *xxiii, xxiv*, 17, 100-101,
162; and concreteness, 29; on
knowing, 21; vs. Zen, 55
Heidegger, Martin, *xxiv*, 82, 117; concrete universal, 100, 111; logic of
the subject, 101
Heraclitus, 59; and paradox, 24;
Nishida and, 24
"here" of immediacy, 1
Herrigal, Eugen, 106
historical world, 103; as dynamic, 119;
as spiritually lined, 124; as the only
real world, 117; historical experience, 112; humans as embodied,
108; not static, 118
history, philosophy of, 116
homo faber, 118
"how" questions, 18-19
Huh, Woo-sung, 116

human mind, and pure experience, 6-7
Hume, David, on fact and value, *xii*
Husserl, Edmund, 60
hypokeímenon, 23, 101, 120; of acting
intuition, 123; as compound, 34;
in time, 38

I-Thou, of Martin Buber, 176
idealists, *xvi*
identity, 69-70
identity of contradiction, 2-3, 54-55,
154
identity of opposites, 60-61
identity of self contradiction, 54-55, 67-
69, 123; and God, 110; as mirroring reality, 109; as mutuality, 104;
as scholarship, 126
ignorance, 132, 155; and enlightenment, 142
Iino Norimoto, 139
imagination, and aesthetic values, 42
immanence and transcendence, 85-89,
148-149
immediate experience, richness of, 135-
136
immortality, 94-95; Kantian, 87
impermanence, 59, 84, 89-90, 157-158
In a Different Voice (Gilligan), 169
inclusiveness, 29
indexicality, 1-2
individual, and environment, 68
individuation, 25-27
ineffability, 9
intellect, vs. feelings, 168
intellectual intuition, the, *xiii*, 11-12,
14-15
intellectual perception, 11-12
intellectual self, 37
intelligible feeling self, 39
intelligible universal, 39-44

intelligible willing self, 39
Intelligible World, The (Nishida), 46-47, 49
interdependent origination (*see* dependent origination), 87-88
interpretation, *xxii*; problems of, *xxiv*
intuition, 3, 121, 125; creative, 106; of the contradictory flow, 104; and field, 29; primacy of, 103
Intuition and Reflection in Self-Consciousness (Nishida), 57
"is" *and yet* "is not" logic, 96
is vs. *ought, xii-xiii*, xvi, 42-43
Isshu Muira, 50
Izutsu Toshihiko, 18

Jaeger, Werner, 20
James, William, *xii-xiii*; on nature of experience, 180-181*n*57; vs. Nishida, 3, 13-14; and pure experience, 1-15 passim, 56, 174; on self-consciousness, 10; and thought and pure experience, 181*n*65
Japan: defeat of China and Russia by, *xi*; as imperialist power, *xi*; in 19th Century, *xi*; pro-Christian contingent, in, *xi-xii*
Japanese: culture of, 163; language of, 163; love of nature among, 163-164; and meditation, 163; mental and emotional training of, 165; spirit of, 157-158; values of, 164-165
Jesus, as paradigm of agapic action, 167
jikaku: defined, 79, 113-14
jiriki, 98
joy, 166; sources of, 166
Judeo-Christian tradition, 129
judgments(s): creation of, 5; defined, 27; and the field, 29; and persona;

morality, 172; and truth values, 41-42

Kahn, Charles H., on predication, 22
kaku (*see jikaku*), 114-116
Kalupahana, David, 64, 67
Kant, Immanuel, *xxiii, xxiv*, 17, 133; antinomies of, 62-63, 94; on duty, 167, 168-169; on fact and value, *xii*; and God, 92-94; practical reason of, 42-43; on religion, 92-93; and unity of perception, 38
Kasulis, Thomas P.: on *A Study of Good, xii*; on completeness and consistency, 65; on development of compassion, 139-140; on enlightenment, 114-116; Foreword of, *ix-xvii*; on Nāgārjuna, 64; on perception of nothingness, 67
Katz, Steven, 48-49
kenshō, 47, 53, 148, 154
kingdom of ends, of Kant, 138-139, 144
Kishimoto Hideo, 162-163
knower/known model, 34
knowing, 38; Aristotle on, 22; Nishida on, 21-22
knowledge: Aristotelian, 20; contradiction in, 33; feeling differentiated from , 83; per Nishida, 20
kōan(s), 49-54; defined, 49; goal of, 84
Kogun, Kanemitzu, 49-50
Kohlberg, Lawrence, 195*n*2
kōiteki chokkan (acting intuition), *xiv*
kokoro, 144-145, 171; aspects of, 196*n*30; defined, 138-139; and Neblett thesis on morality, 169-170
Kyoto School, *xiii*, 71, 81, 167
Kyoto University, 148, 175

language: adequacy (inadequacy) of, 18-20, 19-20, 21-22, 83; and reality, 16-17

life, as continuous self-expression, 93-94

limit concept, a, 8-9

logic (*ronri*), *xiv*; of *basho*, *xv*, 16-57; concrete, 103; dialectical, 112-124; of the East, 16-17; of objects, 136; of opposites, 111; of paradox, 136; of place vs. subject, 31; of predicate, 101, 103, 111-12; of relative approximation, 65; of subject, 101; of the things themselves, 102

"Logic of the Place Nothingness and the Religious Worldview, The" (Nishida), *xxii*, 56-57

love, 77-80, 90; as embrace, 149; Nishida on, 98; as zenith of intelligence, 78-78

MacIntyre, Alasdair, 169

Mahāyāna Buddhists, 85, 122; Nishida as, 96

Maitland, Thomas R., 4-5

Marcel, Gabriel-Honore, 159

martial arts (*see Budo*), 106-107, 125-126

Marxism, 117; Marxists, 126

matter, 25

maya, 61

Mayeroff, Milton, 169

meaning, defined, 5

meditation, 53; and feeling, 84; as source of insight, 143

medium, 77

Meiji period, *x-xi*

metaphysics: an alternative, 109; East Asian, 112; more powerful, 103

Middle Path logic, 64-65

Miki Kiyoshi, 117

Ming chia, 182*n*6

mirroring, 77-80, 110, 119, 124

monad, 110, 194fn62

Moore, C.A., on Zen Buddhism, 18

Moore, Edward I., on James' pure experience, 5

Moore, G.E., *xxiii*

moral development, 191*n*2

"Moral Maxim of Feeling: We Ought to Care About, and We Ought to Act Considerately in Regard to, the Feelings of Others" (Neblett), 170

morality, 43-44, 136-137; of contradictory identity, 145-153; described, 130-131; Eastern, 150; enlightenment and, 145-146; genuine, 137-138; God as source of, 149-150; ground of, 145-146; internalized, 150; and religion, 129-161

multiplicity, 47-48, 75-76

Murti, T.R.V., 64

mutual contradiction, 67-68

mutuality: of influence, 102, 104, 108

myopic perspective, *xxvi*

mystic intuition, 46

mysticism, 47-49, 124

Mysticism and Philosophy (Stace), 48

mythical thinking, 164

Nāgārjuna, influence of, on Nishida, 64-67

Nakamura Hajime, 62, 110, 117, 133, 135

namelessness, 9, 18

nature mysticism, 164

nature/self, change in, 39

Neblett, William, 169-170

Neo-Kantians, *xiii*

Neo-Platonism, 47

Nicholas of Cusa, 134

Niezsche, Friedrich, *xxiii*

nirvana, 54, 66, 75, 86, 132, 137, 140-

141, 155-156, 158

Nishida Kitarō: and Aristotle, 20, 31-32, 55-57; birth of, *x-xi*; on conception of God, 77; criticism of idealists by, *xvi*; debt of, to Descartes, 36-37; as East/West bridge, 173; formless God of, 153; and goal for world, 151-152; and grammatical predicate, 59; vs. James, 3, 14; on Japanese spirit, 157-158; on Kant's ethics, 153; lectures of, at Kyoto University, 148; as *Mahāyāna* Buddhist, 96; on meditation, 143; as practicing philosophy, *xxvi*; and rejection of *A Study of Good*, *xiii-xiv*; self-contradictory sphere of, 134; and social ethics, 144; on sorrow, 95; turn to history, 116-117; use of East and West philosophy by, 171; as world philosopher, *xxiii-xxiv*

Nishidan dialectic, 54-55

Nishitani Keiji, 87-88, 127, 165; and circumsessional inter-penetration, 89, and psychic sympathy, 165

Noda Matao, 100, 103

Noddings, Nell, 169

"no-mind," *xiii, 106*

nonattachment, 64, 143

non-being: beyond, 102; defined, 81

non-dualism, of nothingness, 83

nothingness, 127; absolute, 109; absolute and self-hood, 154; character of, 82-83; as concrete universal, 102; enlightenment of, 90; field of, 101; final field of, 45, 103; as final *hypokeímenon*, 123; as foundation, 112; as identity of self-contradiction, 110; as one and many, 119; as originary, 123; and the ox herder, 71-76; transcendence of, 85-86;

Western meaning of, 81. *See also* absolute nothingness

noumenal, world, 104

now, 162-163; eternal, 87, 104-105; of immediacy, 1

Nygren, Anders, 167

object, as absolute, 131-132

object logic, 69-70

Ohe Seizo, 166

O'Leary, Joseph S., 57

On Caring (Mayeroff), 169

On the Way to Language (Heidegger), *xxiv*

one primal stuff, 3-7

oneness, 48, 58-59

One(ness), 122; absolute, 109; as final *hypokeímenon*, 123; and many, 110, 121

ontological dualism, 8

organicism, 2016n8

Owens, Fr. Joseph, 20

Ox and His Herdsman, The, 70-76, 105-106, 128

Pantheism, 146-147

Paradox: of Buddhist utterance, *xxiii*; of change, 171; dynamic of, 63-64; of dying, 95-96; as expression of Nishida Thesis, 176-177

Parmenides, 59

particular, the, 21-22; characteristics of, 26

perception, per James, 7

Peerenboom, R.P., 109

Perry, Commodore Matthew, *xi*

person, uniqueness of, 154-155

Peters, R.S., 169

phenomenal: world, 104, 105, 194n60

Philosophical Essays, *xxii*

philosophy, and philosophy of religion,

91-92
phrónēsis, 20
place of context (*basho*), *xiv*
Plato, 59, 61, 98; and essential reality,
    19-20; on form and matter, 101;
    on predication, 21-22
plenum, 101, 115
Plotinus, 47
poetry of self-transformation, 89-90
Posterior Analytics (Aristotle), 25
practical wisdom, 20
Prajñāpāramitā Sūtra, 99, 146
predicable, the, characteristics of, 25-26
Prichard, Harold, 168
Principles of Psychology (James), 10
processes-in-experience, 25
psychic sympathy, 165
pure action, 107
pure experience, *xiii, xxii*, 1-15, 109;
    complexity of, 178-179*n*3; de-
    scribed, 174-176; and haiku, 107;
    as negating principle, 114-115; as
    path to understanding nothingness,
    85; as reality, 124, 174-175; and
    thought, 11
Pure Land, 161

reality: as apperception, 6; as being and
    non-being, 90-91; and conception,
    5-6; as a contradiction, 63; defined,
    3-4; in flux, 6; and paradox, 23-24;
    undifferentiated, 14-15
reason, adequacy of, 83
Reason and Compassion (Peters), 169
relative nothingness, *xv*
religion: as contradictory identity, 122;
    goal of, 155-156; and God, 92-96;
    and intuition, 12-13; as killer of
    religiosity, 161; and learning and
    morality, 3, 13; logic of, 96-99; and
    morality, 129-161; as non-stance,

158
religiosity, 155; and self-revelation, 157;
    transformative, 133-134
religious act (itself), 156
religious consciousness, 46
religious experience, 94; ineffableness of,
    91-92
religious intuition, 49
richest experience, 9-15
Rinzai school, 156
Role of Feeling in Morals, The (Neblett),
    169
romanticism, 201*n*8
ronri (logic), *xiv*
Ross, William D., 168
rule-utilitarianism, 168-169
Russel, Bertrand, 28
Russia, Japan's defeat of, *xi*

Sakuma Shosan, *xi*
samsara, 54; as absolute embrace, 137;
    and altruism, 140-141; as fully
    nirvana, 156; as holy, 85-86, 127,
    140-141; and mutuality, 102, 104;
    as self-contradiction, 66, 104; and
    transformation, 132
Santayana, George, *xxiii*
Satan, 101, 102, 130-132
satori, 47, 53, 54
Schinzinger, Robert, 50, 59, 98, 108;
    on Buddhist use of *soku*, 70; on
    transcendence of God, 79-80
School of Names, The, 18
second universal, 37-39
Seigfried, Charlene H., 8, 9
self: absolute negation of, 123; as active
    agency, 37; as center of universe,
    137; deep, 105, 126; of emotions,
    37; as mirror image of God, 132-
    133; as the place, 1-2; as place of
    knowing, 37; as process, *xvi*

self-consciousness (*see also jikaku*), 35-36, 103, 113-114, 116; aspects of, 38; defined, 79; layers of, 37
selfishness, as sin, 160
self-contradiction, unity of, 58-59
self-contradictory identity, 58-80, 93
self-realization, 103, 113-114
sentence/judgement, 26
servant of God, 154
Shintō tradition, 133
Shintōism, 135
Shirk, Evelyn, 167-168
silence, 18, 48; goal of, 84
sincerity, 153, 159
social ethics, 144, 168, 172
soku hi, 59, 63, 112
sophia, 20
sorrow, 95
Sōtō school, 156
space/time identity, 68-69
speaking the unspeakable, 47-49
species/genus model, 34
species-genus relationship, 108-109
spontaneity, 137-138
Stace, W.T., 48; analysis of pantheistic paradox by, 147; on human nature and morality, 169; on paradoxes, 52
Study of Good, A (Nishida), 56-57, 77, 96, 174; central notion of, 1; Kasulis on, *xii-xvi*; and selfless love, 136-138
subject/object dichotomy (nóēsis/*nóema*), 1, 4, 8, 10-11, 44-46, 53-54, 60, 90-91
substance, 23; as compound, 33-34; defined, 26
substance/attribute model, 34
subsumption, 27
subsumptive judgement, 31
subsumptive universal, 34

suchness, 88, 89-90, 166
sūnyatā, 99
sūtras, 71; goal of, 84
Suzuki, D.T., *xiii*, 85, 141
swordsman, 106, 126
syllogistic universal, 34, 35
Symposium (Plato), 98
synthesis, 112

To Te Ching, 17
Taoism, on speaking and knowing, 17
Taoist tradition, 162
tariki, 98
tea-room, symbolism of, 163
technology, effects of, *xvii*
télos of the absolute, 154
Ten Commandments, 140
tension, 70; paradoxical, 97
theoretical thinking, 164
theory of forms, *xxvi*
thing/attribute model, 37
third universal, 39-44
thisness, 21-22
Thomas Aquinas, St., 86
Tillich, Paul: on God as being, 81-83; God-beyond-God of, 153
Timaeus (Plato), *xxii*
time: as awareness of consciousness, 37; and changing, 35; as a form of timeless, 87-88
time/space identity, 68-69
transcendence and immanence, 85-89
transcendent transcendence, 148-149
transformation (moral), 131-132; chart of, 142
transformation of the everyday, 154-156
translation, problems of, *xxiv*
True Pure Land teaching, 157-158
truth, 39, 40-41; as absolute, 124

Ueda Shizuteru, 71, 175; on I-Thou of

Buber, 176-177; *jikaku* and pure experience, 114-116
unborn, the, 132, 144; Fox on, 198*n*50, *n*53
unconditioned, the, 81-82
unconscious(ness), 106; the Unconscious, 107
undifferentiated, the, 53
United States, expansion of, in 19th Century, *xi*
unitive life, 54
universal(s), the, 21-22; abstract 33, 101; of judgment, 34-36; lesser, 34; main, 33; as manifestation of God, 77; nine, 34; as only knowable thing, 22; as predicates, 22; as principles of individuation, 100; of self-consciousness, 37-39, 103; of subject and predicate, 29
universalistic consequentialists, 131
unknown knower, the, 84
utilitarians, 131, 168-169

value (good), 40, 42-44
values: as immediate, 162-166; systemization of, 162
Varieties of Religious Experience, The (James), 9
virtuosity, 146
voluntarism, 201*n*8

Waldenfels, Hans, 113-114
Wargo, Robert Joseph, 27-28; and contradiction in knowledge, 33; on ideas, 40; on judgment, 30
Watson, Walter, *xxii*
Watsuji Tetsurō, 117
"Western techniques, Eastern morality," *xi*
whatness, 21-22
wheel of rebirth, 97

Wheelwright, Philip, on Heraclitus, 24
"why" questions, 18-19
Wilbur, Ken, 147
will, the, *xiii*; and determination of one's nature, 38-39; transparent, 42-43
will self, the, 37
willing, 38
willing self vs. behaving self, 45
Windleband, Wilhelm, 46
wisdom, non-discriminating, 152
Wittgenstein, Ludwig, 54
world, as contradictory identity, 67-69; creative and physical contrasted, 134-135; historical, 94; of objects, 130
"World as Identity of Absolute Contradiction, The" (Nishida), 67

Yokyoku Taisha, 164
Yuasa Yasuo, *xvi; on acting intuition, 105; on genius, 107*
Yusa Michiko, 58, 108

zazen, 156
Zen Buddhism, 117, 124: as distinct from mysticism, 47; experience of immediacy of, *xxiii*; vs. Hegel, 55; ideal of, *xiii*; kōans, 49-54; and language, 18; no-doctrine premise of, 129-130; and notion of "no-mind," 188*n*47; paradoxes of, 51-52; "scandal" of, 140; vs. thinking, 174-175; tradition, 162; ultimate goal of, 129
Zen Action/ Zen Person (Kasulis), *xiii*
Zen in the Art of Archery (Herrigal), 106